James Jennings

The Dialect of the West of England

Salzwasser

James Jennings

The Dialect of the West of England

1. Auflage | ISBN: 978-3-84605-450-5

Erscheinungsort: Frankfurt, Deutschland

Erscheinungsjahr: 2020

Salzwasser Verlag GmbH

Reprint of the original, first published in 1869.

THE DIALECT OF THE WEST OF ENGLAND,

PARTICULARLY

Somersetshire.

"Goo little Reed!
" Aforn tha vawk, an vor me plead :
" Thy wild nawtes, mâ-be, thâ ool hire
" Zooner than zâter vrom a lâre.
" Zâ that thy Maester's pleas'd ta blaw 'em,
" An haups in time thâ'll come ta knaw 'em
" An nif za be thâ'll please ta hear,
" A'll gee zum moor another year."—*The Farewell.*

THE

Dialect of the West of England,

PARTICULARLY

SOMERSETSHIRE;

WITH A GLOSSARY OF WORDS NOW IN USE THERE;
ALSO WITH POEMS AND OTHER PIECES
EXEMPLIFYING THE DIALECT.

By JAMES JENNINGS,

HONORARY SECRETARY OF THE METROPOLITAN LITERARY
INSTITUTION, LONDON.

SECOND EDITION,

THE WHOLE REVISED, CORRECTED, AND ENLARGED, WITH TWO
DISSERTATIONS ON THE ANGLO-SAXON PRONOUNS,
AND OTHER PIECES,

By JAMES KNIGHT JENNINGS, M.A.,

Late Scholar and Librarian, Queens' College, Cambridge;
Vicar of Hagbourn, Berkshire;
and Minister of Catcott Donative, Somersetshire.

LONDON:

JOHN RUSSELL SMITH, 36, SOHO SQUARE.

MDCCCLXIX.

TO

THA DWELLERS O' THA WEST.

THA Fruit o' longvul labour, years,
In theäze veo leaves at last appears.
Ta You, tha DWELLERS o' tha WEST,
I'm pleas'd that thâ shood be addresst :
Vor thaw I now in Lunnun dwell,
I mine ye still—I love ye well ;
And niver, niver sholl vorget
I vust drâw'd breath in *Zummerzet* ;
Amangst ye liv'd, and left ye zorry,
As you'll knaw when you hire my storry.
Theäze little BOOK than take o' ME ;
'Tis âll I hâ just now ta gee.
An when you rade o' *Tommy Gool,*
Or *Tommy Came,* or *Pal* at school,
Or *Mr. Guy,* or *Fanny Fear,*—
(I thenk you'll shod vor her a tear)
Tha Rookery, or *Mary's Crutch,*
Tha cap o' which I love ta touch,
You'll vine that I do not vorget
My naatal swile—dear Zummerzet.

JAS. JENNINGS.

PREFACE TO THE SECOND EDITION.

In preparing this second edition of my relative's work, I have incorporated the results of observations made by me during several years' residence in Somersetshire, in the centre of the district. I have also availed myself by kind permission, of hints and suggestions in two papers, entitled "Somersetshire Dialect," read by T. S. Baynes in 1856, and reprinted from the Taunton Courier, in London, in 1861.

During the forty years which have elapsed since the first edition, very much light has been thrown on the subject of Provincial Dialects, and after all much remains to be discovered. I consider with Mr. Baynes that there is more of the pure Anglo-Saxon in the west of England dialect, as this district was the seat of classical Anglo-Saxon, which first rose here to a national tongue, and lasted longer in a great measure owing to its distance from the Metropolis, from which cause also it was less subject to modern modification.

I shall be happy to receive any suggestions from Philological scholars, which may increase the light thrown on the subject, and by which a third edition may be improved.

Hagbourn Vicarage, August, 1869.

PREFACE.

The usefulness of works like the present is too generally admitted to need any apology for their publication. There is, notwithstanding, in their very nature a dryness, which requires relief: the author trusts, therefore, that, in blending something imaginative with the details of philological precision, his work will afford amusement to the reader.

The Glossary contains the fruit of years of unwearied attention to the subject ; and it is hoped that the book will be of some use in elucidating our old writers, in affording occasional help to the etymology of the Anglo-Saxon portion of our language, and in exhibiting a view of the present state of an important dialect of the western provinces of England.

A late excursion through the West has, however, induced the Author to believe that some valuable information may yet remain to be gathered from our Anglo-Saxon dialect—more especially from that part of it still used by the common people and the yeomanry. He therefore respectfully solicits communications from those who feel an interest in this department of our literature ; by which a second edition may be, materially improved.

To a *native* of the west of England this volume will be found a vade-mecum of reference, and assist the reminiscence of well-known, and too often unnoted peculiarities and words, which are fast receding from the polish of elegance, and the refinement of literature.

In regard to the *Poetical Pieces*, it may be mentioned that most of them are founded on *West Country Stories*, the incidents in which actually occurred. If some of the subjects should be thought trifling, it must not be forgotten that the primary object has been, to exemplify the Dialect, and that common subjects offered the best means of effectuating such an object. Of such Poems as *Good Bwye ta thee Cot*; *the Rookery*; and *Mary Ramsey's Crutch*, it may be observed, that had the Author *felt* less he might, perhaps, have written better.

Metropolitan Literary Institution, London,

March 25, 1825.

CONTENTS.

OBSERVATIONS, &c.

The following Glossary includes the whole of Somerset, *East* of the River Parret, as well as adjoining parts of Wiltshire and Gloucestershire. West of the Parret many of the words are pronounced very differently indeed, so as to mark strongly the people who use them. [This may be seen more fully developed in two papers, by T. Spencer Baynes, read before the Somersetshire Archæological Society, entitled the Somersetshire Dialect, printed 1861, 18mo, to whom I here acknowledge my obligations for several hints and suggestions, of which I avail myself in this edition of my late relative's work].

The chief peculiarity West of the Parret, is the ending of the third person singular, present tense of verbs, in *th* or *eth* : as, he *lov'th*, *zee'th*, &c., for he loves, sees, &c.

In the pronouns, they have *Ise* for *I*, and *er* for *he*. In fact the peculiarities and contractions of the Western District are puzzling to a stranger. Thus, *her* is frequently used for *she.* " *Har'th a doo'd it,*" is, *she has done it,*" (I shall occasionally in the Glossary note such words as distinguishingly characterise that district).

Two of the most remarkable peculiarities of the dialect of the West of England, and particularly of Somersetshire, are the sounds given to the vowels A and E. A, is almost always sounded open, as in *fäther, räther,* or somewhat like the usual sound of *a* in *balloon, calico,* lengthened ; it is so pronounced in bäll, cäll. I shall use for this sound the *circumflex over the a,* thus *â* or *ä.* E, has commonly the same sound as the French gave it, which is, in fact, the slender of A, as heard in *pane fane, cane,* &c. The hard sound given in our polished dialect to the letters *th,* in the majority of words containing those letters [as in *through, three, thing, think*], expressed by the Anglo-Saxon ð, is frequently changed in the Western districts into the sound given in England to the letter *d* :

> as for *three,* we have *dree*
> for *thread, dread, or dird,*
> *through, droo, throng, drong,* or rather *drang*;
> *thrush, dirsh,* &c.

The consonant and vowel following *d*, changing places. The slender or soft sound given to *th* in our polished dialect, is in the West, most commonly converted into the thick or obtuse sound of the same letters as heard in the words *this*, these &c., and this too, whether the letters be at the beginning or end of words. I am much disposed to believe that our Anglo-Saxon ancestors, used indiscriminately the letters Ð and ð for D only, and sounded them as such, as we find now frequently in the West; although our lexicographers usually have given the *two* sounds of *th* to Ð and ð respectively. The vowel O is used for *a*, as *hond, dorke, lorke, hort*, in hand, dark, lark, heart, &c., and other syllables are lengthened, as *voqte, bade, dade*, for foot, bed, dead. The letter O in *no, gold*, &c., is sounded like *aw* in *awful*; I have therefore spelt it with this diphthong instead of *a*. Such word as *jay* for *joy*, and a few others, I have not noted. Another remarkable fact is the disposition to invert the order of some consonants in some words; as the *r* in *thrush, brush, rush, run*, &c., pronouncing them dirsh, birsh, hirsh, hirn; also transposition of *p* and *s* in such words as clasp, hasp, asp, &c., sounded claps, haps, aps, &c. I have not inserted all

these words in the Glossary, as these general remarks
will enable the student to detect the words which
are so inverted. It is by no means improbable
that the order in which such sounds are now
repeated in the West, is the original order in which
they existed in our language, and that our more
polished mode of expressing them is a new and
perhaps a corrupt enunciation. Another peculiarity
is that of joining the letter *y* at the end of some verbs
in the infinitive mood, as well as to parts of different
conjugations, thus, " I can't *sewy, nursy, reapy*, to
sawy, to *sewy*, to *nursy*, &c. A further peculiarity
is the *love of vowel* sound, and opening out mono-
syllables of our polished dialect into two or more
syllables, thus :

ay-er, for air ;	boo-äth, for both ;
fay-er, for fair ;	vi-ër for fire ;
stay-ers for stairs ;	show-er for sure ;
vröo-rst for post ;	boo-ath for both ;
bre-ash for brush ;	chee-ase for cheese ;
kee-ard for card ;	gee-ate for gate ;
mee-ade for mead ;	mee-olk for milk ; &c.

Chaucer gives many of them as dissyllables.

The verb *to be* retains much of its primitive form:
thus *I be, thou*, or *thee, beest*, or *bist, we be, you be,*

they be, thä be, are continually heard for *I am, &c.,* *he be* is rarely used: but *he is.* In the past tense, *war* is used for *was*, and *were*: *I war, thou* or *thee wart*, he *war*, &c., we have besides, *we'm, you'm, they'm*, for *we, you, they, are*, there is a constant tendency to pleonasm in some cases, as well as to contraction, and elision in others. ᐧThus we have *a lost, agone, abought*, &c., for *lost, gone, bought,* &c., Chaucer has many of these prefixes; but he often uses *y* instead of *a*, as *ylost.* The frequent use of Z and V, the softened musical sounds for S and F, together with the frequent increase and multiplication of vowel sounds, give the dialect a by no means inharmonious expression, certainly it would not be difficult to select many words which may for their modulation compete with others of French extraction, and, perhaps be superior to many others which we have borrowed from other languages, much less analogous to the polished dialect of our own. I have added, in pursuance of these ideas, some poetical and prose pieces in the dialect of Somersetshire, in which the idiom is tolerably well preserved, and the pronunciation is conveyed in letters, the nearest to the sound of the words, as there are in truth many sounds for which we have neither letters, nor combinations of letters to express them. [I might at some future period, if thought advisable, go into a comparison between the sound of all the letters of the alphabet pronounced in Somersetshire, and in our polished dialect, but I doubt if the subject is entitled to this degree of criticism]. The reader will bear in mind that these poems are composed in the dialect of Somerset, north east of the Parret, which is by far the most general.

In the Guardian, published about a century ago, is a paper No. 40, concerning pastoral poetry, supposed to have been written by *Pope*, to extol his own pastorals and degrade those of Ambrose Phillips. In this essay there is a quotation from a pretended *Somersetshire* poem. But it is evident Pope knew little or nothing about the Somersetshire dialect. Here are a few lines from "this old West country bard of ours," as Pope calls him:

"*Cicely*. Ah Rager, Rager, cher was zore avraid,
" When in yond vield you kiss'd the parson's maid :
" Is this the love that once to me you zed,
" When from tha wake thou broughtst me gingerbread ?"

Now first, this is a strange admixture of dialects, but neither east, west, north, nor south.

Chez is nowhere used ; but in the southern part *utche* or *iche*, is sometimes spoken contractedly *che*. [See *utchy* in the Glossary].

Vield for *field*, should be *veel*.

Wake is not used in Somersetshire ; but *revel* is the word.

Parson, in Somersetshire, dealer, is *pàson*.

In another line he calls the cows, *kee*, which is not Somersetian ; nor is, *be go* for begone: it should, *be gwon*; nor is *I've a be* ; but *I've a bin*, Somersetian.

The idiomatic expressions in this dialect are numerous, many will be found in the Glossary; the following may be mentioned. *I'd 'sley do it*, for *I would as lief do it*. I have occasionally in the Glossary suggested the etymology of some words; by far the greater part have an Anglo-Saxon, some perhaps a Danish origin; [and when we recollect that *Alfred the Great*, a good Anglo-Saxon scholar, was born at Wantage in Berks, on the border of Wilts, had a palace at Chippenham, and was for some time resident in Athelney, we may presume that traditional remains of him may have influenced the language or dialect of Somersetshire, and I am inclined to think that the present language and pronunciation of Somersetshire were some centuries past, general in the south portion of our island.]

In compiling this Glossary, I give the fruits of twenty-five years' assiduity, and have defined words, not from books, but from actual usage; I have however carefully consulted *Junius, Skinner, Minshew,* and some other old lexicographers, and find many of their definitions correspond with my own; but I avoid *conjectural* etymology. Few dictionaries of our language are to be obtained, published from the invention of printing to the end of the 16th century, a period of about 150 years. They throw much light on our provincial words, yet after all, our *old writers* are our chief resource, [and doubtless many MSS. in various depositories, written at different periods, and recently brought to light, from the Record and State Paper Office, and historical societies, will throw much light on the subject]; and an abundant harvest offers in examining them, by which to make an amusing book, illustrative of our provincial words and ancient manners. I think we cannot avoid arriving at the conclusion, that the Anglo-Saxon dialect, of which I conceive the Western dialect to be a striking portion, has been gradually giving way to our polished idiom; and is considered a barbarism, and yet many of the *sounds* of that dialect are found in Holland and

Germany, as a part of the living language of these countries. I am contented with having thus far elucidated the language of my native county. I have omitted several words, which I supposed provincial, and which are frequent to the west, as they are found in the modern dictionaries, still I have allowed a few, which are in Richardson's Johnson.

Thee is used for the nominative *thou*; which latter word is seldom used, diphthong sounds used in this dialect are :

uai, uoa, uoi, uoy, as

guain, (gwain), quoat, buoil, buoy ;

such is the disposition to pleonasm in the use of the demonstrative pronouns, that they are very often used with the adverb *there*. *Theäze here, thick there, [thicky there, west of the Parret]* theäsam here, *theazamy here, them there, themmy there.* The substitution of V for F, and Z (*Izzard, Shard,* for S, is one of the strongest words of numerous dialects.)

In words ending with *p* followed by *s*, the letters change places as :

hasp—haps ;   clasp—claps.

wasp—waps ;

In a paper by General Vallancey in the second

volume of the *Transactions of the Royal Irish Academy*, read Dec. 27, 1788, it appears that a colony of English soldiers settled in the *Baronies* of *Forth Bargie*, in the county of Wexford, in Ireland, in 1167, 1168, and 1169 ; and that colony preserved their customs, manners, and language to 1788. There is added in that paper a *vocabulary* of their language, and a *song*, handed down by tradition from the arrival of the colony more than 600 years since.   I think there can be no question that these Irish colonists were from the West of England, from the apparent admixture of dialects in the *vocabulary* and *song*, although the language is much altered from the Anglo-Saxon of Somersetshire.*   The words *nouth*, knoweth ; *zin*, sin, *vrast*, frost ; *die*, day ; *Zathardie*, Saturday ; *Zindii*, Sunday ; and a few others, indicate an origin west of the Parret.   There are many words which with a trifling alteration in spelling, would suit at the present time the north eastern portion

---

* This subject has been more fully treated in the following work : A Glossary, with some pieces of verse of the old dialect of the English colony in the Baronies of Forth and Bargy, Co. Wexford, Ireland.   Formerly collected by Jacob Poole, of Growton, now edited with Notes and Introduction by the Rev. W. Barnes, author of the Dorset Poems and Glossary, fcap. 8vo, 1867.

of the county : as *blauther*, bladder : *crwest*, crust ; *smill*, smell ; *skir*, to rise in the air [see *skeer*]; *vier*, fire ; *vier*, a weasel ; *zar*, to serve ; *zatch*, such, &c. From such words as *ch'am*, add *ch'uh*, the southern part of the county is clearly indicated. I think the disposition to elision and contraction is as, evident here as it is at present in Somersetshire In the song, there are marks of its having undergone change since its first introduction.

Lowthee is evidently derived from *lewth* [see Glossary] *lewthy*, will be, *abounding in lewth*, i. e. *sheltered.*

The line

" *As by mizluck wus I pit t' drive in.*"

would in the present Somerset dialect stand thus :

" *That by misluck war a put ta dreav in.*"

That by mis luck was placed to drive in.

In the line

" *Chote well ar aim wai t' yie ouz n'eer a blowe.*"

the word *chete* is, I suspect, compounded of *'ch'* [*iche*] and *knew*, implying *I knew*, or rather *I knew'd*, or *knewt.**

---

* The following is from an amatory poem, written in or about the reign of Henry II., during which the colony of the English was established in the county of Wexford.
" Ichoz from heune iz is me senz."

The modern English of the line will then be,

I knew well their aim was to give us ne'r a blow.

I suspect *zitckel* is compounded of *zitch*, such, and the auxiliary verb *will.* *I view ame*, is *a veo o'm*; that is, *a few of them.* *Emethee*, is *emmtey*, that is, abounding with ants. *Meulten away*, is melting away.

Th'ast ee pait it, thee'st a paid it; thou hast paid it.

In the *English translation* which accompanies the original *song* in *General Vallancey's* paper, some of the words are, I think, beyond controversy misinterpreted, but I have not room to go critically through it. All I desire should be inferred from these remarks is, that, although this *Anglo-Saxon* curiosity is well worthy the attention of those who take an interest in our early literature, we must be careful not to assume that it is a pure specimen of the language of the period to which, and of the people to whom, it is said to relate.

In Johnson's *History of the English Language*, page liii. it is thus translated—

" I wot (believe) it is sent me from heaven."

To an admirer of our Anglo-Saxon all the lines, twelve in number, quoted by M. Todd with the above, will be found a rich treat : want of space only prevents my giving them here.

A

GLOSSARY OF WORDS

COMMONLY USED IN THE

County of Somerset,

BUT WHICH ARE NOT ACCCEPTED AS LEGITIMATE WORDS OF

THE ENGLISH LANGUAGE;

OR

WORDS

WHICH, ALTHOUGH ONCE USED GENERALLY, ARE NOW

BECOME PROVINCIAL.

A GLOSSARY OF WORDS

USED IN

SOMERSETSHIRE.

A.

A. *adv.* Yes; or *pron.* He: as *a zed a'd do it*; he said he'd do it.

Aa'th, *s.* earth.

Ab'bey. *s.* The great white poplar: one of the varieties of the *populus alba.*

Ab'bey-lubber. *s.* A lazy, idle fellow.

Abought. *part.* Bought. *See* VAUGHT.

Abrood'. *adv.* When a hen is sitting on her eggs she is said to be *abrood.*

Ad'dle. *s.* A swelling with matter in it.

Ad'dled. *a.* Having pus or corruption ; hence

Ad'dled-egg. *s.* An egg in a state of putrefaction.

Affeard'. *a.* Afraid.

Afo're.
Afo'rn. } *prep.* and *adv.* Before ; *afore, Chaucer.*

Again. *prep.* Against.

Agon'. { *adv.* [these words literally mean *gone.*]
Agoo'. { Ago ; *agoo, Chaucer ;* from the verb to *goo,* i.e. to go ; *he is up and agoo ;* he is up and gone.

Alas-a-dây. *interj*. A-lack-a-day.

Ale. *s*. A liquor, brewed with a proportion of malt from about four to six bushels to the hogshead of 63 gallons; if it contain more malt it is called *beer*; if less, it is usually called *small beer*.

Al'ler. *s*. The alder tree.

Allès. *adv*. Always.

All'once. *pron*. [all ones] or rather (all o'n's) All of us; *Let's go allonce*; let us go all of us.

All o's. *pron*. All of us.

Alost'. *part*. Lost: *ylost, Chaucer*.

Amang. *prep*. Among.

Amawst'. ⎫
Amoo'äst ⎬ *adv*. Almost.

Amper. *s*. A small red pimple.

Anby'. *adv*. Some time hence; in the evening.

Anear'. ⎫
Ane'ast. ⎬ *prep*. Nigh to; *aneast en*, near him.
Aneoust', ⎭

Aneen. On end, upright.

An'passy. *s*. The sign &, corrupted from *and per se*.

Anty. *adj*. Empty.

Apast'. *part*. and *prep*. Past; *apast. Chaucer*.

A'pricock. *s*. An apricot.

Aps. *s*. The asp tree; *populus tremula*.

Aps'en. *a*. Made of the wood of the asp; belonging to the asp.

To Arg. *v. n*. To argue.

To Ar'gufy. *v. n.*. To hold an argument; to argue.

Ascri'de. *adv.* Across; astride.

Aslen'. *adv.* Aslope.

Assu'e. *adj.* When a cow is *let up* in order that she may calve, she is said to be *assue*—having no milk.

Ater. *prep.* After. *Goo ater'n*: go after him.

Athin. *adv.* Within.

Athout. *prep.* Without.

Auverdro. *v. a.* Overthrow.

Avaur'.
Avaur'en. } *prep.* Before.
Avaurn'.

Avoordin. *part.* Affording.

Avraur'. *adj.* Frozen; stiff with frost.

Awa kid. *adj.* Awake; *awakid, Chaucer.*

To Ax. *v. a.* To ask; *ax, Chaucer.*

Ax'en. *s. pl.* Ashes.

Axing. *s.* and *part.* Asking; *axing, Chaucer.*

Ay'ir. *s.* Air.

B.

Back'sid. *s.* A barton.

Back'y. *s.* Tobacco.

Bad. *adv.* Badly.

Bade. *s.* Bed.

Ba'ginet. *s.* Bayonet.

Bai'ly. *s.* A bailiff; a superintendent of an estate.

Ball. *adj.* Bald.

Bal'let. *s.* Ballad.

Ball'rib. *s.* A sparerib.

To Bal'lirag. *v. a.* To abuse with foul words; to scold.

To Ban. *v. a.* To shut out; to stop.

To Bane. *v. a.* To afflict with a mortal disease; applied to sheep. *See* to COATHE.

To Barenhond'. } *v. n.* (used chiefly in the third person
To Banehond'. } singular) to signify intention; to intimate.

These words are in very common use in the West of England. It is curious to note their gradation from Chaucer, whose expression is *Beren hem on hond,* or *bare him on hond;* implying always, it appears to me, the same meaning as I have given to the words above. There is, I think, no doubt, that these expressions of Chaucer, which he has used several times in his works, are figurative; when Chaucer tells us he *beren hem in hond,* the literal meaning is, he carried it in, or on, his hand so that it might be readily seen. "*To bear on hand,* to affirm, to relate."—JAMIESON's Etymological Scots Dictionary. But, whatever be the meaning of these words in Chaucer, and at the present time in Scotland, the above is the meaning of them in the west of England.

Banes. *s. pl.* The banns of matrimony.

Ban'nin. *s.* That which is used for shutting out or stopping.

Ban'nut. *s.* A walnut. [Only used in northern parts of county.]

Barrow-pig. *s.* A gelt pig.

Baw'ker. ⎱ *s.* A stone used for whetting scythes;
Baw'ker-stone. ⎰ a kind of sand-stone.

To Becall'. *v. a.* To censure; to reprove; to chide.

Bee'äs. ⎱ *s. pl.* [*Beasts*] Cattle. Applied only to *Oxen*
Bease. ⎰ not Sheep.

Bee-but. ⎱
Bee-lippen. ⎰ *s.* A bee-hive.

Bee'dy. *s.* A chick.

Beedy's-eyes. *s. pl.* Pansy, love-in-idleness.

Beer. *s. See* ALE.

Befor'n. *prep.* Before.

To Begird'ge, ⎱
To Begrud'ge. ⎰ *v. a.* To grudge; to envy.

LORD BYRON has used the verb *begrudge* in his notes to the 2nd canto of Childe Harold.

Begor'z. ⎱
Begum'mer s ⎰ *interj.*

These words are, most probably, oaths of asseveration. The last appears to be a corruption of *by godmothers.* Both are thrown into discourse very frequently: *Begummers, I ont tell; I cant do it begorz.*

Begr um pled. *part.* Soured; offended.

To Belg. *v. n.* To cry aloud; to bellow.

Bell-flower. *s.* A daffodil.

To Belsh. *v. a.* To cut off dung, &c., from the tails of sheep.

Beneäpt. *part.* Left aground by the recess of the spring tides.

To Benge. *v. n.* To remain long in drinking; to drink to excess.

Ben'net. *v.* Long coarse grass.

Ben'nety. *adj.* Abounding in bennets.

Ber'rin. *s.* [burying] A funeral procession.

To Beskum'mer. *v. a.* To foul with a dirty liquid; to besmear.

To Bethink' *v. a.* To grudge.

Bettermost. *adj.* The best of the better; not quite amounting to the best.

Betwat'tled. *part.* In a distressing and confused state of mind.

To Betwit'. *v. a.* To upbraid; to repeat a past circumstance aggravatingly.

To Bib'ble. *v. n.* To drink often; to tope.

Bib'bler. *s.* One who drinks often; a toper.

Bil'lid. *adj.* Distracted; mad.

Billy. *s.* A bundle of wheat straw.

Bi'meby. *adv.* By-and-by; some time hence.

Bin. *conj.* Because; probably corrupted from, being.

Bin'nick. *s.* A small fish; minnow; *Cyprinus phloxinus.*

Bird-battin. *s.* The catching of birds with a net and lights by night. Fielding uses the expression.

Bird-battin-net. *s.* The net used in bird-battin.

Birch'en. *adj.* Made of birch ; relating to birch.

Bis'gee. *s.* (g hard), A rooting axe.

Bisky. *s.* Biscuit.

> The pronunciation of this word approximates nearer to the sound of the French *cuit* ["twice baked "] the *t* being omitted in this dialect.

To Bi'ver. *v. n.* To quiver; to shake.

Black-pot. *s.* Black-pudding.

Black'ymoor. *s.* A negro.

Blackymoor's-beauty. *s.* Sweet scabious; the musk-flower.

Blanker. *s.* A spark of fire.

Blans'cue. *s.* Misfortune; unexpected accident.

Blather. *s.* Bladder. To blather. *v. n.* To talk fast, and nonsensically [*to talk so fast that bladders form at the mouth*]

Bleáchy. *adj.* Brackish; saltish : applied to water.

Blind-buck-and-Davy. *s.* Blind-man's buff. *Blindbuck and have ye,* is no doubt the origin of this appellation for a well-known amusement.

Blis'som. *ad.* Blithesome.

Blood-sucker. *s.* A leech.

Bloody-warrior. *s.* The wall-flower.

Boar. *s.* The peculiar head or first flowing of water from one to two feet high at spring tides, in the

river Parret a few miles below and at Bridgewater, and in some other rivers.

[In Johnson's Dictionary this is spelt *bore*; I prefer the above spelling. I believe the word is derived from the animal *Boar*, from the noise, rushing, and impetuosity of the water, Todd gives it " a tide swelling above another tide." Writers vary in their opinions on the causes of this phenomenon. St. Pierre. Ouvres, tom vi., p. 234, Ed. Hamburgh, 1797, describes it not exactly the same in the Seine as in the Parret :—" Cette montagne d'eau est produite par les marèes qui entrent, de la mer dans la Seine, et la font refluer contre son cours. On l'appelle la *Barre*, parce-qu'elle *barre* le cours de la Seine. Cette barre est suivée d'une seconde barre plus elevèe, qui la suit a cent toises de distance. Elles courent beaucoup plus vîte qu'un cheval au galop." He says it is called *Bar*, because it *bars* the current. In the Encyclop. Metropol., art. *Bore*, the editor did not seem more fortunate in his derivation.

Bobbish. *adj.* In health and spirits. [*Pirty bobbish*, pretty well.]

Bonk. *s.* Bank.

Booät. *s.* Boat.

Booäth. *pron.* Both. " *Boo'äth o' ye*; both of you.

Bor'rid. *adj.* A sow is said to be borrid when she wants the male.

Bote. *part.* Bought.

Bow. *s.* A small arched bridge.

Boy's-love. *s.* Southernwood; a species of mugwort; *artemisia abrotonum.*

Brave. *adj.* Well; recovering.

Bran. *s.* A brand; a stump of a tree, or other irregular and large piece of wood, fit only for burning.

Bran-viër. *s.* A fire made with brands.

Bran'dis. *s.* A semicircular implement of iron, made to be suspended over the fire, on which various things may be prepared; it is much used for warming milk.

Brash. *s.* Any sudden development; a crash.

Brick'le,
Brick'ly, } *adj.* Brittle; easily broken.

Brim'mle. *s.* A bramble.

To Bring gwain. *v. a.* [*To bring going.*] To spend; to accompany some distance on a journey.

To Brit. *v. a.* To indent; to make an impression: applied to solid bodies.

Brock. *s.* An irregular piece of peat dried for fuel; a piece of turf. *See* TURF.

Bruck'le,
Bruck'ly, } *adj.* Not coherent; easily separable: applied to solid bodies. "My things are but in a bruckle state." Waverley, v. 2, p. 328, edit. 1821. *See* BRICKLE.

Bruck'leness. *s.* The state of being bruckle.

To Buck. *v. n.* To swell out.

To Bud'dle. *v.* To suffocate in mud.

To Bulge. *v. a.* To indent; to make an irregular impression on a solid body; to bruise. It is also used in a neuter sense.

Bulge. *s.* An indentation; an irregular impression made on some solid body; a swelling outwards or depression inwards.

Bul'len. *adj.* Wanting the bull.

Bul'lins. *s. pl.* Large black sloes; a variety of the wild plum.

Bun'gee. *s.* (g hard), Any thing thick and squat.

Bunt,
Bunting, } *s.* Bolting cloth.

Bunt. *s.* A bolting-mill.

To Bunt. *v. a.* To separate flour from the bran.

Bur'cot. *s.* A load.

Buss. *s.* A half grown calf.

But. *s.* A conical and peculiar kind of basket or trap used in large numbers for catching salmon in the river Parret. The term *but*, would seem to be a generic one, the actual meaning of which I do not know; it implies, however, some containing vessel or utensil. *See* BEE-BUT. *But*, applied to beef, always means *buttock*.

Butter-and-eggs. *s.* A variety of the daffodil.

Bwile. *v.* Boil.

Bwye. *interj.* Bye! adieu. This, as well as *good-bye* and *good-bwye*, is evidently corrupted from *God be with you;* God-be-wi' ye, equivalent to the French *à Dieu*, to God. Bwye, and good-bwye, are, therefore, how vulgar soever they may seem, more analogous than *bye* and *good-bye*.

C.

CALLYVAN'. *s.* A pyramidal trap for catching birds.

Car'riter. *s.* Character.

Câs. Because.

Cass'n, Cass'n't. Canst not: as, *Thee cass'n do it*, thou canst not do it.

Catch corner. A game commonly called elsewhere puss in the corner.

Cat'terpillar. *s.* The cockchafer; *Scarabeus melolontha.*

West of the Parret this insect is called *wock-web*, oak-web, because it infests the *oak*, and spins its web on it in great numbers.

Chaíty. *adj.* Careful; nice; delicate.

To Cham. *v. a.* To chew.

Chámer. *s.* A chamber.

Change. *s.* A shift; the garment worn by females next the skin.

Chay'er. *s.* A chair; chayer—*Chaucer.*

Chick-a-beedy. *s.* A chick.

'Chill. I will.

Chim'ley. *s.* A chimney.

Chine. *s.* The prominence of the staves beyond the head of a cask. This word is well known to coopers throughout England, and ought to be in our dictionaries.

To Chis'som. *v. n.* To bud ; to shoot out.

Chis'som. *s.* a small shoot ; a budding out.

Chit'terlins. *s. pl.* The frills around the bosom of shirt.

Choor. *s.* A job ; any dirty household work ; a troublesome job.

Choor'er,   } *s.* A woman who goes out to do any
Choor'-woman, } kind of odd and dirty work ; hence the term *char-woman* in our polished dialect ; but it ought to be *choor-woman.*

To Choóry. *v.* To do any kind of dirty household work.

Chub'by. *adj.* Full, swelling ; as *chubby-faced.*

Claps. *s.* A clasp.

To claps. *v. a.* To clasp.

Clávy and Clávy-piece. *s.* A mantel-piecce.
 [*Clavy* was probably given to that piece of wood or other material laid over the front of the fire-place, because in many houses the keys are often hung on nails or pins driven into it ; hence from *clavis* (Latin) *a key,* comes *clavy,* the place where the keys are hung.]

Clavy-tack. *s.* The shelf over [tacked on to] the mantel-piece.

Clear-and-sheer. *adv.* Completely ; totally.

Cleve-pink. *s.* A species of Carnation which grows wild in the crannies of Cheddar-cliffs : a variety of the *Dianthus deltoides ;* it has an elegant smell.

To Clim.
To Climmer. } *v. a.* To climb; *to clamber.*

Clin'kers. *s. pl.* Bricks or other earthy matter run into irregular shapes by action of heat.

Clinker-bell. *s.* An icicle.

Clint. *v.a.* To clench; to finish; to fasten firmly.

Cliver-and-Shiver. *adv.* Completely; totally.

Clit. *v. n.* To be imperfectly fermented : applied to bread.

Clit'ty. *adj.* Imperfectly fermented.

Clize. *s.* A place or drain for the discharge of water regulated by a valve or door, which permits a free outlet, but no inlet for return of water.

Coäse. *adj.* Coarse.

Coathe. *v. a.* To bane : applied to sheep.

Cob-wall. *s.* Mud-wall; a wall made of clay mixed with straw.

Cockygee. *s.* Cockagee; a rough sour apple.

Cocklawt. *s.* A garret; cock-loft.

 Originally, most probably, a place where the fowls roosted.

Cock-squailing. *s.* A barbarous game, consisting in tying a cock to a stake, and throwing a stick at him from a distance till he is killed.

Cock-and-Mwile. *s.* A jail.

Col'ley. *s.* A blackbird.

To Collogue. *v. n.* To associate in order to carry out some improper purpose, as *thieves.*

[Two such rascals *collogue* together for mischief. Rob Roy, p. 319, ed. 1821.]

Collo′gin. *s.* (g *hard*). An association for some improper purpose.

(*Johnson* defines it *flattery* ; *wheedling* ; which does not convey the correct meaning.)

Colt-ale. *s.* (Sometimes called *footing* or foot-ale) literally ale given, or money paid for ale, by a person entering on a new employment, to those already in it.

Comforts (comfits.) *s. pl.* Sugared corianders, cinnamon, &c.

Com′ical. *adj.* Odd ; singular.

Contraption. *s.* Contrivance ; management.

Coop. *interj.* Come up ! a word of call to fowls to be fed.

To Cork. *v. a.* Cawk ; calk ; to set on a horse's shoes sharp points of iron to prevent slipping on ice.

To Count. *v. n.* To think ; to esteem.

Cow-baby. *s.* A coward ; a timid person.

To Crap. } *v. n.* to snap ; to break with a sudden
To Crappy. } sound ; to crack.

Crap. *s.* A smart sudden sound.

Craup. *preterite* of creep.

Cre′aped.   Crept.

Creem. *s.* Sudden shivering.

Creémy. *adj.* Affected with sudden shivering.

Creeplin. *part.* Creeping.

Crips. *adj.* Crisp.

Criss-cross-lain. *s.* The alphabet; so called in consequence of its being formerly preceded in the *horn-book* by a ✛ to remind us of the cross of Christ; hence the term *Christ-Cross-line* came at last to mean nothing more than the alphabet.

Crock. *s.* A bellied pot, of iron or other metal, for boiling food.

Croom. *s.* A crumb; a small bit.

Crowd-string. *s.* A fiddle-string.

Crowdy-kit. *s.* A small fiddle.

Crow'ner. *s.* A coroner.

To be Crowned. *v. pass.* To have an inquest held over a dead body by the coroner.

Crowst. *s.* Crust.

Crow'sty. *adj.* Crusty, snappish, surly.

Crub.
Crubbin. } *s.* Food; particularly bread and cheese.

Cubby-hole. *s.* A snug, confined place.

Cuckold *s.* The plant burdock.

To Cull. *v. n.* To take hold round the neck with the arms.

Cute. *adj.* [Acute] sharp; clever.

Cutty. *adj.* Small; diminutive.

Cutty.
Cutty-wren. } *s.* A wren.

D.

Da`. *s.* Day.

Dàyze. Days.

Dade. Dead.

Dad'dick. *s.* Rotten wood.

Dad'dicky. *adj.* Rotten, like daddick.

Dame. *s.* This word is originally French, and means in that language, *lady ;* but in this dialect it means a mistress ; an old woman ; and never a lady ; nor is it applied to persons in the upper ranks of society, nor to the very lowest ; when we say *dame* Hurman, or *dame* Bennet, we mean the wife of some farmer ; a school-mistress is also sometimes called dame (dame-schools).

Dang. *interj.* Generally followed by pronoun, as *dang it ; dang êm ; od dang it :* [an imprecation, a corruption of *God dang it* (*God hang it*) or more likely corruption of *damn*].

Dap, *v. n.* To hop ; to rebound.

Dap. *s.* A hop ; a turn. *To know the daps of a person* is, to know his disposition, his habits, his peculiarities.

Dap'ster. *s.* A proficient.

To Daver. *v. n.* To fade ; to fall down ; to droop.

Dav'ison. *s.* A species of wild plum, superior to the bullin.

Daw'zin. *s.* The passing over land with a bent hazel rod, held in a certain direction, to discover whether veins of metal or springs are below, is called *Dawzin*, which is still practised in the mining districts of Somersetshire. There is an impression among the vulgar, that certain persons only have the gift of the *divining rod*, as it has been sometimes called; by the French, *Baguette Devinatoire*.

Ray, in his *Catalogus Plantarum Angliæ, &c.*, Art. *Corylus*, speaks of the divining rod : "Vulgus metallicorum ad virgulam divinum, ut vocant, quâ venas metallorum inquirit præ cæteris furcam eligit colurnam." More may be seen in John Bauhin.

Des'perd. *adj.* [Corrupted from desperate.] Very, extremely ; used in a good as well as a bad sense : *desperd good*; *desperd bad*.

Dewberry. *s.* A species of blackberry.

Dibs. *s. pl.* Money.

Did'dlecome. *adj.* Half-mad ; sorely vexed.

Dig'ence. *s.* [g hard, *diggunce*, Dickens] a vulgar word for the *Devil*.

Dird. *s,* Thread.

Dirsh, *s.* A thrush.

Dirten. *adj.* Made of dirt.

Dock. *s.* A crupper.

Doe. *part.* Done.

To Doff. *v. a.* To put off.

To Don. *v. a.* To put on.

Donnins. *s. pl.* Dress ; clothes.

Dough-fig. *s.* A fig; so called, most probably, from its feeling like *dough*. JUNIUS has *dotefig* : I know not where he found it. *See* FIG.

To Dout. *v. a.* To extinguish; to put out.

To Downarg. *v. a.* [To *argue* one *down*]; to contradict; to contend with.

Dowst. *s.* Dust; money; *Down wi' tha dowst !* Put down the money !

Dowsty. *adj.* Dusty.

[*Dr* used for *thr* in many words :] as *droo* for *through.*

Draf'fit. *s.* [I suppose from draught-vat.] A vessel to hold pot-liquor and other refuse from the kitchen for pigs.

Drang. *s.* A narrow path.

To Drash. *v. a.* To thresh.

Dras'hel. *s.* The threshold; a flail.

Dras'her. *s.* A thresher.

Drauve. *s.* A drove, or road to fields.

Drawt. *s.* Throat.

To Drean. *v. n.* To drawl in reading or speaking.

Drean. *s.* A drawling in reading or speaking.

Dreaten. *v.* Threaten.

Dree. *a.* Three.

To Dring. *v. n.* To throng; to press, as in a crowd; to thrust.

Dring'et. *s.* A crowd; a throng.

To Droa. *v. a.* To throw.

Droa. Throw.

Drooäte. Throat.

Drob. *v.* Rob.

Drode (*throw'd*). *part.* Threw, thrown.

Droo. *prep.* Through.

To drool. *v. n.* To drivel.

To Drow. $\left\{ \begin{array}{l} v.\ n. \\ v.\ a. \end{array} \right\}$ To dry.

> *The hay do'nt drowy at all.* See the observations which precede this vocabulary.

Drowth. *s.* Dryness; thirst.

Drow'thy. *adj.* Dry; thirsty.

Drove. *s.* A road leading to fields, and sometimes from one village to another. Derived from its being a way along which cattle are driven. RAY uses the word in his *Catalogus Plantarum Angliæ, &c.*, Art. *Chondrilla.*

To Drub. $\left\{ \begin{array}{l} v.\ n. \\ v.\ a \end{array} \right\}$ To throb; to beat.

Drubbin. *s.* A beating.

To Druck. *v. a.* To thrust down; to cram; to press.

Dub, Dub'bed, Dub'by. *adj.* Blunt; not pointed; squat.

Dub'bin. *s.* Suet.

Duck-an-Mallard. *s.* (Duck and Drake) a play of throwing slates or flat stones horizontally along the water so as to skim the surface and rise several times before they sink. "*Hen pen, Duck-an-Mallard, Amen.*"

To Dud'der. *v. a.* To deafen with noise; to render the head confused.

Duds. *s. pl.* Dirty cloaths.

Dum'bledore. *s.* A humble-bee; a stupid fellow.

Dunch, (Dunce?). *adj.* Deaf.

As a deaf person is very often, apparently at least, stupid; a stupid, intractable person is, therefore, called a DUNCE: one who is deaf and intractable. What now becomes of *Duns Scotus*, and all the rest of the recondite observations bestowed upon DUNCE?—*See* GROSE.

I have no doubt that *Dunch* is Anglo-Saxon, although I cannot find it in any of our old dictionaries, except Bailey's. But it ought not to be forgotten, that many words are floating about which are being arrested by our etymologists in the present advancing age of investigation.

Durns. *s. pl.* A door-frame.

Dwon't.
Dwon. } *v.* (Don't) do not.

E.

EAKE. *adv.* Also.

Ear-wrig. *s.* Earwig.

This word ought to be spelled *Earwrig*, as it is derived, doubtless, from wriggle. *See* WRIGGLE.

Eese. *adv.* Yes.

Eet. *adv.* Yet.

El'men. *adj.* Of or belonging to elm; made of elm.

El'ver. *s.* A young eel.

Em'mers. *s. pl.* Embers.

Emmet-batch. *s.* An ant-hill.

To Empt. *v. a.* To empty.

En. *pron.* Him; *a zid en*; he saw him.

Er. *pron.* He. [Used West of the Parret.]

Eth. *s.* Earth.

To Eve. *v. n.* To become damp; to absorb moisture from the air.

Evet. *s.* A lizard.

Ex. *s.* An axle.

F.

Fags! *interj.* Truly; indeed.

Fayer. *s.* and *adj.* Fair.

To Fell. *v. a.* To sew in a particular manner; to inseam.

> This word is well known to the ladies, I believe, all over the kingdom; it ought to be in our dictionaries.

Fes'ter. *s.* An inflammatory tumour.

Few. ⎱ *adj.* More commonly pronounced *veo*. Little;
Veo. ⎰   as a *few broth.*

Fig. *s.* A raisin.

Figged-pudding. *s.* a pudding with raisins in it; plum-pudding.

Fildèfare. *s.* A Fieldfare. "Farewell fieldèfare." *Chaucer.* Meaning that, as fieldfares disappear at a particular season, *the season is over, the bird is flown.*

Fil'try. *s.* Filth; nastiness; rubbish.

Firnd. *v.* To find.

Firnd. *s.* Friend.

Fitch. }
Fitchet. } *s.* A pole-cat. *As cross as a fitchet.*

Fit'ten. }
Vit'ten. } *s.* A feint; a pretence.

Flap-jack. *s.* A fried cake made of batter, apples, &c.; a fritter.

To Flick. *v. a.* To pull out suddenly with some pointed instrument.

Flick-tooth-comb. *s.* A comb with coarse teeth for combing the hair.

Flick. *s.* The membrane loaded with fat, in the bellies of animals: a term used by butchers.

Flook. *s.* An animal found in the liver of sheep, similar in shape to a flook or flounder.

Flush. *adj.* Fledged; able to fly: (applied to young birds.)

Fooäse. *s.* Force. *See* Vooäse.

To Fooäse. *v. a.* To force.

Foo'ter. *s.* [Fr. *foutre*] A scurvy fellow; a term of contempt.

Foo'ty. *adj*. Insignificant ; paltry ; of no account.

For'rel. *s*. the cover of a book.

Forweend'. *adj*. Humoursome ; difficult to please : (applied to children).

Fout. *preterite*. of to fight.

French-nut. *s*. A walnut.

To Frump. *v. a*. To trump up.

To Frunt. *v. a*. To affront.

To Fur. *v. a*. To throw.

Fur'cum. *s*. The bottom : the whole.

Fur'nis. *s*. A large vessel or boiler, used for brewing, and other purposes ; fixed with bricks and mortar, and surrounded with flues, for the circulation of heat, and exit of smoke.

G.

GAERN. *s*. A garden.

Gale. *s*. An old bull castrated.

Gal'libagger. *s*. [From *gally* and *beggar*] A bug-bear.

Gal'lise. *s*. The gallows.

Gallid. *adj*. Frightened.

To Gal'ly. *v. a*. To frighten.

Gallant'ing.　　} *part*. Wandering about in gaiety and
Galligant'ing. } enjoyment : applied chiefly to associa-
tions of the sexes.

Gam'bril. *s*. A crooked piece of wood used by butchers to spread, and by which to suspend the carcase.

Gan'ny-cock. *s.* A turkey-cock.

Ganny-cock's Snob. *s.* The long membranous appendage at the beak, by which the cock-turkey is distinguished.

Gare. *s.* The iron work for wheels, waggons, &c., is called ire-gare; accoutrements.

Gate-shord. *s.* A gate-way; a place for a gate.

Gat'fer. *s.* An old man.

Gaw'cum. *s.* A simpleton; a gawkey.

Gawl-cup. *s.* Gold cup.

To Gee. *v. n.* [g soft] To agree; to go on well together.

To Gee. *v. n.* [g hard; part. and past tense, *gid.*] To give. *Gee* often includes the pronoun, thus, " I'll gee" means I'll give you; the *gee*, and *ye* for *you*, combining into *gee*.

To G'auf. *v. n.* To go off.

To G'auver. *v. n.* To go over.

To G'in. *v. n.* To go in.

To G'on. *v. n.* To go on.

To G'out. *v. n.* To go out.

To G'under. *v. n.* To go under,

To G'up. *v. n.* To go up.

Gib'bol. *s.* [g soft] The sprout of an onion of the second year.

Gid. *pret. v.* Gave.

Gifts. *s. pl.* The white spots frequently seen on the finger nails.

Gig'letin. *adj.* Wanton; trifling; applied to the female sex.

Gil'awfer. *s.* A term applied to all the kinds of flowers termed *stocks*; and also to a few others: as a *Whitsuntide gilawfer*, a species of *Lychnidea*.

Gim'mace. *s.* A hinge.

Gim'maces. *s. pl.* When a criminal is gibbeted, or hung in irons or chains, he is said to be hung in *Gimmaces*, most probably because the apparatus swings about as if on hinges.

Ginnin. *s.* Beginning.

Girnin. *part.* Grinning.

Girt. *adj.* Great.

Gird'l. Contracted from *great deal*; as, gird'l o' work; great deal of work.

To Glare. *v. a.* To glaze earthenware.

Glare. *s.* The glaze of earthenware.

G'lore. *adv.* In plenty.

This word, without the apostrophe, *Glore*, is to be found in Todd's Johnson, and there defined *fat*. The true meaning is, I doubt not, as above; *fat g'lore*, is *fat in plenty*.

Gold. *s.* The shrub called sweet-willow or wild myrtle; *Myrica gale*.

This plant grows only in peat soils; it is abundant in the boggy moors of Somersetshire; it has a powerful and fragrant smell.

Gold-cup. *s.* A species of crow-foot, or ranunculus,

growing plentifully in pastures ; *ranunculus pratensis*.

To Goo. *v.n.* [*Gwain*, going ; *gwon*, gone.] To go.

Gookoo. *s.* Cookoo.

Goo'ner. *interj.* Goodnow !

Good'-Hussey. *s.* A thread-case.

Goose-cap. *s.* A silly person.

Graint'ed. *adj.* Fixed in the grain ; difficult to be removed ; dirty.

Gram'fer. *s.* Grandfather.

Gram'mer. *s.* Grandmother.

To Gree. *v. n.* To agree.

Gribble. *s.* A young apple-tree raised from seed.

To Gripe. *v. a.* To cut into gripes. *See* GRIPE.

Gripe. *s.* [from Dutch, *groep.*] A small drain, or ditch, about a foot deep, and six or eight inches wide.

In English Dictionaries spelled *grip*.

Griping-line. *s.* A line to direct the spade in cutting gripes.

Groan'in. *s.* Parturition ; the time at which a woman is in labour.

Ground. *s.* A field.

Gro'zens. *s. pl.* The green minute round-leaved plants growing upon the surface of water in ditches ; duck's-meat ; the *Lens palustris* of Ray.

Gruff. *s.* A mine.

Gruf'fer. Gruf'fier. *s.* A miner.

To Gud'dle. *v. n.* To drink much and greedily.

Gud'dler. *s.* A greedy drinker; one who is fond of liquor.

To Gulch. *v. n.* To swallow greedily.

Gulch. *s.* A sudden swallowing.

Gump'tion. *s.* Contrivance; common sense.

Gum'py. *adj.* Abounding in protuberances.

Gurds. *s. pl.* Eructations. [By *Fits and gurds.*]

Guss. *s.* A girth.

To Guss. *v. a.* To girth.

Gwain. *part.* Going.

Gwon. *part.* Gone.

H.

HACK. *s.* The place whereon bricks newly made are arranged to dry.

To Hain. *v. a.* To exclude cattle from a field in order that the grass may grow, so that it may be mowed.

Hal'lantide. *s.* All Saints' day.

Ham. *s.* A pasture generally rich, and also unsheltered, applied only to level land.

Hame. *sing.* } *s.* Two moveable pieces of wood or
Hames. *pl.* } iron fastened upon the collar, with suitable appendages for attaching a horse to the shafts. Called sometimes *a pair of hames.*

Han'dy. *adv.* Near, adjoining.

Hang-gallise. *adj.* Deserving the gallows, felonious, vile; as, *a hang-gallise fellow.*

Hange. *s.* The heart, liver, lungs, &c., of a pig, calf, or sheep.

Hang′kicher. *s.* Handkerchief.

Hangles. *s. pl. A pair of hangles* is the iron crook, &c., composed of teeth, and hung over the fire, to be moved up and down at pleasure for the purpose of cookery, &c.

To Happer. *v.n.* To crackle; to make repeated smart noises.

To Haps. *v. a.* To Hasp.

Haps. *s.* A hasp.

Hard. *adj.* Full grown. *Hard people,* adults.

Harm. *s.* Any contagious or epidemic disease not distinguished by a specific name.

Har′ras. *s.* Harvest.

Hart. *s* A haft; a handle.

 Applied to such instruments as knives, awls, etc.

Hathe. *s. To be in a hathe,* is to be set thick and close like the pustules of the small-pox or other eruptive disease; to be matted closely together.

To Have. *v. n.* To behave.

Haw. See *ho.*

Hay-maidens. *s. pl.* Ground ivy.

Hay′ty-tay′ty.) *interj.* What's here!
Highty-tity.) *s.* [*height* and *tite,* weight].

A board or pole, balanced in the middle on some prop, so that two persons, one sitting at each end, may move up and down in turn by striking the ground with the feet. Sometimes called *Tayty* [See-saw].

In Hay'digees. [g soft] *adv.* To be in high spirits; to be frolicsome.

Heät *s.* Pronounced He-at, dissyllable, heat.

Hea'ram-skearam. *adj.* Wild; romantic.

To Heel. *v. a.* To hide; to cover. Chaucer, "*hele.*" Hence, no doubt, the origin of *to heal*, to cure, as applied to wounds; *to cover over.*

Heeler. *s.* One who hides or covers. Hence the very common expression, *The healer is as bad as the stealer;* that is, the receiver is as bad as the thief.

Heft. *s.* Weight.

To Hell. *v. a.* To pour.

Hel'lier. *s.* A person who lays on the tiles of a roof; a tiler. A Devonshire word.

Helm. *s.* Wheat straw prepared for thatching.

To Hen. *v. a.* To throw.

To Hent. *v. n.* To wither; to become slightly dry.

Herd *s.* A keeper of cattle.

Hereawa.
Hereaway. } *adv.* Hereabout.

Herence. *adv.* From this place; hence.

Hereright. *adv.* Directly; in this place.

Het. *pron.* It. *Het o'nt*, it will not.

To Het. *v. a.* To hit, to strike; *part. het* and *hut.*

To Hick. *v.n.* To hop on one leg.

Hick. *s.* A hop on one leg.

 Hick-step and jump. Hop-step and jump. A well known exercise.

To Hike of. *v. n.* To go away; to go off. Used generally in a bad sense.

Hine. *adj.* (Hind) Posterior; relating to the back part. Used only in composition, as, a *hine* quarter.

To Hire tell. *v. n.* To hear tell; to learn by report; to be told.

Hip'pety-hoppety. *adv.* In a limping and hobbling manner.

Hirches. *s.* riches.

Hir'd. *v.* [i long] heard.

To Hirn. *v. n.* [*hirnd*, pret. and part.] To run.

To Hitch. *v. n.* To become entangled or hooked together; to *hitch up*, to hang up or be suspended. *See the next word.*

To Hitch up. *v. a.* To suspend or attach slightly' or temporarily.

 The following will exemplify the active meaning of this verb:

> Sir Strut, for so the witling throng
> Oft called him when at school,
> And *hitch'd* him *up* in many a song
> To sport and ridicule.

Hiz'en. Used for *his* when not followed by a substantive, as, whose house is that ? *Hiz'en.* [His own].

Hi'zy Pi'zy. A corruption of *Nisi Prius.* a well known law assize.

To Ho for, } *v. a.* To provide for ; to take care of ;
To Haw vor, } to desire; to wish for.

Hob'blers. *s. pl.* Men employed in towing vessels by a rope on the land.

Hod. *s.* A sheath or covering ; perhaps from *hood.*

Hog. *s.* A sheep one year old.

To Hoke. *v. a.* To wound with horns ; to gore.

Hod'medod. *adj.* Short ; squat.

Hol'lar. *adj.* Hollow.

To Hol'lar. *v. a.* To halloo.

Hol'lar. *s.* A halloo.

Hol'lardy. *s.* A holiday.

Hol'lardy-day. *s.* Holy-rood day ; the third of May.

Hollabeloo'. *s.* A noise ; confusion ; riot.

Hol'men. *adj.* Made of holm.

Holt. *interj.* Hold ; stop. *Holt-a-blow,* give over fighting

Ho'mescreech. *s.* A bird which builds chiefly in apple-trees ; I believe it is the *Turdus viscivorus,* or missel.

Hon. *s.* hand.

Honey-suck, } *s.* The wodbine.
Honey-suckle, }

Honey-suckle. *s.* Red Clover.

Hoo'say. *See* WHOSAY.

Hoop. *s.* A bullfinch.

Hor'nen. *adj.* Made of horn.

Hornen-book. *s.* Hornbook.

Horse-stinger. *s* The dragon-fly.

Hoss. *s.* horse.

Hoss-plâs *s. pl.* Horse-plays; rough sports.

Houzen. *s. pl.* Houses.

Howsomiver. *adv.* However; howsoever.

Huck'muck. *s.* A strainer placed before the faucet in the mashing-tub.

Hud. *s.* A hull, or husk.

Huf. *s* A hoof.

Huf-cap *s.* A plant, or rather weed, found in fields, and with difficulty eradicated.

I regret that I cannot identify this plant with any known botanical name.

Graced with *huff-cap* terms and thundering threats,
That his poor hearers' hair quite upright sets.

Bp. Hall, Book I, *Sat.* iii.

Some editor of Hall has endeavoured to explain the term huff-cap by *blustering, swaggering.* I think it simply means *difficult.*

Hug. *s.* The itch. *See* SHAB (applied to brutes.)

Hug-water. *s.* Water to cure the hug. *See* SHAB.

To Hul'der. *v. a.* To hide; conceal.

Hul'ly. *s.* A peculiarly shaped long wicker trap used for catching eels.

To Hulve. *v. a.* To turn over ; to turn upside down.

Hum'drum. *s.* A small low three-wheeled cart, drawn usually by one horse : used occasionally in agriculture.

From the peculiarity of its construction, it makes a kind of humming noise when it is drawn along; hence, the origin of the adjective *humdrum*.

Hunt-the-slipper. *s.* A well-known play.

I.

I. *ad.* Yes ; *I, I,* yes, yes : most probably a corrupt pronunciation of *ay.*

Inin. *s.* Onion.

Ire. *s.* Iron.

Ire-gare. *s.* *See* GARE.

Ise. *pron.* I. *See* UTCHY, [West of the Parret].

Ist. [i long]. *s.* East.

Istard. [i long]. *adv.* Eastward.

It. *adv.* Yet, [pronouced both *it* and *eet*]. see N'eet.

J.

Jack-in-the-Lanthorn and Joan-in-the-Wad. } *s.* The meteor usually called a *Will with the Wisp.*

Ignis Fatuus. — Arising from ignition of phosphorus from rotten leaves and decayed vegetable matters.

Jaunders. *s.* The jaundice.

To Jee. *v. n.* To go on well together ; *see* To GEE.

Jif'fey. *s.* A short time : an instant.

Jist. *adv.* Just.

Jitch.
Jitchy. } *adj.* Such.

Jod. *s.* The letter J.

Jorum. *s.* A large jug, bowl, &c., full of something to be eaten or drank.

To Jot. *v. a.* To disturb in writing ; to strike the elbow.

K.

THE sound K is often displaced by substituting *qu*, as for coat, corn, corner, cost ; *quoat* or (*quôt*) *quoin, quiner, quost.*

Keck'er. *s.* The windpipe ; the trachea.

Keep. *s.* A basket, applied only to large baskets.

To Keeve. *v. a.* To put the wort in a keeve for some time to ferment.

Keeve. *s.* A large tub or vessel used in brewing. A mashing-tub is sometimes called a *keeve*.

Kef'fel. *s.* A bad and worn out horse.

To Kern. *v. n.* To turn from blossom to fruit : the process of turning from blossom to fruit is called *kerning.*

Kex. } *s.* The dry stalks of some plants, such as
Kexy. } Cows-parsley and Hemlock, are called Kexies. *As dry as a kexy* is a common simile.

Kill. *s.* A Kiln.

Kil'ter. *s.* Money.

King'bow, or rather, a-kingbow. *adv.* Kimbo.

Chaucer has this word *kenebow*, which is, perhaps, the true one—a *kenebow*, implying a bow with a keen or sharp angle.

"He set his arms in *kenebow.*"
CHAUCER, *Second Merchant's Tale.*

Or place the arms *a-Kingbow*, may be to place them in a consequential manner of commanding, like a king.

Kir'cher. *s.* The midriff; the diaphragm.

Kirsmas. *s.* Christmas.

Kirsen. *v. a.* To Christen.

[These two words are instances of the change of place of certain letters, particularly *r.*]

Kit. *s.* A tribe; a collection; a gang.

Kit'tle.
Kittle-smock. } *s.* A smock frock.

Knack-kneed. *adj.* In-kneed; having the knees so grown that they strike [*knock*] against each other.

Knot'tlins. *s. pl.* The intestines of a pig or calf prepared for food by being tied in knots and afterwards boiled.

L.

LADE-PAIL. *s.* A small pail, with a long handle, used for the purpose of filling other vessels.

Ládeshrides. *s. pl.* The sides of the waggon which project over the wheels. *See* SHRIDE.

Ladies-smock. *s.* A species of bindweed; *Convolvulus sepium.* *See* WITHY-WINE.

Lady Buddick. *s.* A rich and early ripe apple.

Lady-cow. *s.* A lady-bird; the insect *Coccinella Septempunctata.*

Lady's-hole. *s.* A game at cards.

Lai'ter. *s.* The thing laid; the whole quantity of eggs which a hen lays successively.
She has laid out her laiter.

Lamager. *adj.* Lame; crippled; laid up.

Larks-leers. *s. pl.* Arable land not in use; such is much frequented by larks; any land which is poor and bare of grass.

Lart. } *s.* The floor : never applied to a stone floor,
Lawt. } but only to *wooden* floors ; and those up stairs.

Las-charg'eable! *interj.* Be quiet ! *The last chargeable* : that is, he who last strikes or speaks in contention is most blamable.

Lât. *s.* A lath.

Lat'itat. *s.* A noise ; a scolding.

Lat'tin. *s.* Iron plates covered with tin.

Lattin. *adj.* Made of lattin ; as a lattin saucepan, a lattin teakettle, &c.

Laugh-and-lie-down. *s.* A common game at cards.

To Lave. *v. a.* To throw water from one place to another.

To Le'ät. *v. n.* To leak.

Le'ät. *s.* A leak ; a place where water is occasionally let out.

Leath'er. *v. a.* To beat.

Leathern-mouse. *s.* A bat.

Leer. *adj.* Empty.

Leer. *s.* The flank.

Leers. *s. pl.* Leas ; rarely used : but I think it always means stubble land, or land similar to stubble land.

Lent. *s.* Loan ; the use of any thing borrowed.

Lew. *adj.* Sheltered ; defended from storms, or wind

Lew.
Lewth. } *s.* Shelter ; defence from storm or wind.

Lib'et. *s.* A piece ; a tatter.

Lid'den. *s.* A story ; a song.

Lie-lip. *s.* A square wooden vessel having holes in its bottom, to contain wood-ashes for making lie.

Lights. *s. pl.* The lungs.

Lighting-stock. *s.* A horse-block ; steps of wood or stone, made to ascend and descend from a horse.

Lim'bers.
Lim'mers. } *s. pl.* The shafts of a waggon, cart, &c.

Linch. *s.* A ledge ; a rectangular projection ; whence the term *linch-pin* (a pin with a linch), which JOHNSON has, but not *linch*.

The derivations of this word, *linch-pin* by our etymologists, it will be seen, are now inadmissable.

To Line. *v. n.* To lean; to incline towards or against something.

Lin'ny. *s.* An open shed, attached to barns, outhouses, &c.

Lip.   } *s.* A generic term for several containing
Lip'pen. } vessels, as *bee-lippen, lie-lip, seed-lip, &c.,* which see.

Lip'ary. *adj.* Wet, rainy. Applied to the seasons: *a lipary time.*

To Lir'rop. *v. a.* To beat.

    This is said to be a corruption of the sea term, *lee-rope.*

Lis'som. *adj.* Lithe; pliant. Contracted from *light-some,* or *lithe-some.*

List.   }
Lis'tin. } *s.* The strip or border on woollen cloth.

Lis'tin. *adj.* Made of list.

To Lob. *v. n.* To hang down; to droop.

Lock. *s.* A small quantity; as a *lock* of hay, a *lock* of straw.

Lock-a-Daisy. *interj.* of surprise or of pleasure.

Lockyzee. *interj.* Look, behold! *Look you, see!*

To Long. *v. n.* To belong.

Long'ful. *adj.* Long in regard to time.

Lose-Leather. To be galled by riding.

Lowance. *s.* Allowance: portion.

Lug. *s.* A heavy pole; a pole; a long rod.

    I incline to think this is the original of log.

Lug-lain. *s.* Full measure; the measure by the lug or pole.

Lump′er. *v. n.* To lumber; to move heavily; to stumble.

M.

Mace. *s. pl.* Acorns.

Madam. *s.* Applied to the most respectable classes of society: as, Madam Greenwood, Madam Saunders, &c.

Mal′lard. *s.* A male duck.

To Manche. ⎫ *v. a.* To chew. Probably from *manger*,
To Munche. ⎰ French.

Man′der. *s.* A corruption of the word, *manner*, used only in the sense of *sort* or *kind*: as, *all mander o' things*; all sorts of things.

To Mang. *v. a.* To mix.

Mang-hangle. *adj.* Mixed in a wild and confused manner.

To maw. *v. a.* To mow.

Maw′kin. *s.* A cloth, usually wetted and attached to a pole, to sweep clean a baker's oven. *See* Slo-making.

May. *s.* The blossom of the white thorn.

May-be. ⎫
Mâ-be. ⎰ *adv.* Perhaps; it may be.

May-fool. *s.* Same as *April fool.*

May-game. }
Mâ-game. } *s.* A frolic ; a whim.

To Meech. *v. n.* To play truant; to absent from school without leave.

Meech'er. *s.* A truant.

To Mell. *v. a.* To meddle : to touch. *I'll neither mell nor make* : that is, I will have nothing to do with it. *I ont mell o't,* I will not touch it.
" Of eche mattir thei wollin mell."
CHAUCER's *Plowman's Tale.*

Mesh. *s.* Moss ; a species of lichen which grows plentifully on apple trees.

To Mess. }
To Messy. } *v. a.* To serve cattle with hay.

Messin. *s.* The act of serving cattle with hay.

Mid. *v. aux.* Might, may.

To Miff. *v. a.* To give a slight offence ; to displease.

Miff. *s.* A slight offence ; displeasure.

Mig. *s.* *As sweet as mig* is a common simile ; I suspect that *mig* means *mead,* the liquor made from honey.

Milt. *s.* The spleen.

Mi'lemas. Michaelmas.

Min. A low word, implying contempt, addressed to the person to whom we speak, instead of Sir. I'll do it, *min.*

Mine. *v.* Mind; remember.

Mix'en *s.* A dunghill.

Miz'maze. *s.* Confusion.

Mom'macks. *s. pl.* Pieces; fragments.

Mom'met.   }   *s.* A scarecrow; something dressed up
Mom'mick.   }   in clothes to personate a human being.

Moor-coot. *s.* A moor hen.

To Moot. *v. a.* To root up.

Moot. *s.* A stump, or root of a tree.

To More. *v. n.* To root; to become fixed by rooting.

More. *s.* A root.

Mought. *v. aux.* Might.

Mouse-snap. *s.* A mouse trap.

Mug'gets. *s. pl.* The intestines of a calf or sheep.
    Derived, most probably, from *maw* and *guts.*

To Mult. *v.* To melt.

Mus' goo. must go.

'Mus'd. Amused.

N.

MANY words beginning with a vowel, following the article *an*, take the *n* from an; as, *an inch*, pronounced *a ninch.*

Na'atal. *adj.* natural.

Na'atally. *adv.* naturally.

Naìse. *s.* noise.

Nan. *interjec.* Used in reply, in conversation or address, the same as *Sir*, when you do not understand.

Nânt. *s.* Aunt.

Nap. *s.* A small rising; a hillock.

Nâtion. *adv.* Very, extremely : as *nation* good ; *nation* bad.

Nawl. *s.* An awl.

Nawl. *s.* The navel.

Nawl-cut. *s.* A piece cut out at the navel : a term used by butchers.

N'eet. ⎫
N'it. ⎬ *adv.* Not yet.

Nestle Tripe. *s.* The weakest and poorest bird in the nest ; applied, also, to the last-born, and usually the weakest child of a family ; any young, weak, and puny child, or bird

New-qut-and-jerkin. *s.* A game at cards   in a more refined dialect *new-coat and jerkin.*

Nif. *conj.* If.

Nill. *s.* A needle.

Nist. ⎫
Nuost. ⎬ *prep.* Nigh, near.

Niver-tha-near. *adv.* (Never-the-near), To no purpose, uselessly.

Nona'tion. *adj.* Difficult to be understood ; not intelligent ; incoherent, wild.

Nor'ad. *adv.* Northward.

Nora'tion. *s.* Rumour ; clamour.

Nor'ra un. ⎫
Nor'ry un. ⎬ Never a one.

Norn. *pron.* Neither.   *Norn o'm,* neither of them.

Nor'thering. *adj.* Wild, incoherent, foolish.

Nort. *s.* Nothing.   West of the Parret.

Not-sheep. *s.* A sheep without horns.

Not. *s.* The place where flowers are planted is usually called the *flower not*, or rather, perhaps, knot; a flower bed.

Not'tamy. *s.* Corrupted from *anatomy* : it means very often the state of body, *mere skin and bone.*

Nottlins. *s. pl. See* KNOTTLINS.

Num'met. *s.* A short meal between breakfast and dinner; nunchion, luncheon.

Nuncle. *s.* An uncle.

To Nuncle. *v. a.* To cheat.

Nuth'er. *adv.* Neither.

O.

O'. *prep.* for of.

Obstrop'ilous. *adj.* Obstinate, resisting [obstreperous.]

Odments. *s. pl.* Odd things, offals.

Office. *s.* The eaves of a house.

Old-qut-and-jerkin. *s.* A game at cards; in a more refined dialect, *old-coat-and-jerkin*; called also *five cards.*

To Onlight.   *v. n.* To alight; to get off a horse.

O'änt (for w'on't). Will not.   This expression is used in almost all the persons, as *I önt, he önt, we önt, they*, or *thå önt* ; I will not, he will not, etc.

Ont. } Of it. I a done ont; I a done o't : I have done
O't. } of it.

Ool. *v. aux.* Will.

Ope. *s.* An opening—the distance between bodies arranged in order.

Or'chit. *s.* An orchard.

Ornd. *pret.* Ordained, fated.

Orn. *pron.* Either. *Orn o'm,* either of them.

Or'ra one. } Any one ; ever a one.
Or'ry one. }

Ort. *s.* Any thing. [West of the Parret.]

Ort. *s.* Art.

Oten. *adv.* Often.

Ourn. *pron.* Ours.

To Overget. *v. a.* To overtake.

To Overlook. *v. a.* To bewitch.

Overlookt. *part.* Bewitched.

Over-right. } *adv.* Opposite ; fronting.
Auver-right. }

Overs. *s. pl.* The perpendicular edge, usually covered
with grass, on the sides of salt-water rivers is
called *overs.*

P.

Pack-an-Penny-Day. *s.* The last day of a fair when
bargains are usually sold. [*Pack, and sell for
pennies.*]

Parfit. *adj.* Perfect.

Parfitly. *adv.* Perfectly.

To Par'get. *v.a.* To plaster the inside of a chimney with mortar of cowdung and lime.

Par'rick. *s.* A paddock.

To Payze. *v. a.* To force, or raise up, with a lever.

To Peach. *v. a.* To inform against ; to impeach.

Peel. *s.* A pillow, or bolster.

To Peer. *v. n.* To appear.

Pen'nin. *s.* The enclosed place where oxen and other animals are fed and watered ; any temporary place erected to contain cattle.

Pick. *s.* A pitch-fork : a two pronged fork for making hay.

Pigs-Hales. *s. pl.* Haws; the seed of the white thorn.

Pigs-looze. *s.* A pigsty.

Pilch. ⎱
Pilcher. ⎰ *s.* A baby's woollen clout.

Pill-coal. *v.* A kind of peat, dug most commonly out of rivers : peat obtained at a great depth, beneath a stratum of clay.

Pil'ler. *s.* a pillow.

Pilm. *s.* Dust ; or rather fine dust, which readily floats in air.

Pink. *s.* A chaffinch.

Pip. *s.* A seed; applied to those seeds which have the shape of apple, cucumber seed, &c. ; never to round, or minute seeds.

To Pitch. *v. a.* To lay unhewn and unshaped stones together, so as to make a road or way.

To Pitch, in the West of England, is not synonymous with *to pave*. *To pave*, means to lay flat, square, and hewn stones or bricks down, for a floor or other pavement or footway. A *paved* way is always smooth and even; a *pitched* way always rough and irregular. Hence the distinguishing terms of *Pitching* and *Paving*.

Pit'is. *adj.* Piteous; exciting compassion.

Pit'hole. *s.* The grave.

To Pix. } *v. a.* To pick up apples after the main crop
To Pixy. } is taken in; to glean, applied to an orchard only.

Pix'y. *s.* A sort of fairy; an imaginary being.

Pix'y-led. *part.* Led astray by pixies.

Plâd. *v.* Played.

Pla'zen. *s. pl.* Places.

To Plim. *v. n.* To swell; to increase in bulk.

Plough. *s.* The cattle or horses used for ploughing; also a waggon and horses or oxen.

Pock'fredden. *adj.* Marked in the face with small pox.

To Pog. *v. n.* and *v. a.* To thrust with the fist; to push.

Pog. *s.* A thrust with the fist; a push; an obtuse blow.

Pollyantice. *s.* Polyanthus.

To Pom'ster. *v. n.* To tamper with, particularly in curing diseases; to quack.

Pont'ed. *part.* Bruised with indentation.

Any person whose skin or body is puffed up by disease, and subject to occasional pitting by pressure, is said to be *ponted* ; but the primary meaning is applied to fruit, as, a *ponted* apple ; in both meanings incipient decay is implied.

Pook. *s.* The belly ; the stomach ; a vell.

Popple. *s.* A pebble : that is, a stone worn smooth, and more or less round, by the action of the waves of the sea.

Pottle-bellied. *adj.* Potbellied.

To Pooät. ⎱ *v. a.* To push through any confined open-
To Pote. ⎰ ing, or hole.

Pooät-hole. ⎱ *s.* A small hole through which anything
Pote-hole. ⎰ is pushed with a stick ; a confined place.

Pooäty. *adj.* Confined, close, crammed.

Port'mantle. *s.* A portmanteau.

Poti'cary. *s.* An apothecary.

To Poun. *v.* To pound [to put into the pound, to " lock up"].

A Power of rain. A great deal of rain.

Pruv'd. *v.* Proved.

To pray. *v. a.* To drive all the cattle into one herd in a moor ; *to pray the moor,* to search for lost cattle.

Prankin. *s.* Pranks.

Pud. *s.* The hand ; the fist.

Pulk. ⎱ *s.* A small shallow-place, containing water.
Pulker. ⎰

Pull-reed. *s.* [Pool reed.] A long reed growing in ditches and pools, used for ceiling instead of laths.

Pul try. . Poultry.

Pum'ple. *adj.* Applied only, as far as I know, in the compound word *pumple-voot*, a club-foot.

Put. *s.* A two-wheeled cart used in husbandry, and so constructed as to be turned up at the axle to discharge the load.

Pux'ie. *s.* A place on which you cannot tread without danger of sinking into it ; applied most commonly to places in roads or fields where springs break out.

Pwint. *s.* Point.

Pwine-end. ⎫ The sharp-pointed end of a house, where
Pwinin-end. ⎬ the wall rises perpendicularly from the foundation.

Py'e *s.* A wooden guide, or rail to hold by, in passing over a narrow wooden bridge.

Q.

Qu is in many words used instead of K.

Quare. *adj.* Queer ; odd.

Quar'rel. *s.* [*Quarré*, French.] A square of window glass.

To Quar. *v. a.* To raise stones from a quarry.

Quar-man. *s.* A man who works in a quarry [*quar*].

Quine. *s.* Coin, money. A corner.

To Quine. *v. a.* To coin.

Quoin. Coin.

Quoit. Coit.
Qût (Quut). *s.* Coat.

R.

R in many words is wholly omitted, as, *Arth. Coäse, Guth, He'äth, Pason, Vooäth,. Wuss,* &c., for Earth, Coarse, Girth, Hearth, Parson, Forth, Worse.

To RAKE UP. *v. a.* To cover; to bury. To rake the vier. To cover up the fire with ashes, that it may remain burning all night.

Rames. *s. pl.* The dead stalks of potatoes, cucumbers, and such plants; a skeleton.

Rams-claws. *s. pl.* The plant called gold cups; *ranunculus pratensis*.

Ram'shackle. *adj.* Loose; disjointed.

Ram'pin. *part.* Distracted, obstreperous : *rampin mad,* outrageously mad.

Ran'dy. ⎫
Ran'din. ⎬ *s.* A merry-making; riotous living.

Range. *s.* A sieve.

To Rangle. *v. n.* To twine, or move in an irregular or sinuous manner. *Rangling plants* are plants which entwine round other plants, as the woodbine, hops, etc.

Ran'gle. *s.* A sinuous winding.

Ras'ty. *adj.* Rancid : gross; obscene.

Rathe-ripe. *adj.* Ripening early. [*Rath. English Dictionary.*

"The rathe-ripe wits prevent their own perfection."
BP. HALL..

Raught. *part.* Reached.

Rawd. *part.* Rode.

To Rawn. *v. a.* To devour greedily.

Raw'ny. *adj.* Having little flesh: a thin person, whose bones are conspicuous, is said to be rawny.

To Ray. *v. a.* To dress.

To Read. *v. a.* To strip the fat from the intestines; *to read the inward.*

Read'ship. *s.* Confidence, trust, truth.

To Ream. *v. a.* To widen; to open.

Reamer. *s.* An instrument used to make a hole larger.

Re'balling. *s.* The catching of eels with earthworms attached to a ball of lead, hung by a string from a pole.

Reed. *s.* Wheat straw prepared for thatching.

Reen.
Rhine. } *s.* A water-course; an open drain.

To Reeve. *v. a.* To rivel; to draw into wrinkles.

Rem'let. *s.* A remnant.

Rev'el. *s.* A wake.

To Rig. *v. n.* To climb about; to get up and down a thing in wantonness or sport.

Hence the substantive *rig*, as used in *John Gilpin*, by Cowper.

"He little dreamt of running such a *rig.*"

To Rig. *v. a.* To dress.

Hence, I suspect, the origin of the *rigging* of a vessel.

Righting-lawn. Adjusting the ridges after the wheat is sown.

Rip. *s.* A vulgar, old, unchaste woman.

Hence, most probably, the origin of *Demirip*.

Robin-Riddick. *s.* A redbreast. [Also *Rabbin Hirddick*; the *r* and *i* transposed.]

Rode. *s. To go to rode*, means, late at night or early in the morning, to go out to shoot wild fowl which pass over head on the wing.

To Rose. *v n.* To drop out from the pod, or other seed vessel, when the seeds are over-ripe.

To Rough. *v. a.* To roughen ; to make rough.

Round-dock. *s.* The common mallow; *malva sylvestris.*

Called round-dock from the *roundness* of its leaves. CHAUCER has the following expression which has a good deal puzzled the glossarists :

" But canst thou playin raket to and fro,

" *Nettle in, Docke out*, now this, now that, Pandare ?"
Troilus and Cressida, Book IV.

The round-dock leaves are used at this day as a supposed remedy or charm for the sting of a nettle, by being rubbed on the stung part, with the following words :—

In dock, out nettle,
Nettle have a sting'd me.

That is, *Go in dock, go out nettle.* Now, to play *Nettle in Docke out,* is to make use of such expedients as shall drive away or remove some previous evil, similar to that of driving out the venom of the nettle by the juice or charm of the dock.

Roz'im. $\begin{cases} s. \text{ A quaint saying; a low proverb.} \\ s. \text{ Rosin.} \end{cases}$

Rud'derish. *adj.* Hasty, rude, without care.

Ruf. *s.* A roof.

Rum. *s.* Room; space.

Rum'pus. *s.* A great noise.

   This word ought to be in our English Dictionaries.

Rungs. *s. pl.* The round steps of a ladder.

S.

THE sound of S is very often converted into the sound of Z. Thus many of the following words, *Sand-tot, Sar, Seed-lip, Silker, Sim, &c.*, are often pronounced *Zand-tot, Zar, Zeeäd-lip, Zilker, Zim, &c.*

Sâ'cer-eyes. Very large and prominent eyes. [Saucer eyes.

Sand-tot. *s.* A sandhill.

To Sar. *v. a.* To serve—Toearn; as, *I can sar but zixpence* a day.

Sar'ment. *s.* A sermon.

Sar'rant. *s.* A servant.

Sar'tin. *adj.* Certain.

Sar'tinly. *adv.* Certainly.

Scad. *s.* A short shower.

Schol'ard. *s.* A scholar.

Scissis-sheer. *s.* A scissors-sheath.

Scollop. *s.* An indentation; notch; collop.

To Scollop. *v. a.* To indent; to notch.

Scoose wi'. *Discourse* or talk with you.

To Scot'tle. *v. a.* To cut into pieces in a wasteful manner.

Scrawf. *s.* Refuse.

Scrawv'lin. *adj.* Poor and mean, like scrawf.

Screed. *s.* A shred.

To Scrunch. *v. a.* and *v. n.* The act of crushing and bringing closer together is implied, accompanied with some kind of noise. A person may be said to scrunch an apple or a biscuit, if in eating it he made a noise; so a pig in eating acorns. Mr. SOUTHEY has used the word in *Thalaba* without the *s.*

"No sound but the wild, wild wind,
"And the snow *crunching* under his feet."

And, again, in the *Anthology*, vol 2, p. 240.

"Grunting as they *crunch'd* the mast."

Scud. *s.* A scab.

Sea-Bottle. *s.* Many of the species of the sea-wrack, or *fucus*, are called *sea-bottles*, in consequence of the stalks having round or oval vesicles or pods in them; the pod itself.

Sea-crow. *s.* A cormorant.

Seed-lip. *s.* A vessel of a particular construction, in which the sower carries the seed.

Sel'times. *adv.* Not often; seldom.

Shab. *s.* The itch; the hug. Applied to brutes only.

Shab-water. *s.* A water prepared with tobacco, and some mercurial, to cure the shab.

Shabby. *adv.* Affected with the shab. Hence the origin of the common word *shabby*, mean, paltry.

Shackle. *s.* A twisted band.

Shal'der. *s.* A kind of broad flat rush, growing in ditches.

Sharp. *s.* A shaft of a waggon, &c.

Shatt'n. Shalt not.

Sheer. *s.* A sheath.

Shil'lith. *s.* A shilling's worth.

Shine. *s.* Every *shine o'm*, is, every one of them.

To Shod. *v. a.* To shed : to spill.

Sholl. *v.* Shall.

Shord. *s.* A sherd ; a gap in a hedge. A *stop-shord*, a stop-gap.

hower. *adj.* Sure.

Showl. s. A shovel.

To Showl. *v. a.* To shovel.

To Shride. } *v. a.* To cut off wood from the sides of
To Shroud. } trees ; or from trees generally.

Shride. } *s.* Wood cut off from growing trees. It
Shroud. } sometimes means a pole so cut ; *ladeshrides* —shrides placed for holding the load. *See* LADE-SHRIDES.

To Shug. *v. a.* To shrug ; to scratch ; to rub against.

Shut'tle. *adj.* Slippery, sliding : applied only to solid bodies.

From this word is derived the *shuttle* (*s.*) of the weaver.

Sig. *s.* Urine.

Sil'ker. *s.* A court-card.

To Sim. *v. n.* To seem, to appear. This verb is used personally, as, *I sim, you sim,* for *it seems to me,* etc.

Sim-like-it. *interj.* (Seems like it.) Ironically, for *very improbable.*

Sine. *conj.* [Probably from *seeing* or *seen.*] Since, because.

Single-guss. *s.* The plant orchis.

Single-stick. *s.* A game; sometimes called *backsword.*

Sizes. *s. pl.* The assizes.

To Skag. To give an accidental blow, so as to tear the clothes or the flesh; to wound slightly.

Skag. *s.* An accidental blow, as of the heel of the shoe, so as to tear the clothes or the flesh; any slight wound or rent.

To Skeer. *v. a.* To mow lightly over: applied to pastures which have been summer-eaten, never to meadows. In a neuter sense, to move along quickly, and slightly touching. Hence, from its mode of flight,

Skeer-devil. *s.* The black martin, or Swift.

Skeer'ings. *s. pl.* Hay made from pasture land.

Skent'in. *adj.* When cattle, although well fed, do not become fat, they are called skentin.

Skenter. *s.* An animal which will not fatten.

To Skew.
To Skiv'er. } *v. a.* To skewer.

Skiff-handed. *adj.* Left-handed, awkward.

Skills.
Skittles. } *s. pl.* The play called nine-pins.

Skim'merton. *s.* To ride Skimmerton, is an exhibition
of riding by two persons on a horse, back to back;
or of several persons in a cart, having *skimmers*
and *ladles*, with which they carry on a sort of
warfare or gambols, designed to ridicule some one
who, unfortunately, possesses an unfaithful wife.
This *may-game* is played upon some other occasion
besides the one here mentioned: it occurs, however, very rarely, and will soon, I apprehend, be
quite obsolete. *See* SKIMMINGTON, in *Johnson.*

Skiv'er. *s.* A skewer.

To Skram. *v. a.* To benumb with cold.

Skram. *adj.* Awkward: stiff, as if benumbed.

> "With hondis al *forskramyd.*"
> CHAUCER, *Second Merchant's Tale.*

Skram-handed. *adj.* Having the fingers or joints of the
hand in such a state that it can with difficulty be
used; an imperfect hand.

To Skrent. *v. a.* [An irregular verb.] To burn, to
scorch.
Part. *Skrent.* Scorched.

Skum'mer. *s.* A foulness made with a dirty liquid, or with soft dirt.

To Skum'mer. *v.a.* To foul with a dirty liquid, or to daub with soft dirt.

Slait. *s.* An accustomed run for sheep; hence the place to which a person is accustomed, is called slait.

To Slait. *v. a.* To accustom.

To Slait. *v. a.* To make quick-lime in a fit state for use, by throwing water on it; to slack.

To Slat. *v. a.* To split; to crack; to cleave.

To Sleeze. *v. n.* To separate; to come apart; applied to cloth, when the warp and woof readily separate from each other.

Sleezy. *adj.* Disposed to sleeze; badly woven.

Slen. *adj.* Slope.

'Slike. It is like.

Slipper-slopper. *adj.* Having shoes or slippers down at the heel; loose.

To Slitter. *v.n.* To slide.

To Slock. *v. a.* To obtain clandestinely.

To Slock'ster. *v. a.* To waste.

Slom'aking. *adj.* Untidy; slatternly (applied to females.)

This word is, probably, derived from *slow* and *mawkin.*

Slop'per. *adj.* Loose; not fixed : applied only to solid bodies.

To Slot'ter. *v.n* To dirty ; to spill.

Slot'tering. *adj.* Filthy, wasteful.

Slot'ter. *s.* Any liquid thrown about, or accidentally spilled on a table, or the ground.

Slug'gardy-guise. *s.* The habit of a sluggard.

> *Sluggardy-guise ;*
> *Loth to go to bed,*
> *And loth to rise.*

WYAT says—" Arise, for shame ; do away your *sluggardy.*"

Sluck'-a-bed.
Sluck'-a-trice. } *s.* A slug-a-bed ; a sluggard.
Slock'-a-trice.

Smash. *s.* A blow or fall, by which any thing is broken. *All to smash,* all to pieces.

Smeech. *s.* Fine dust raised in the air.

To Smoor. *v. a.* To smooth ; to pat.

Snags. *s.* Small sloes : *prunus spinosa.*

Snag.
Snagn. } *s.* A tooth.

Snaggle'tooth. *s.* A tooth growing irregularly.

Snarl. *s.* A tangle ; a quarrel. There is also the verb *to snarl,* to entangle.

Sneäd. *s.* The crooked handle of a mowing scythe.

Snip'py. *adj.* Mean, parsimonious.

Snock. *s.* A knock ; a smart blow.

Snowl. *s.* The head.

Soce. *s. pl.* Vocative case. Friends ! Companions ! Most probably derived from the Latin *socius.*

To Soss. *v. a.* To throw a liquid from one vessel to another.

Sour-dock. *s.* Sorrel : *rumex acetosa.*

Souse. *s. pl. Sousen.* The ears. *Pigs sousen,* pig's ears.

Spar. *s.* The pointed sticks, doubled and twisted in the middle, and used for fixing the thatch of a roof, are called *spars :* they are commonly made of split willow rods.

Spar'kid. *adj.* Speckled.

Spar'ticles. *s. pl.* Spectacles : glasses to assist the sight.

Spawl. *s.* A chip from a stone.

Spill. *s.* A stalk ; particularly that which is long and straight. *To run to spill,* is to run to seed ; it sometimes also means to be unproductive.

Spill. *s. See* WORRA.

To Spit. *v. a.* To dig with a spade ; to cut up with a spitter. *See* the next word.

Spitter. *s.* A small tool with a long handle, used for cutting up weeds, thistles, &c.

To Spit'tle. *v. a.* To move the earth lightly with a spade or spitter.

Spit'tle. *adj.* Spiteful ; disposed to spit in anger.

To Spring. *v. a.* To moisten ; to sprinkle.

To Spry. *v. n.* To become chapped by cold.

Spry. *adj.* Nimble ; active.

To Squail. *v. a.* To fling a stick at a cock, or other bird. *See* COCK-SQUAILLING.

To Squitter. *v. n.* To Squirt.

To Squot. *v. n.* To bruise; to compress. *v. n.* To squat.

Squot. *s.* A bruise, by some blow or compression; a squeeze.

Stad'dle. *s.* The wooden frame, or logs, &c., with stone or other support on which ricks of corn are usually placed.

Stake-Hang. *s.* Sometimes called only a *hang.* A kind of circular hedge, made of stakes, forced into the sea-shore, and standing about 6 feet above it, for the purpose of catching salmon, and other fish.

Stang. *s.* A long pole.

Stay'ers. *s. pl.* Stairs.

Steän. *s.* A large jar made of stone ware.

Steänin. *s.* A ford made with stones at the bottom of a river.

Steeple. *s.* Invariably means a spire.

Steert. *s.* A point.

Stem. *s.* A long round shaft, used as a handle for various tools.

Stick'le. *adj. Steep,* applied to hills; *rapid,* applied to water: a *stickle* path, is a steep path; a *stickle* stream, a rapid stream.

Stick'ler. *s.* A person who presides at backsword or singlestick, to regulate the game; an umpire: a person who settles disputes.

Stitch. *s.* Ten sheaves of corn set up on end in the field after it is cut ; a shock of corn.

To Stive. *v. a.* To close and warm.

To Stiv′er. *v. n.* To stand up in a wild manner like hair ; to tremble.

Stodge. *s.* Any very thick liquid mixture.

Stonen.
Stwonen. } *adj.* Made of stone ; consisting of stone.

Stom′achy. *adj.* Obstinate, proud ; haughty.

Stook. *s.* A sort of stile beneath which water is discharged.

To Stoor. *v. a.* and *v. n.* To stir.

Stout. *s.* A gnat.

Strad. *s.* A piece of leather tied round the leg to defend it from thorns, &c. A *pair* of strads, is two such pieces of leather.

Stritch. A strickle : a piece of wood used for striking off the surplus from a corn measure.

To Strout. *v. n.* To strut.

Strouter. *s.* Any thing which projects ; a strutter.

To Stud. *v. n.* To study.

Su′ent. *adj.* Even, smooth, plain.

Su′ently. *adj.* Evenly, smoothly, plainly.

To Sulsh. *v. a.* To soil ; to dirty.

Sulsh. *s.* A spot ; a stain.

Sum. *s.* A question in arithmetic.

Sum′min. *s.* (Summing) Arithmetic.

To Sum'my. *v. n.* To work by arithmetical rules.

Summer-voy. *s.* The yellow freckles in the face.

To Suf'fy. } *v. n.* To inspire deeply and quickly. Such
To Zuffy. } an action occurs more particularly upon immersing the body in cold water.

Suth'ard. *adv.* Southward.

To Swan'kum. *v. n.* To walk to and fro in an idle and careless manner.

To Swell. } *v. a.* To swallow.
To Zwell. }

To Sweetort. *v. a.* To court; to woo.

Sweetortin. *s.* Courtship.

T.

TACK. *s.* A shelf.

Tac'ker. *s.* The waxed thread used by shoemakers.

Ta'ëty. *s.* A potato.

Taf'fety. *adj.* Dainty, nice: used chiefly in regard to food.

Tal'let. *s.* The upper room next the roof; used chiefly of out-houses, as a hay-*tallet*.

Tan. *adv.* Then, *now an Tan;* now and then.

To Tang. *v. a.* To tie.

Tap and Cannel. *s.* A spigot and faucet.

Tay'ty. *s. See* A hayty-tayty.

Tees'ty-totsy. *s.* The blossoms of cowslips, tied into a ball and tossed to and fro for an amusement called *teesty-tosty.* It is sometimes called simply a *tosty.*

Tee'ry. *adj.* Faint weak.

Tem'tious. *adj.* Tempting; inviting. [Used also in Wiltshire].

Thâ. *pron.* They.

Than. *adv.* Then.

Thauf. *conj.* Though, although.

Theäze. *pron.* This.

Theeäzam.
Theeäzamy. } *pron.* These.

Them.
Them'my. } *pron.* Those.

The'rence. *adv.* From that place.

Thereawâ.
Thereaway. } *adv.* Thereabout.

Therevor-i-sayt! *interj.* Therefore I say it!

Thic. *pron.* That. (Thilk, *Chaucer.*) [West of the Parret, *thecky.*]

Tho. *adv.* Then.

Thornen. *adj.* Made of thorn; having the quality or nature of thorn.

Thorough. *prep.* Through.

Thread the Needle.
Dird the Needle. } *s.* A play.

"Throwing batches," cutting up and destroying ant-hills.

Tiff. *s.* A small draught of liquor.

To tile. *v. a.* To set a thing in such a situation that it may easily fall.

Til'ty. *adj.* Testy, soon offended.

Tim'mer. *s.* Timber; wood.

Tim'mern. *adj.* Wooden; as a timmern bowl; a wooden bowl.

Tim'mersom. *adj.* Fearful; needlessly uneasy.

To Tine. *v. a.* To shut, to close; as, *tine the door;* shut the door. To inclose; to *tine in the moor,* is to divide it into several allotments. To light, to kindle; as, to *tine the candle,* is to light the candle.

QUARLES uses this verb:

"What is my soul the better to be *tin'd*
" With holy fire ?"

Emblem XII.

To Tip. *v. a.* To turn or raise on one side.

Tip. *s.* A draught of liquor. Hence the word *tipple,* because the cup must be *tipped* when you drink.

To Tite. *v. a.* To weigh.

Tite. *s.* Weight. *The tite of a pin,* the weight of a pin.

Todo'. *s.* A bustle; a confusion.

To Toll. *v. a.* To entice; to allure.

Toor. *s.* The toe.

Tosty. *s. See* TEESTY-TOSTY.

Tote. *s.* The whole. This word is commonly used for intensity, as the *whol tote,* from *totus,* Latin.

To Tot'tle. *v. n.* To walk in a tottering manner, like a child.

Touse. *s.* A blow on some part of the head.

Towards. *prep.* is, in Somersetshire, invariably pronounced as a dissyllable, with the accent on the last : *to-ward's.* Our polite pronunciation, *tordz,* is clearly a corruption.

Tramp. *s.* A walk ; a journey.

   To Tramp. v. n. and *Tramper. s.* will be found in *Johnson*, where also this word ought to be.

To Trapes. *v. n.* To go to and fro in the dirt.

Trapes. *s.* A slattern.

Trim. *v. a.* To beat.

Trub'agully. *s.* A short dirty, ragged fellow, accustomed to perform the most menial offices.

To Truckle. *v. a.* and *v. n.* To roll.

Truckle. *s.* A globular or circular piece of wood or iron, placed under another body, in order to move it readily from place. A *Truckle-bed,* is a small bed placed upon truckles, so that it may be readily moved about.

   These are the primary and the common meanings in the West, of To *truckle, v. Truckle, s.* and *Truckle-bed.*

Tun. *s.* A chimney.

Tun'negar. *s.* A Funnel.

Turf. *s. pl.* Turves. Peat cut into pieces and dried for fuel.

Tur'mit. *s.* A turnip.

Tur'ney. *s.* An attorney.

Turn-string. *s.* A string made of twisted gut, much used in spinning. *See* WORRA.

To Tus'sle. *v. n.* To struggle with ; to contend.

Tut. *s.* A hassock.

Tut-work. *s.* Work done by the piece or contract ; not work by the day.

Tuth'er. *pron.* The other.

Tuth'eram.
Tuth'ermy. } *pron.* The others.

Tut'ty. *s.* A flower ; a nosegay.

'Tword'n. It was not.

To Twick. *v. a.* To twist or jerk suddenly.

Twick. *s.* A sudden twist or jerk.

Twi'ly. *adj.* Restless ; wearisome.

Twi'ripe. *adj.* Imperfectly ripe.

U.

Unk'et. *adj.* Dreary, dismal, lonely.

To Unray'. *v. a.* To undress.

To Untang'. *v. a.* To untie.

To Up. *v. a.* To arise.

Up'pin-stock. *s.* A horse-block. *See* LIGHTING-STOCK.

Upsi'des. *adv.* On an equal or superior footing. *To be upsides* with a person, is to do something which shall be equivalent to, or of greater importance or value than what has been done by such person to us.

Utch'y. *pron.* I. This word is not used in the Western or Eastern, but only in the Southern parts of the County of Somerset. It is, manifestly, a corrupt pronunciation of *Ich,* or *Ichè,* pronounced as two syllables., the Anglo-Saxon word for I. *What shall utchy do ?* What shall I do.

I think Chaucer sometimes uses *iche* as a dissyllable ; *vide* his Poems *passim.* *Ch'am,* is I am, that is, *ich am ;* *ch'ill,* is I will, *ich will.* See Shakespeare's King Lear, Act IV., Scene IV. What is very remarkable, and which confirms me greatly in the opinion which I here state, upon examining the first folio edition of Shakespeare, at the London Institution, I find that *ch* is printed, in one instance, with a mark of elision before it thus, *'ch,* a proof that the *i* in *iche* was sometimes dropped in a common and rapid pronunciation. In short, this mark of elision ought always so to have been printed, which would, most probably, have prevented the conjectures which have been hazarded upon the origin of the mean- of such words *chudd, chill,* and *cham.* It is singular enough that Shakespeare has the *ch* for *iche* I, and *Ise for I,* within the distance of a few lines in the passage above alluded to, in King Lear. But, perhaps, not more singular than that in Somersetshire may, at the present time, be heard for the pronoun I, *Utchy,* or *iché,* and *Ise.* In the Western parts of Somersetshire, as well as in Devonshire, *Ise* is now used very generally for I.

The Germans of the present day pronounce, I understand, their *ich* sometimes as it is pronounced in the West, *Ise*, which is the sound we give to frozen water, *ice*. See MISS HAM's letter, towards the conclusion of this work.

V.

[The V is often substituted for f, as *vor*, for, *veo*, few, &c.

Vage. ⎱ *s.* A voyage; but more commonly applied to
Vaze. ⎰ the distance employed to increase the intensity of motion or action from a given point.

To Vang. *v. a.* To receive; to earn.

Varden. *s.* Farthing.

Vare, *s.* A species of weasel.

To Vare. *v. n.* To bring forth young: applied to pigs and some other animals.

Var'mint. *s.* A vermin.

Vaught. *part.* Fetched.

> *Vur vaught,*
> *And dear a-bought.*

(*i. e.*) Far-fetched, and dear bought.

Vawth. *s.* A bank of dung or earth prepared for manure.

To Vay. *v. n.* To succeed; to turn out well; to go. This word is, most probably, derived from *vais*, part of the French verb *aller*, to go.

It don't vay; it does not go on well.

To **Vaze.** *v. n.* To move about a room, or a house, so as to agitate the air.

Veel'vare. *s.* A fieldfare.

Veel. *s.* A field; corn land unenclosed.

To **Veel.** *v.* To feel.

Veel'd. *part.* Felt.

Vell. *s.* The salted stomach of a calf used for making cheese; a membrane.

Veö. *adj.* Few, little.

Ver'di.
Ver'dit. } *s.* Opinion.

To **Ves'sy.** *v. n.* When two or more persons read verses alternately, they are said to *vessy.*

Ves'ter. *s.* A pin or wire to point out the letters to children to read; a fescue.

Viër. *s.* Fire. Some of our old writers make this word of two syllables : " *Fy-er.*"

Vin'e. *v.* Find.

Vine. *adj.* Fine.

Vin'ned. *adj.* Mouldy; humoursome; affected.

Vist.
Vice. } *s.* [*i* long.] The Fist.

Vitious. *adj.* Spiteful; revengeful.

Vitten. *s. See* FITTEN.

Vit'ty. *adv.* Properly, aptly.

Vlare. *v. n.* To burn wildly; to flare.

Vleër. *s.* A flea.

Vlan'nin. *s.* Flannel.

Vleng'd. *part.* Flung.

Vloth'er. *s.* Incoherent talk ; nonsense.

Voc'ating. *part.* Going about from place to place in an idle manner. From *voco*, Latin. The verb to *voc'ate*, to go about from place to place in an idle manner, is also occasionally used.

Voke. *s.* Folk.

To Vol'ly. *v. a.* To follow.

Vol'lier. *s.* Something which follows ; a follower.

Vooäth. *adv.* Forth ; out. *To goo vooäth*, is to go out.

To Vooäse. *v. a.* To force.

Vorad. *adv. adj.* Forward.

Vor'n. *pron.* For him.

Voreright. *adj.* Blunt ; candidly rude.

Voun. Found.

Vouse. *adj.* Strong, nervous, forward.

Vroäst. *s.* Frost.

To Vug. *v. a.* To strike with the elbow.

Vug. *s.* A thrust or blow with the elbow.

Vur. *adv.* Far.

Vur'der. *adv.* Farther.

Vurdest. *adv.* Farthest.

Vur'vooäth. *adv.* Far-forth.

Vust. *adj.* First.

W.

To Wal'lup. *v. a.* To beat.

Walnut. *s.* The *double* large walnut. The ordinary walnuts are called *French nuts.*

To Wam'mel. } *v. n.* To move to and fro in an irregu-
To Wamble. } lar and awkward manner; to move out of a regular course or motion.

Applied chiefly to mechanical operations.

War. *interj.* Beware! take care! *War-whing !* Take care of yourself.

War. *v.* This is used for the preterite of the verb *to be,* in almost all the persons, as *1 war, he war, we war,* &c.

To Ward. *v. n.* To wade.

To Warnt. } *v. a.* To warrant.
To Warnd. }

Wash-dish. *s.* The bird called wagtail.

To Way-zalt. *v. n.* [To weigh salt.] To play at the game of wayzaltin. *See the next article.*

Way-zaltin. *s.* A game, or exercise, in which two persons stand back to back, with their arms interlaced, and lift each other up alternately.

Weepy. *adj.* Abounding with springs ; moist.

Well-apaid. *adj.* Appeased; satisfied.

Well-at-ease. } *adj.* Hearty, healthy.
Well-at-eased. }

Wetshod. *adj.* Wet in the feet.

Wev'et. *s.* A spider's web.

To Whack. *v. a.* To beat with violence.

Whack. *s.* A loud blow.

Whatsomiver. *pron.* Whatsoever.

Whaur. *adv.* Where.

To Whec'ker. *v. n.* To laugh in a low vulgar manner; to neigh.

Where. *adv.* Whether.

Wherewi'. *s.* Property, estate; money.

Whim. *s.* Home.

Whing. *s.* Wing.

Whipper-snapper. *adj.* Active, nimble, sharp.

Whipswhile. *s.* A short time; the time between the strokes of a whip.

Whir'ra. *See* WORRA.

Whister-twister. *s.* A smart blow on the side of the head.

To Whiv'er. *v. n.* To hover.

Whiz'bird. *s.* A term of reproach.

To Whop. *v. a.* To strike with heavy blows.

Whop. *s.* A heavy blow.

Who'say, or Hoosay. *s.* A wandering report; an observation of no weight.

Whot. *adj.* Hot.

Whun. *adv.* When.

Wi'. With ye.

Wid'ver. *s.* A widower.

Willy. *s.* A term applied to baskets of various sizes, but generally to those holding about a bushel. So called from their being made commonly of *willow*: sometimes called also *willy-basket*.

To Wim. *v. a.* To winnow.

Wim-sheet. } *s.* A sheet upon which corn is
Wimmin-sheet. } winnowed.

Wimmin-dust. *s.* Chaff.

Win'dor. *s.* A window.

Wine. *s.* Wind.

With'er. *pron.* Other.

With'erguess. *adj.* Different.

With'y-wine. *s.* The plant bindweed: *convolvulus.*

Witt. *adj.* Fit.

With'erwise. *adj.* Otherwise.

Wock. *s.* Oak.

Wocks. *s. pl.* The cards called *clubs;* most probably
from having the shape of an oak leaf : *oaks.*

Wont. *s.* A Mole.

Wont-heave. *s.* A mole-hill.

Wont-snap. *s.* A mole-trap.

Wont-wriggle. *s.* The sinuous path made by moles
under ground.

Wood-quist. *s.* A wood-pigeon.

Wordle. *s.* World.   [Transposition of *l* and *d.*]

Wor'ra. *s.* A small round moveable nut or pinion,
with grooves in it, and having a hole in its
centre, through which the end of a round stick or
spill may be thrust. The *spill and worra* are
attached to the common spinning-wheel, which,
with those and the *turn-string,* form the apparatus
for spinning wool, &c.   Most probably this word,
as well as whir'on, is used for *whir,* to turn round
rapidly with a noise.

Wrassly. Wrestle.

To Wride. *v. n.* To spread abroad ; to expand.

Wriggle. *s.* Any narrow, sinuous hole.

Wrine. *s.* A mark occasioned by wringing cloth, or by folding it in an irregular manner.

Wring. *s.* A Press. A *cyder-wring*, a cyder-press.

To Wrumple. *v. a.* To discompose : to rumple.

Wrumple. *s.* A rumple.

Wust. *adj.* Worst.

Y.

Yack'er. *s.* An acre.

Yal. *s.* Ale.

Yaller. *adj.* Yellow.

Yal'house. *s.* An ale-house.

Yap'ern. *s.* An apron.

Yarly. *adj.* Early.

Yarm. *s.* Arm.

Yarth. *s.* Earth.

Yel. *s.* An eel.

Yel-spear. *s.* An instrument for catching eels.

Yes. *s.* An earthworm.

Yezy. *adj.* Easy.

Yokes. *s. pl.* Hiccups.

Yourn. *pron.* Yours.

Z.

See the observations which precede the letter S, relative to the change of that letter to Z.

Za. *adv.* So.

Zâ. *v.* Say.

Zât. *adj.* Soft.

Za'tenfare. *adj.* Softish : applied to the intellects.

To Zam. *v. a.* To heat for some time over the fire, but not to boil.

Zam'zod. } *adj.* Any thing heated for a long time
Zam'zodden. } time in a low heat so as to be in part spoiled, is said to be zamzodden.

> Conjecture, in etymology, may be always busy. It is not improbable that this word is a compound of *semi*, Latin, half ; and to *seethe*, to boil : so that Zamzodden will then mean, literally, *half-boiled*.

Zand. *s.* Sand.

Zandy. *adj.* Sandy.

Zand-tot. *s.* A sand-hill.

To Zee. *v. a. pret.* and *part. Zid, Zeed.* To see.

Zeeäd. *s.* Seed.

Zeeäd-lip. *See* SEED-LIP.

Zel. *pron.* Self.

Zen'vy. *s.* Wild mustard.

> The true etymology will be seen at once in *séneve*, French, from *sinapi*, Latin, contracted and corrupted into *Zenvy*, Somersetian.

Zil'ker. *See* SILKER.

Zim, Zim'd. *v.* Seem, seemed.

Zitch. *adj.* Such.

Zooäp. *s.* Soap.

Zog. *s.* Soft, boggy land ; moist land.

Zog'gy. *adj.* Boggy ; wet.

Zoon'er. *adv.* Rather.

To Zound.   }
To Zoun'dy.   } *v. n.* To swoon.

To Zuf'fy. *v. n. See* To Suffy.

Zug'gers! *interj.* This is a word, like others of the same class, the precise meaning of which it is not easy to define. I dare say it is a composition of two, or more words, greatly corrupted in pronunciation.

Zull. *s.* The instrument used for ploughing land ; a plough.

Zum. *pron.* Some.

Zum'met. *pron.* Somewhat ; something.

Zunz. *adv.* Since.

To Zwail. *v. n.* To move about with the arms extended, and up and down.

To Zwang. *v. n.* and *v. n.* To swing ; to move to and fro.

Zwang. *s.* A swing.

To Zwell. *v. a.* To swell ; to swallow. *See* To Swell.

Zwird. *s.* Sword.

Zwod'der. *s.* A drowsy and stupid state of body or mind.

Derived, most probably, from *sudor*, Latin, a sweat.

POEMS

AND

OTHER PIECES

EXEMPLIFYING THE

DIALECT

OF THE

County of Somersetshire.

Notwithstanding the Author has endeavoured, in the Observations on the Dialects of the West, and in The Glossary, to obviate the difficulties under which strangers to the dialect of Somersetshire may, very possibly, labour in the perusal of the following Poems, it may be, perhaps, useful here to remind the reader, that many mere inversions of sound, and differences in pronunciation, are not noted in the Glossary.   That it did not appear necessary to explain such words as wine, *wind;* zâ, *say;* qut, *coat;* bwile, *boil;* hoss, *horse;* hirches, *riches; and many others, which it is presumed the* context, *the* Observations, *or the* Glossary, *will sufficiently explain.   The Author, therefore, trusts, that by a careful attention to these, the reader will soon become* au fait *at the interpretation of these West-country* LIDDENS.

GOOD BWYE TA THEE COT!

Good bwye ta thee Cot! whaur tha dâs o' my childhood
   Glaw'd bright as tha zun in a mornin o' mâ;
When tha dumbledores hummin, craup out o' tha cob-
    wâll,
   An' shakin ther whings, thâ vleed vooäth an' awâ.*

Good bwye ta the Cot!—on thy drashel, a-mâ-be,
   I niver naw moor sholl my voot again zet;
Tha jessamy awver thy porch zweetly bloomin,
   Whauriver I goo, I sholl niver vorget.

Tha rawzes, tha lillies, that blaw in tha borders—
   The gilawfers, too, that I us'd ta behawld—
Tha trees, wi' tha honeyzucks ranglin âll awver,
   I âlways sholl think o' nif I shood be awld.

Tha tutties that oten I pick'd on a zunday,
   And stickt in my qut—thâ war thawted za fine:
Aw how sholl I tell o'm—vor âll pirty maidens
   When I pass'd 'em look'd back—ther smill rawze on
    tha wine.

* The humble-bee, *bombilius major*, or *dumbledore*, makes holes
very commonly in mud walls, in which it deposits a kind of farina:
in this bee will be found, on dissection, a considerable portion of
honey, although it never deposits any.

Good bwye ta thee Ash ! which my Father beforne me,
  A planted, wi' pleasure, tha dâ I was born ;
Zâ, oolt thou drap a tear when I cease to behawld thee,
  An wander awâ droo tha wordle vorlorn.

Good bwye ta thee Tree ! an thy cawld shade in zummer ;
  Thy apples, aw who ool be lotted ta shake ?
When tha wine, mangst thy boughs sifes at Milemas in sorrow,
  Zâ oolt thou sife for me, or one wild wish awake ?

Good bwye ye dun Elves ! who, on whings made o' leather,
  Still roun my poorch whiver an' whiver at night ;
Aw mâ naw hord-horted, unveelin disturber,
  Destrây your snug nests, an your plâ by moonlight.

Good bwye ta thee Bower !—ta thy moss an thy ivy—
  To tha flowers that aroun thee âll blossomin graw ;
When I'm gwon, oolt thou grieve ?—bit 'tis foolish to ax it ;
  What is ther that's shower in this wordle belaw ?

Good bwye ta thee Cot ! whaur my mother za thought-vul,
  As zumtimes she war droo er care vor us âll,
Er lessins wi' kindness, wi' tenderness gid us ;
  An ax'd, war she dead, what ood us bevâll.

Good bwye ta thee Cot! whaur tha nightingale's music,
  In tha midnight o' Mâ-time, rawze loud on the ear;
Whaur tha colley awâk'd, wi' tha zun, an a zingin
  A went, wi' tha dirsh, in a voice vull and clear.

Good bwye ta thee Cot! I must goo ta tha city.
  Whaur, I'm tawld, that the smawk makes it dork at
    noon dâ;
Bit nif it is true, I'm afeard that I âlways,
  And iver sholl thenk on tha cot thatch'd wi' strâ.

Good bwye ta thee Cot! there is One that râins awver,
  An wâtches tha wordle, wi' wisdom divine;
Than why shood I mang, wi' tha many, my ma-bes;
  Bin there's readship in Him, an to him I resign.

Good bwye ta thee Cot! shood I niver behauld thee
  Again; still I thank thee vor âll that is past!
Thy friendly ruf shelter'd—while mother wâtch'd
  awver.
  An haw'd vor my comfort vrom vust unto last.

Good bwye ta thee Cot; vor the time mâ be longful
  Beforn I on thy drashall again zet my eye;
Thy tutties ool blossom, an daver an blossom
  Again and again—zaw good bwye, an good bwye!

FANNY FEAR.

The melancholy incident related in the following story, actually
occurred a few years ago at Shapwick.

Good Gennel-vawk! an if you please
    To lissen to my storry,
A mâ-be 'tis a jitch a one,
    Ool make ye zummet zorry.

'Tis not a hoozay tale of grief,
    A put wi' ort together,
That where you cry, or where you laugh,
    Da matter not a veather;

Bit 'tis a tale vor sartin true,
    Wi' readship be it spawken;
I knaw it âll, begummers! well,
    By tale, eese, an by tawken.

The maid's right name war FANNY FEAR,
    A tidy body lookin;
An she cood brew, and she cood bake,
An dumplins bwile, and skimmer cake;
    An âll the like o' cookin.

Upon a Zunday âternoon,
    Beforne the door a stanin,
To zee er chubby cheaks za hird,
An whitist lilies roun 'em spird,
    A damas rawze her han in,

Ood do your hort good ; an er eyes,
　Dork, vull, an bright, an sporklin ;
Tha country lads could not goo by,
Bit look thâ must—she iver shy,
　Ood blish—tha timid lorklin !

Her dame war to her desperd kind ;
　She knaw'd er well dezarvin :
She gid her good advice an claws,
At which she niver toss'd her naws,
　As zum ool, thawf pon starvin.

She oten yarly upp'd to goo
　A milkin o' tha dairy ;
The meads ring'd loudly wi' er zong ;
Aw how she birshed the grass along,
　As lissom as a vairy !

She war as happy as a prince ;
　Naw princess moor o' pleasure
When well-at-eased cood iver veel ;
She ly'd her head upon her peel,
　An vound athin a treasure.

There war a dessent comly youth,
　Who took'd to her a likin ;
An when a don'd in zunday claws,
You'd thenk en zummet I suppaws,
　A look'd so desperd strikin.

His vace war like a zummer dâ,
  When âll the birds be zingin;
Smiles an good nature dimplin stood,
An moor besides, an âll za good,
  Much pleasant promise bringin.

Now Jan war sawber, and afeard
  Nif he in haste shood morry,
That he mid long repent thereof;
An zo a thwart 'twar best not, thawf
  To stâ mid make en zorry.

Jan oten pass'd the happy door,
  There Fanny stood a scrubbin;
An Fanny hired hiz pleasant voice,
An thawt—"An if she had er choice !"
  An veel'd athin a drubbin.

Bit Jan did'n hulder long iz thawts;
  Vor thorough iv'ry cranny,
Hirn'd of iz hort tha warm hird tide;
An a cood na moor iz veelins bide,
  Bit tell 'em must to Fanny.

To Fanny, than, one Whitsun eve,
  A tawld er how a lov'd er;
Naw dove, a zed to er cood be
Moor faithvul than to her ood he;
  His hort had long appruv'd er.

Wi' timourous blishin, Fanny zed,
  "A maid mist not believe ye;
" Vor men ool tell ther lovin tale,
" And awver seely maids prevail—
  " Bit I dwont like ta grieve ye :

"Vor nif za be you now zâ true—
  "That you've for I a fancy :
" (Aw Jan ! I dwont veel desperd well,
" An what's tha câze, I cannot tell),
  " You'll zâ na moor to Nancy."

Twar zaw begin'd their zweetortin ;
  Booäth still liv'd in their places :
Zometimes thâ met bezides tha stile ;
Wi' pleasant look an tender smile
  Gaz'd in each wither's faces.

In spreng-time oten on tha nap
  Ood Jan and Fanny linger ;
An when war vooäs'd to zâ " good bwye,"
Ood meet again, wi' draps in eye,
  While haup ood pwint er vinger.

Zo pass'd tha dâs—tha moons awâ,
  An haup still whiver'd nigh ;
Nif Fanny's dreams high pleasures vill,
Of her Jan's thawts the lidden still,
  An oten too the zigh.

Bit still Jan had not got wherewi'
   To venter eet to morry ;
Alas-a-dâ ! when poor vawk love,
How much restraint how many pruv ;
   How zick zum an how zorry.

Aw you who live in houzen grate,
   An wherewi' much possessin,
You knaw not, mâ-be, care not you,
What pangs jitch tender horts pursue,
   How grate nor how distressin.

Jan sar'd a varmer vour long years,
   An now iz haups da brighten :
A gennelman of high degree
Choos'd en iz hunsman vor to be ;
   His Fanny's hort da lighten !

" Now, Fan," zed he, " nif I da live,
   " Nex zummer thee bist mine ;
" Sir John ool gee me wauges good,
" Amâ-be too zum viër ood ! "
   His Fan's dork eyes did shine.

" To haw vor thee, my Fan," a cried,
   " I iver sholl delight ;
" Thawf I be poor, 'tool be my pride
" To ha my Fan vor a buxom bride—
   " My lidden dâ an night."

A took er gently in iz orms
  Aṅ kiss'd er za zweetly too ;
His Fan, vor jay, not a word cood speak,
Bit a big roun tear rawl'd down er cheak,
It zimm'd as thawf er hort ood break—
  She cood hordly thenk it true.

To zee our hunsman goo abroad,
  His houns behind en volly ;
His tossel'd cap—his whip's smort smack,
His hoss a prancin wi' tha crack,
His whissle, horn, an holler, back !
  Ood cure âll malancholy.

It happ'd on a dork an wintry night,
  Tha stormy wine a blawin ;
Tha houns made a naise an a dismal yell ;
Jitch as zum vawk zâ da death vaurtell,
  The cattle loud war lawin.

Tha hunsman wâkid an down a went ;
  A thawt ta keep 'em quiet ;
A niver stopped izzel ta dress,
Bit a went in iz shirt vor readiness
    A voun a dirdful riot.

Bit âll thic night a did not come back ;
  All night tha dogs did raur ;
In tha mornin thâ look'd on tha kannel stwons
An zeed 'em cover'd wi' gaur an bwons,
  The vlesh âll vrom 'em a taur.

His head war left—the head o' Jan
  Who lov'd hiz Fanny za well;
An a bizzy gossip, as gossips be
Who've work o' ther awn bit vrom it vlee,
  To Fanny went ta tell.

She hirn'd, she vleed ta meet tha man
  Who corr'd er dear Jan's head :
An when she zeed en âll blood an gaur,
She drapp'd down speechless jist avaur,
  As thauf she had bin dead.

Poor Fanny com'd ta erzel again,
  Bit her senses left her vor iver !
An âll she zed, ba dâ or night—
Vor sleep it left her eye-lids quite—
War, " why did he goo in the cawld ta shiver ?—
  " Niver, O Jan ! sholl I zee the, niver ! "*

JERRRY NUTTY;

OR

THE MAN OF MORK.

Awa wi' âll yer tales o' grief,
  An dismal storry writin ;

* See a letter by Edward Band, on this subject, in the prose
pieces.

A mâ-be zumthin I mâ zing
  Ool be as much delightin.

Zumtime agoo, bevaur tha moors
  War tin'd in, lived at Mork
One JERRY NUTTY—spry a war;
  A upp'd avaur the lork.

Iz vather in a little cot
  Liv'd, auver-right tha moor,
An thaw a kipt a vlock o' geese,
  A war a thoughted poor.

A niver teach'd tha cris-cross-lain
  Ta any of his bways,
An Jerry, mangst the rest o'm, did
  Not much appruv his ways.

Vor Jerry zumtimes went ta church
  Ta hire tha Pâson preach,
An thawt what pity that ta read
  Izzel a cood'n teach.

Vor than, a zunday âternoon,
  Tha Bible, or good book
Would be companion vit vor'm âll
  Who choos'd therein ta look.

Bit Jerry than tha naise o' geese
  Bit little moor could hire ;

An dâly goose-aggs ta pick up
    Droo-out tha moor did tire.

A ôten look'd upon tha hills
    An stickle mountains roun,
An wished izzel upon their taps :
    What zights a ood be bôun !

Bit what did mooäst iz fancy strick
    War Glassenberry Torr :
A âlways zeed it when tha zun
    Gleam'd wi' tha mornin stor.

O' Well's grate church a ôten hired,
    Iz fancy war awake ;
An zaw a thawt that zoon a ood
    A journey ta it make.

An Glassenberry's Torr, an Thorn
    The hawly blowth of which
A hired from one and tother too ;
    Tha like war never jitch !

Bit moor o' this I need not zâ,
    Vor off went Jerry Nutty,
In hiz right hon a wâkin stick,
    An in hiz qut a tutty.

Now, lock-y-zee ! in whimly dress
    Trudg'd chearful Jerry on ;

Bit on tha moor not vur a went—
  A made a zudden ston.

Which wâ ta goo a cood not thenk,
  Vor there war many a wâ ;
A put upright iz walking stick ;
  A vâll'd ta tha zon o' dâ.

Ta tha suthard than iz wâ a took
  Athert tha turfy moors,
An zoon o' blissom Cuzziton,*
  A pass'd tha cottage doors.

Tha maidens o' tha cottages,
  Not us'd strange vawk to zee,
Com'd vooäth and stood avaur tha door ;
  Jer wonder'd what cood be.

Zum smil'd, zum whecker'd, zum o'm blish'd.
  "Od dang it !" Jerry zed,
"What do tha think that I be like?"
  An nodded to 'm iz head.

" Which is tha wâ to Glassenberry ?
  " I've hired tha hawly thorn
" War zet there by zum hawly hons
  " Zoon âter Christ war born ;

* Cossington.

" An I've a mine ta zee it too,
  " An o' tha blowth ta take."
" An how can you, a seely man,
  " Jitch seely journey make ?

" What ! dwont ye knaw that now about
  " It is the midst o' June ?
" Tha hawly thorn at Kirsmas blaws—
  "'You be zix months too zoon.

" Goo whim again, yea gâwky ! goo !"
  Zaw zed a damsel vair
As dewy mornin late in Mâ ;
  An Jerry wide did stare.

" Lord Miss !" zed he, " I niver thawt,
  " O' Kirsmas !—while I've shoes,
" To goo back now I be zet out,
  " Is what I sholl not choose.

" I'll zee the Torr an hawly thorn,
  " An Glassenberry too ;
" An, nif you'll put me in tha wâ,
  " I'll gee grate thanks ta you."

" Goo droo thic veel an up thic lane,
  " An take tha lift hon path,
" Than droo Miss Crossman's backzid strait,
  " Ool bring ye up ta Wrath.

"Now mine, whaur you do turn again
  "At varmer Veal's long yacker,
"Clooäse whaur Jan Lide, tha cobler, lives.
  "Who makes tha best o' tacker ;

"You mist turn short behine tha house
  "An goo right droo tha shord,
"An than you'll pass a zummer lodge,
  "A builded by tha lord.

"Tha turnpick than is jist belaw,
  "An Cock-hill strait avaur ye."
Za Jerry doff'd his hat an bow'd,
  An thank'd er vor er storry.

Bit moor o' this I need not zâ,
  Vor off went Jerry Nutty ;
In his right hand a wâkin stick,
  An in hiz qut a tutty.

Bit I vorgot to zâ that Jer
  A zatchel wi' en took
To hauld zum bird an cheese ta ate ;—
  Iz drink war o' tha brook.

Za when a got upon Cock-hill
  Upon a linch a zawt ;
The zun had climmer'd up tha sky ;
  A voun it very hot.

An, as iz stomick war za good,
  A made a horty meal ;
An werry war wi' wâkin, zaw
  A sleepid zoon did veel.

That blessed power o' bâmy sleep,
  Which auver ivery sense
Da wi' wild whiverin whings extend
  A happy influence ;

Now auver Jerry Nutty drow'd
  Er lissom mantle wide ;
An down a drapp'd in zweetest zleep,
  Iz zatchel by iz zide.

Not âll tha nasty stouts could wâke
  En vrom iz happy zleep,
Nor emmets thick, nor vlies that buz,
  An on iz hons da creep.

Naw dreams a had ; or nif a had
  Mooäst pleasant dreams war thâ :
O' geese an goose-aggs, ducks and jitch ;
  Or Mally, vur awâ,

Zum gennelmen war dreavin by
  In a gilded cawch za gâ ;
Thâ zeed en lyin down asleep ;
  Thâ bid the cawchman stâ.

Thâ bâll'd thâ hoop'd—a niver wâk'd ;
  Naw houzen there war handy ;
Zed one o'm, "Nif you like, my bways,
  " We'll ha a little randy ! "

" Jist put en zâtly in tha cawch
  " An dreav en ta Bejwâter ;
" An as we âll can't g'in wi'n here,
  " I'll come mysel zoon âter."

Twar done at once : vor norn o'm car'd
  A strâ vor wine or weather ;
Than gently rawl'd the cawch along,
  As zât as any veather.

Bit Jerry snaur'd za loud, tha naise
  Tha gennelmen did gally ;
Thâ'd hâf a mind ta turn en out ;
  A war dreamin o' his Mally !

It war the morkit dâ as rawl'd
  Tha cawch athin Bejwâter ;
Thâ drauv up ta the Crown-Inn door,
  Ther Mâ-game man com'd âter.

" Here Maester Wâter ! Lock-y-zee !
  " A-mâ-be you mid thenk
" Thic mon a snauren in tha cawch
  " Is auvercome wi' drenk.

" Bit 'tis not not jitchy theng we knaw ;
  " A is a cunjerin mon,
" Vor on Cock-hill we vound en ly'd
  " Iz stick stif in his hon.

" Iz vace war cover'd thick wi' vlies
  " An bloody stouts a plenty ;
" Nif he'd o pumple voot bezide,
" An a brumstick vor'n to zit ascride,
" O' wizards a mid be thawt tha pride,
  " Amangst a kit o' twenty."

" Lord zur ! an why d'ye bring en here
  " To gally âll tha people ?
" Why zuggers ! nif we frunt en than,
  " He'll auver-dro tha steeple.

" I bag ye, zur, to take en vooäth ;
  " There ! how iz teeth da chatter ;
" Lawk zur ! vor Christ—look there again !
  " A'll witchify Bejwâter !"

Tha gennelman stood by an smiled
  To zee tha bussle risin :
Vor zoon, droo-out tha morkit wide
  Tha news wor gwon saprisin.

An round about tha cawch thâ dring'd—
  Tha countryman and townsman ;
An young an awld, an man an maid—
Wi' now an tan, an here an there,
Amang tha crowd to gape an stare,
  A doctor and a gownsman.

Jitch naise an bother wâkid zoon
    Poor hormless Jerry Nutty,
A look'd astunn'd ;—a cood'n speak !
    An daver'd war iz tutty.

A niver in his life avaur
    'ad been athin Bejwâter ;
A thawt, an if a war alive,
    That zummet war tha matter.

Tha houzen cling'd together zaw !
    Tha gennelmen an ladies !
Tha blacksmith's, brazier's hammers too !
    An smauk whauriver trade is.

Bit how a com'd athin a cawch
    A war amaz'd at thenkin ;
A thawt, vor sartin, a must be
    A auvercome wi' drenkin.

Thâ ax'd en nif a'd please to g'out
    An ta tha yalhouse g'in ;
Bit thâ zo clooäse about en dring'd
    A cood'n goo athin.

Ta g'under 'em or g'auver 'em
    A try'd booâth grate and smâll ;
Bit g'under, g'auver, g'in, or g'out,
    A cood'n than at âll.

" Lord bless ye ! gennel-vawk !" zed he,
  " I'm come to Glassenberry
" To zee tha Torr an Hawly Thorn ;
  " What makes ye look za merry ?"

" Why mister wizard ? dwont ye knaw,
  " Theäse town is câll'd Bejwâter !
Cried out a whipper-snapper man :
  Thâ âll bust out in lâughter.

" I be'nt a wizard, zur !" a zed ;
  " Bit I'm a little titch'd ;*
" Or, witherwise, you mid well thenk
  I'm, zure anow, bewitch'd !"

Thaw Jerry war, vor âll tha wordle,
  Like very zel o' quiet,
A veel'd iz blood ta bwile athin
  At jitchy zort o' riot ;

Za out a jump'd amangst 'em âll !
  A made a desperd bussle ;
Zum hirn'd awâ—zum made a ston ;
  Wi' zum a had a tussle.

Iz stick now sar'd 'em justice good ;
  It war a tough groun ash ;
Upon ther heads a plâ'd awâ,
  An round about did drash.

* Touched.

Thâ belg'd, thâ raur'd, thâ scamper'd âll.
  A zoon voun rum ta stoory;
A thawt a'd be reveng'd at once,
  Athout a judge or jury.

An, thaw a brawk naw-body's bwons,
  A gid zum bloody nawzes;
Tha pirty maids war fainty too;
  Hirn'd vrom ther cheaks tha rawzes.

Thinks he, me gennelmen! when nex
  I goo to Glassenbery,
Yea shant ha jitch a rig wi' I,
  Nor at my cost be merry.

Zaw, havin clear'd izzel a wâ.
  Right whim went Jerry Nutty;
A flourished roun iz wâkin stick;
  An vleng'd awâ iz tutty.

A LEGEND OF GLASTONBURY.

[First Printed in " Graphic Illustrator, p. 124.]

I cannot do better than introduce here " *A Legend of Glastonbury*," made up, not from books, but from oral tradition once
very prevalent in and near Glastonbury, which had formerly one
of the richest Abbeys in England ; the ruins are still attractive.

WHO hath not hir'd o' *Avalon ?*[*]
'Twar talked o' much an long agon,—

* " The Isle of ancient Avelon."—DRAYTON.

Tha wonders o' tha *Holy Thorn*,
Tha wich, zoon âter Christ war born,
Here a planted war by *Arimathé*,
Thic Joseph that com'd auver sea,
An planted Kirstianity.
Thâ zâ that whun a landed vust,
(Zich plazen war in God's own trust)
A stuck iz staff into tha groun
An auver iz shoulder lookin roun,
Whatever mid iz lot bevâll,
A cried aloud " *Now, weary âll* ! "
Tha staff het budded an het grew,
An at Kirsmas bloom'd tha whol dâ droo.
An still het blooms at Kirsmas bright,
But best thâ zâ at dork midnight,
A pruf o' this nif pruf you will,
Iz voun in tha name o' *Weary-âll-hill* !
Let tell *Pumparles* or lazy *Brue*.
That what iz tauld iz vor sartin true !

[" The story of the Holy Thorn was a long time credited by
the vulgar and credulous. There is a species of White Thorn which
blossoms about Christmas ; it is well known to naturalists so as
to excite no surprise."]

MR. GUY.

The incident on which this story is founded, occurred in the rly part of the last century; hence the allusion to making a ʉ before making a journey to the metropolis.

> Mr. Guy war a gennelman
>   O' Huntspill, well knawn
> As a grazier, a hirch one,
>   Wi' lons o' hiz awn.
>
> A ôten went ta Lunnun
>   Hiz cattle vor ta zill ;
> All tha horses that a rawd
>   Niver minded hadge or hill.
>
> A war afeard o' naw one ;
>   A niver made hiz will,
> Like wither vawk, avaur a went
>   His cattle vor ta zill.
>
> One time a'd bin ta Lunnun
>   An zawld iz cattle well ;
> A brought awâ a power o' gawld,
>   As I've a hired tell.
>
> As late at night a rawd along
>   All droo a unket ood,
> A ooman rawze vrom off tha groun
>   An right avaur en stood :

She look'd za pitis Mr. Guy
　　At once hiz hoss's pace
Stapt short, a wonderin how, at night,
　　She com'd in jitch a place.

A little trunk war in her hon ;
　　She zim'd vur gwon wi' chile.
She ax'd en nif a'd take her up
　　And cor her a veo mile.

Mr. Guy, a man o' veelin
　　For a ooman in distress,
Than took er up behind en :
　　A cood'n do na less.

A corr'd er trunk avaur en,
　　An by hiz belt o' leather
A bid er hawld vast ; on thâ rawd,
　　Athout much tâk, together.

Not vur thâ went avaur she gid
　　A whissle loud an long ;
Which Mr. Guy, thawt very strânge ;
　　Er voice too zim'd za strong !

She'd lost er dog, she zed ; an than
　　Another whissle blaw'd,
That stortled Mr. Guy ;—a stapt
　　Hiz hoss upon tha rawd.

Goo on, zed she ; bit Mr. Guy
   Zum rig beginn'd ta fear :
Vor voices rawze upon tha wine,
   An zim'd a comin near.

Again thâ rawd along ; again
   She whissled. Mr. Guy
Whipt out hiz knife an cut tha belt,
   Then push'd er off !—Vor why ?

Tha ooman he took up behine,
   Begummers, war a *man !*
Tha rubbers zaw ad lâd ther plots
   Our grazier to trepan.

I shall not stap ta tell what zed
   Tha man in ooman's clawze ;
Bit he, and all o'm jist behine,
   War what you mid suppawze.

Thâ cust, thâ swaur, thâ dreaten'd too,
   An ater Mr. Guy
Thâ gallop'd âll ; 'twar niver-tha-near :
   Hiz hoss along did vly.

Auver downs, droo dales, awâ a went,
   'Twar dâ-light now amawst,
Till at an inn a stapt, at last,
   Ta thenk what he'd a lost.

A lost ?—why, nothin—but hiz belt !—
A zummet moor ad gain'd :
Thic little trunk a corr'd awâ—
It gawld g'lore contain'd !

Nif Mr. Guy war hirch avaur,
A now war hircher still :
Tha plunder o' tha highwâmen
Hiz coffers went ta vill.

In sâfety Mr. Guy rawd whim ;
A ôten tawld tha storry.
Ta meet wi' jitch a rig myzel
I shood'n, soce, be zorry.

THE ROOKERY.

THE ROOK, *corvus frugilegus*, is a bird of considerable intelligence, and is, besides, extremely useful in destroying large quantities of worms and larvæ of destructive insects. It will, it is true, if not watched, pick out, after they are dibbled, both pease and beans from the holes with a precision truly astonishing : a very moderate degree of care is, however, sufficient to prevent this evil, which is greatly overbalanced by the positive good which it effects in the destruction of insects. It is a remarkable fact, and not, perhaps, generally known, that this bird rarely roosts at the rookery; except for a few months during the period of incubation, and rearing its young. In the winter season it more commonly takes flights of no ordinary length, to roost on the trees of some remote and sequestered wood. The *Elm* is its favorite, on which it usually builds ; but such is its attachment to locality that since the incident alluded to in the following Poem took place the Rooks have, many of them, built in *fir* trees at a little distance from their former habitation. The habits of the Rook are well worthy the attention of all who delight in the study of Natural History.

MY zong is o' tha ROOKERY,
   Not jitch as I a zeed
On stunted trees wi' leaves a veo,
   A very veo indeed,

In thic girt place thâ *Lunnun* câll ;—
   Tha Tower an tha Pork
Hâ booäth a got a Rookery,
   Althaw thâ han't a Lork.

I zeng not o' jitch Rookeries,
   Jitch plazen, pump or banners ;
Bit town-berd Rooks, vor âll that, hâ,
   I warnt ye, curious *manners*.

My zong is o' a Rookery
   My Father's cot bezide,
Avaur, years âter, I war born
   'Twar long tha porish pride.

Tha elms look'd up like giants tâll
   Ther branchy yarms aspread ;
An green plumes wavin wi' tha wine,
   Made gâ each lofty head.

Ta drâ tha pectur out—ther war
    At distance, zid between
Tha trees, a thatch'd Form-house, an geese
    A cacklin on tha green.

A river, too, clooäse by tha trees,
    Its stickle coose on slid,
Whaur yells an trout an wither fish
    Mid ôtentimes be zid.

Tha rooks voun this a pleasant place—
    A whim ther young ta rear;
An I a ôten pleas'd a bin
    Ta wâtch 'em droo tha year.

'Tis on tha dâ o' Valentine
    Or there or thereabout,
Tha rooks da vust begin ta build,
    An cawin, make a rout.

Bit aw! when May's a come, ta zee
    Ther young tha gunner's shut
Vor SPOORT, an bin, as zum da zâ,
    (Naw readship in't I put)

That nif thâ did'n shut tha rooks
    Thâ'd zoon desert tha trees!
Wise vawk! Thic reason vor ther SPOORT
    Gee thâ mid nif thâ please!

Still zeng I o' tha Rookery,
  Vor years it war tha pride
Of âll tha place, bit 'twor ta I
  A zumthin moor bezide.

A hired tha Rooks avaur I upp'd ;
  I hired 'em droo tha dâ ;
I hired ther young while gittin flush
  An ginnin jist ta câ.

I hired 'em when my mother gid
  Er lessins kind ta I,
In jitch a wâ when I war young,
  That I war fit ta cry.

I hired 'em at tha cottage door,
  When mornin, in tha spreng,
Wâk'd vooäth in youth an beauty too,
  An birds beginn'd ta zeng.

I hired 'em in tha winter-time
  When, roustin vur awâ,
Thâ visited tha Rookery
  A whiverin by dâ.

My childhood, youth, and manood too,
  My Father's cot recâll
Thic Rookery.   Bit I mist now
  Tell what it did bevâll.

' Twar Mâ-time—heavy wi' tha nests
    War laden âll tha trees ;
An to an fraw, wi' creekin loud,
    Thâ sway'd ta iv'ry breeze.

One night tha wine—a thundrin wine,
    Jitch as war hired o' niver,
Blaw'd two o' thic girt giant trees
    Flat down into tha river.

Nests, aggs, an young uns, âll awâ
    War zweept into tha wâter ;
An zaw war spwiled tha Rookery
    Vor iver and iver âter.

I visited my Father's cot :
    Tha Rooks war âll a gwon ;
Whaur stood tha trees in lofty pride
    I zid there norra one.

My Father's cot war desolate ;
    An âll look'd wild, vorlorn ;
Tha Ash war stunted that war zet
    Tha dâ that I war born.

My Father, Mother, Rooks, âll gwon !
    My Charlotte an my Lizzy !—
Tha gorden wi' tha tutties too !—
    Jitch thawts why be za bizzy !—

Behawld tha wâ o' human thengs !
  Rooks, lofty trees, an Friends—
A kill'd, taur up, like leaves drap off !—
  Zaw feaver'd bein ends.

TOM GOOL,

AND

LUCK IN THA BAG.

" Luck, Luck in tha Bag ! Good Luck !
  " Put in an try yer fortin ;
" Come, try yer luck in tha Lucky Bag !
  " You'll git a prize vor sartin."

Mooäst plazen hâ their customs
  Ther manners an ther men ;
We too a got our customs,
  Our manners and our men.

He who a bin ta Huntspill Fâyer
  Or Highbridge—Pawlet Revel—
Or Burtle Sassions, whaur thâ plâ
  Zumtimes tha very devil,

Mist mine once a man well
  That war a câll'd Tom Gool ;
Zum thawt en mazed, while withers thawt
  En moor a knave than fool.

At âll tha fâyers an revels too
  Tom Gool war shower ta be,
A tâkin vlother vast awâ,—
  A hoopin who bit he.

Vor'âll that a had a zoort o' wit
  That zet tha vawk a laughin ;
An mooäst o' that, when he tha yal
  Ad at tha fâyer bin quaffin.

A corr'd a kit o' pedlar's waur,
  Like awld *Joannah Martin ;**
An nif you hân't a hired o' her,
  You zumtime sholl vor sartin.

* This Lady, who was for many years known in Somerset-shire as an itinerant dealer in earthenware, rags, &c., and occasionally a *fortune-teller*, died a few years since at Huntspill, where she had resided for the greater part of a century. She was extremely illiterate, so much so, as not to be able to write, and, I think, could scarcely read. She lived for some years in a house belonging to my father, and while a boy, I was very often her gratuitous amanuensis, in writing letters for her to her children. She possessed, however, considerable shrewdness, energy, and perseverance, and amassed property to the amount of several hundred pounds. She had three husbands ; the name of the first was, I believe, *Gool* or *Gould*, a relation of *Thomas Gool*, the subject of the above Poem ; the name of the second was *Martin*, of the third *Pain*; but as the last lived a short time only after having married her, she always continued to be called *Joannah Martin*.

Joannah was first brought into public notice by the Rev. Mr. Warner, in his *Walks through the Western Counties*, published in 1800, in which work will be found a lively and interesting description of her; but she often said that she should wish me to write her life, as I was, of course, more

" Luck, Luck in tha Bag !" Tom, cried
   " Put in and try yer fortin ;
" Come try yer luck in tha lucky bag ;
   " You'll git a prize vor sartin.

" All prizes, norra blank,
   " Norra blank, âll prizes !
" A waiter—knife—or scissis sheer—
" A splat o' pins—put in my dear !—
   " Whitechapel nills âll sizes.

" Luck, Luck in tha Bag !—only a penny vor a
venter—you mid get, a-ma-be, a girt prize—a *Rawman
waiter !*—I can avoord it as cheep as thic that stawl it
—I a bote it ta trust, an niver intend to pâ vor't.
Luck, Luck in tha bag ! âll prizes; norra blank !

intimately acquainted with it than any casual inquirer could
possibly be. An additional notice of Joannah was inserted by
me in the *Monthly Magazine*, for Nov. 1816, page 310. I had
among my papers, the *original song composed* by her, which I
copied from her dictation many years ago,—the only, copy in
existence ; I regret that I cannot lay my hand upon it ;
as it contains much of the Somersetshire idiom. I have
more than once heard her sing this song, which was satirical,
and related to the conduct of a female, one of her neighbours,
who had become a thief.

Such was JOANNAH MARTIN, a woman whose name (had
she moved in a sphere where her original talents could have
been improved by education,) might have been added to the
list of distinguished female worthies of our country.

[The MS. song was never, that I am aware of, discovered
after my relative's death.—Editor, J. K. J.]

" Luck, Luck in tha Bag ! Good Luck !
    " Put in an try yer fortin ;
" Come, try yer luck in tha lucky bag !
    " You'll git a prize vor sartin.

" Come, niver mine tha single-sticks,
    " Tha whoppin or tha stickler,
" You dwon't want now a brawken head,
    " Nor jitchy zoort o' tickler !

" Now Lady ! yer prize is—'A Snuff-Box,'
    " A treble-japann'd Pontypool !
" You'll shower come again ta my luck in tha bag,
    " Or niver trust me—Tommy Gool.

" Luck, Luck in tha bag ! Good Luck !
    " Put in an try yer fortin ;
" Come, try yer luck in tha lucky bag !
    " You'll git a prize for sartin !

TEDDY BAND.

"THE short and simple annals ot the poor."

GRAY.

Miss Hanson to Miss Mortimer. Ashcot, July 21st.

My Dear Jane.

Will you do me the favour to amuse yourself and your friends with the enclosed epistle? it is certainly an original—written in the dialect of the County. You will easily understand it, and, I do not doubt, the " moril " too.

Edward Band, or as he is more commonly called here, Teddy Band, is a poor, but honest and industrious cottager, but I am, nevertheless, disposed to think that " if ignorance is bliss, 'tis folly to be wise."

My dear Jane, affectionately yours,

MARIA HANSON.

Teddy Band to Miss Hanson.

Mâm,

I da thenk you'll smile at theeäzam here veo lains that I write ta you, bin I be naw scholard; vor vather coud'n avoord ta put I ta school. Bit nif

you'll vorgee me vor my bauldniss, a-mâ-be, I mid
not be afeard ta zâ zummet ta you that you, mâm your-
zell mid like ta hire. Bit how be I ta knaw that? I
knaw that you be a goodhorted Lady, an da like ta
zee poor vawk well-at-eased an happy. You axt I
tother dâ ta zing a zong : now I dwont much like zum
o' thâ zongs that I hired thic night at squire Reevs's
when we made an end o' Hâ-corrin : vor, zim ta I,
there war naw moril to 'em. I like zongs wi' a moril
to 'em. Tha nawtes, ta be shower, war zât anow, bit,
vor âll that, I war looking vor tha moril, mâm. Zo,
when I cum'd whim, I tawld our Pall, that you axt I
ta zing : an I war zorry âterward that I did'n, bin you
be âlways zo desperd good ta poor vowk. Bit I thawt,
a-mâ-be, you mid be angry wi' my country lidden.
Why Teddy, zed Pall, dwont ye zend Miss Hanson thic
zong which ye made yerzel ; I thenk ther is a moril in
thic. An zo, mâm, nif you please, I a zent tha zong.
I haup you'll vorgee me.

Mâm, your humble sarvant,

TEDDY BAND.

ZONG.

I HAVE a cot o' Cob-wâll
    Roun which tha ivy clims ;
My Pally at tha night-vâll
    Er crappin viër trims.

A comin vrom tha plow-veel
  I zee tha blankers rise,
Wi' blue smauk cloudy curlin,
  An whivering up tha skies.

When tha winter wines be crousty,
  An snaws dreav vast along,
I hurry whim—tha door tine,
  An cheer er wi' a zong.

When spreng, adresst in tutties,
  Câlls âll tha birds abroad;
An wrans an robin-riddicks,
  Tell âll the cares o' God,

I zit bezides my cot-door
  After my work is done,
While Pally, bizzy knittin,
  Looks at tha zettin zun.

When zummertime is passin,
  An harras dâs be vine,
I drenk tha sporklin cider,
  An wish naw wither wine.

How zweet tha smill o' clawver,
  How zweet tha smill o' hâ;
How zweet is haulsom labour,
  Bit zweeter Pall than thâ.

An who d'ye thenk I envy ?—
Tha nawbles o' tha land ?
Thâ can't be moor than happy,
An *that* is Teddy Band.

Mister Ginnins ;

I a red thic ballet o' yourn câlled Fanny Fear, an, zim ta I, there's naw moril to it.   Nif zaw be you da thenk zo well o't, I'll gee one.

I dwont want to frunt any ov the gennelmen o' tha country, bit I âlways a thawt it desperd odd, that dogs should be keept in a kannel, and keept a hungered too, zaw that thâ mid be moor eager to hunt thic poor little theng câlled a hare. I dwon' naw, bit I da thenk, nif I war a gennelman, that I'd vine better spoort than huntin ; bezides, zim ta I 'tis desperd wicked to hunt animals vor one's spoort. Now, jitch a horrid blanscue as what happened at Shapick, niver could a bin but vor tha hungry houns. I haup that gennelmen ool thenk o't oten ; an when thâ da hire tha yell o' tha houns thâ'll not vorgit Fanny Fear ; a-mâ-be thâ mid be zummet tha wiser an better vor't ; I'm shower jitch a storry desarves ta be remimbered. This is the moril.

I am, sur, your sarvant,,

TEDDY BAND.

THE CHURCHWARDEN.

Upon a time, naw matter whaur,
Jitch plazen there be many a scaur
  In Zummerzet's girt gorden ;
(Ive hir'd 'twar handy ta tha zea,
Not vur vrom whaur tha zantots be)
  There liv'd a young churchwarden.

A zim'd delighted when put in.
An zaw a thawt a ood begin
  Ta do hiz office duly :
Bit zum o'm, girt vawk in ther wâ—
  Tha *Porish* o'ten câlled,—a girt bell sheep
  Or two that lead the rest an quiet keep—
Put vooäth ther hons iz coose to stâ,
  Which made en quite unruly.

A went, of coose, ta Visitâtion
Ta be sworn in ;—an than 'twar nâtion
Hord that a man his power should doubt,—
An moor—ta try ta turn en out !
"Naw, Naw !" exclaim'd our young churchwarden,
"I dwon't care vor ye âll a copper varden !"

Tha church war durty.—Wevets here
Hang'd danglin vrom tha ruf ; an there
  Tha plaisterin shaw'd a crazy wâll ;

Tha âltar-piece war dim and dowsty too,
That Peter's maricle thâ scase cood view.
Tha Ten Commandments nawbody cood rade ;*
Tha Lord's Prayer ad nuthin in't bit " Brade ; "†
　Nor had tha Creed
A lain or letter parfit, grate or smâll.
'Twar time vor zum one ta renew 'em âll.

I've tawld o' wevets—zum o'm odd enow ;
Thâ look'd tha colour of a dork dun cow,
　An like a skin war stratched across tha corners ;
Tha knitters o' tha porish tâk'd o knittin
Stockins wi' 'em !—Bit aw, how unbevittin
　All tâk like this !—aw fie, tha wicked scorners !

Ta work went tha Churchwarden ; wevets tummel'd
Down by tha bushel, an tha pride o' dowst war
　　hummel'd.
　Tha wâlls once moor look'd bright.
Tha Painter, fags, a war a Plummer
　An Glazier too,
　Put vooäth his powers,
(His workin made naw little scummer !)
In zentences, in flourishes, and flowers.
Tha chancel, church and âll look'd new,
　An war well suited to avoord delight.

Tha Ten Commandments glitter'd wi' tha vornish ;
Compleat now, tha Lord's Prayer, what cood tornish.

　　　　* Read　　　　　　　　† Bread

'As vor tha Creed 'twar made bran new
Vrom top ta bottom ; I tell ye true !
Tha âltar piece wi' Peter war now naw libel
  Upon tha church,
Which booäth athin an, tower an all, athout
Look'd like a well-dressed maid in pride about ;
Tha walls rejâic'd wi' texts took vrom tha Bible.
  Bit vor âll that, thâ left en in tha lurch ;
    I bag your pardon.
I meän, of âll tha expense thâ ood'n pâ a varden.

Jitch zweepin, birshin, paintin, scrubbin ;
Tha tuts ad niver jitch a drubbin ;
  Jitch white-washin and jitch brought gwâin
A power of money.—Tha Painter's bill
Made of itzel a pirty pill,
  Ta zwell which âll o'm tried in vain !
Ther stomicks turn'd, ther drawts were norry ; *
Jitch gillded pills thâ cood'n corry.
An when our young churchwarden ax'd em why,
Thâ laugh'd at en, an zed, ther drawts war dry.

Tha keeper o' tha church war wrong;
(Churchwarden still the burden o' my zong)
  A should at vust
A câll'd a Vestry : vor 'tis hord ta trust
  To Porish generasity ; an zaw
  A voun it : I dwon' knaw

* Narrow.

Whaur or who war his advisers ;
  Zum zed a Lâyer gid en bad advice ;
  A-mâ-be saw ; jitch vawk ben't always nice.
Lâyers o' advice be seltimes misers
  Nif there's wherewi' ta pâ ;
Or, witherwise, good bwye ta Lâyers an tha Lâ.

A Vestry than at last war cried—
A Vestry's power let noäne deride—
When tha church war auver tha clork bal'd out,
  Aw eese ! aw eese ! aw eese !
All wonder'd what cood be about,
  An stratch'd ther necks like a vlock o' geese ;
  Why—*ta make a Rate*
  Vor tha church's late
    Repairâtion.
    A grate norâtion,
A nâtion naise tha nawtice made,
About tha cost ta be defray'd
  Vor tha church's repairâtion.

Tha Vestry met, âll naise an bother ;
One ood'n wait ta hire tha tuther.
When thâ war tir'd o' jitch a gabble,
Ta bâl na moor not one war yable,
A man, a little zâtenfare,
Got up hiz verdi ta delcare.
Now Soce, zed he, why we be gwâin
Ta meet in Vestry here in vâin.

Let's come to some determination,
An not tâk âll in jitch a fashion.
Let's zee tha 'counts.   A snatch'd tha book
Vrom tha Churchwarden in't ta look.
Tha book war chain'd clooäse to his wrist ;
A gid en slily jitch a twist !
That the young Churchwarden loud raur'd out,
" You'll break my yarm !—what be about ?"

Tha man a little zâtenfare,
An âll tha Vestry wide did stare!
Bit Soce, zed he again, I niver zeed
Money brought gwâin zaw bad.   What need
War ther tha âltar-piece ta titch ?
What good war paintin, vornishin, an jitch ?
What good war't vor'n ta mend
Tha Ten Commandments ?—Why did he
Mell o' tha Lord's Prayer ?   Lockyzee !
    Ther war naw need
To mell or make wi' thic awld Creed.
I'm zorry vor'n ; eesse zorry as a friend ;
Bit can't conzent our wherewi' zaw ta spend.

    Thâ âll, wi one accord,
    At tha little zâtenfare's word,
        Agreed, that, not one varden,
            By Rate,
      Should be collected vor tha late
            Repairâtion
Of tha church by tha young Churchwarden.

THE FISHERMAN

AND

THE PLAYERS.

Now who is ther that han't a hir'd
  O' one young TOM CAME?
A Fisherman of Huntspill,
  An a well-knawn name.

A knaw'd much moor o' fishin
  Than many vawk bezides ;
An a knaw'd much moor than mooäst about
  Tha zea an âll tha tides.

A knaw'd well how ta make buts,
  An hullies too an jitch,
An up an down tha river whaur
  Tha best place vor ta pitch.

A knaw'd âll about tha stake-hangs
  Tha zâlmon vor ta catch;—
Tha pitchin an tha dippin net,—
  Tha Slime an tha Mud-Batch.*

* Two islands well known in the River Parret, near its mouth.
Several words will be found in this Poem which I have not
placed in the *Glossary*, because they seem too local and technical
to deserve a place there : they shall be here expl ained,

A handled too iz gads well
    His paddle and iz oor ;*
A war âlways bawld an fearless—
    A, when upon tha Goor.†

O' heerins, sprats, an porpuses—
    O' âll fish a cood tell ;
Who bit he amangst tha Fishermen—
    A âlways bear'd tha bell.

Tommy Came ad hired o' Plâyers,
    Bit niver zeed 'em plâ ;
Thâ war actin at Bejwâter ;
    There a went wi' Sally Dâ.

To Pitch. v. n. To fish with a boat and a pitchin-net in a proper position across the current so that the fish may be caught.

Pitchin-net. s. A large triangular net attached to two poles, and used with a boat for the purpose, chiefly, of catching salmon. —The fishing boats in the Parret, are *flat-bottomed,* in length about seventeen feet, about four feet and a half wide, and pointed at both ends : the are easily managed by *one* person, and rarely, if ever, known to overturn.

Dippen-net. s. A small net somewhat semicircular, and attached to two round sticks for sides, and a long pole for a handle. It is used for the purpose of *dipping salmon* and some other fish, as the *shad,* out of water.

Gad. s. A long pole, having an iron point to it, so that it may be easily thrust into the ground. Two gads are used for each boats. Their uses are to keep the boat steady across the current in order that the net may be in a proper position

* Oar.

† The Gore. Dangerous sands so called, at the mouth of the River Parret, in the Bristol Channel.

When tha curtain first drâw'd up, than
  Sapriz'd war Tommy Came ;
A'd hâf a mine ta hirn awâ,
  Bit stapp'd vor very shame.

Tha vust act bein auver
  Tha zecond jist begun,
Tommy Came still wonder'd grately,
  Ta him it war naw fun.

Zaw âter lookin on zumtime,
  Ta understond did strive ;
There now, zed he, *I'll gee my woth**
That thâ be âll alive !

———◦———

MARY RAMSEY'S CRUTCH.

I ZENG o' *Mary Ramsey's Crutch !*
"Thic little theng !"—Why 'tis'n much
It's true, but still I like ta touch
Tha cap o' *Mary Ramsey's Crutch !*
She zed, wheniver she shood die,
Er little crutch she'd gee ta I.
Did Mary love me ? eese a b'leeve.
She died—a veo vor her did grieve,—
An *but* a veo—vor Mary awld,

* Oath.

Outliv'd er friends, or voun 'em cawld.
Thic crutch I had—I ha it still,
An port wi't wont—nor niver will.
O' her I lorn'd tha cris-cross-lâin ;
I haup that 'tword'n quite in vâin !
'Twar her who teach'd me vust ta read
· Jitch little words as *beef* an *bread* ;
An I da thenk 'twar her that, âter,
Lorn'd I ta read tha single zâter.
Poor Mary ôten used ta tell
O' das a past that pleas'd er well ;
An mangst tha rest war zum o' jay
When I look'd up a little bway.
She zed I war a good one too,
An lorn'd my book athout tha *rue*.*
Poor Mary's gwon !—a longful time
Zunz now !—er little scholard's prime
A-mâ-be's past.—It must be zaw ;—
There's nothin stable here belaw !
O' Mary—âll left is—er *crutch !*
An thaw a gift, an 'tword'n much
'Tis true, still I da like ta touch
Tha cap o' *Mary Ramsey's Crutch !*
That I lov'd Mary, this ool tell.
I'll zâ na moor—zaw, forè well !†

---

* This Lady, when her scholars neglected their duty, or
ɔehaved ill, rubbed their fingers with the leaves of *rue !*
† Fare ye well.

--------oo¿o¿oo--------

HANNAH VERRIOR.

THA zâ I'm maz'd,—my Husband's dead,
  My chile, (hush ! hush ! Lord love er face !)
Tha pit-hawl had at Milemas, when
  Thâ put me in theäze pooät-hawl place.

Thâ zâ I'm maz'd.—I veel—I thenk·—
I tâk—I ate, an oten drenk.—
Tha *thenk*, a-mâ-be, zumtimes, *veel*—
An gee me stra vor bed an peel !

Thâ zâ I'm maz'd.—Hush ! Babby, dear !
Thâ shan't come to er ·!—niver fear !
Thâ zâ thy Father's dead !—Naw, naw !
A'll niver die while I'm belaw.

Thâ zâ I'm maz'd.—Why dwont you speak ?
Fie James !—or else my hort ool break !—
James *is* not dead ! nor Babby !—naw !
Thâ'll niver die while I'm belaw !

REMEMBRANCE.

An shall I drap tha Reed—an shall I,
Athout one nawte about my SALLY?
Althaw we Pawets âll be zingers,
We like, wi' enk, ta dye our vingers;
Bit mooäst we like in vess ta pruv
That we remimber those we love.
Sim-like-it than, that I should iver
Vorgit my SALLY.—Niver, niver!
Vor, while I've wander'd in tha West—
At mornin tide—at evenin rest—
On Quantock's hills—in Mendip's vales—
On Parret's banks—in zight o' Wales—
In thic awld mansion whaur tha bâll
Once vrighten'd Lady Drake an âll;—
When wi' tha Ladies o' thic dell
Whaur witches spird ther 'ticin spell—*
Amangst tha rocks on Watchet shaur
When did tha wine an wâters raur—
In Banwell's cave—on Loxton hill—
At Clifton gâ—at Rickford rill—
In Compton ood—in Hartree coom—
At Crispin's cot wi' little room;—

* COMBE SYDENHAM, the residence of my Friend, GEORGE
NOTLEY, Esq. The history of the *Magic Ball*, as it has been
called, is now pretty generally known, and therefore need not
be here repeated.

At Upton—Lansdown's lofty brow—
At Bath, whaur pleasure flânts enow ;
At Trowbridge, whaur by Friendship's heed,
I blaw'd again my silent Reed,
An there enjay'd, wi' quiet, rest,
Jitch recollections o' tha West ;
Whauriver stapp'd my voot along
I thawt o' HER.—Here ends my zong.

DOCTOR COX; A BLANSCUE.

(First printed in the Graphic Illustrator.)

The catastrophe described in the following sketch, occurred near *Highbridge*, in Somersetshire, about the year 1779.—Mr. or *Doctor Cox*, as surgeons are usually called in the west, was the only medical resident at Huntspill, and in actual practice for many miles around that village. The conduct of Mr. Robert Evans, the friend and associate of Cox, can only be accounted for by one of those unfortunate infatuations to which the minds of some are sometimes liable. Had an immediate alarm been given when we children first discovered that Cox was missing, he might, probably, have been saved. The real cause of his death was, a too great abstraction of heat from the body; as the water was fresh and still, and of considerable depth, and, under the surface, much beneath the usual temperature of the human body. This fact ought to be a lesson to those who bathe in still and deep fresh water; and to warn them to continue only a short time in such a cold medium.*

> The BRUE war bright, and deep and clear;†
> And Lammas dâ and harras near:
> The zun upon the waters drode
> Girt sheets of light as on a rode;
> From zultry heät the cattle hirn'd
> To shade or water as to firnd:
> Men, too, in yarly âternoon
> Doff'd quick ther cloaths and dash'd in zoon

* Various efforts to restore the suspended animation of *Cox*, such as shaking him, rolling him on a cask, attempts to get out the water which it was then presumed had got into the stomach or the lungs, or both, in the drowning; strewing salt over the body, and many other equally ineffectual and improper methods to restore the circulation were, I believe, pursued. Instead of which, had the body been laid in a natural position, and the lost heat gradually administered, by the application of warm frictions, a warm bed, &c., how easily in all probability, would animation have been restored!

† The reader must not suppose that the *river Brue*, is generally a clear stream, or always rapid. I have elsewhere called it "lazy Brue." It is sometimes, at and above the floodgates at *Highbridge*, when they are not closed by the tide, a rapid stream; but through the moors, generally, its course is slow. In the summer-time, and at the period to which allusion is made, the floodgates were closed.

To thic deep river, whaur the trout,
In all ther prankin, plâd about ;
And yels wi' zilver skins war zid,
While gudgeons droo the wâter slid,
Wi' carp sumtimes and wither fish
Avoordon many a dainty dish.
Whaur elvers* too in spring time plâd,
And pailvuls mid o' them be had.
The wâter cold—the zunshine bright,
To zwimmers than what high delight !
'Tis long agwon whun youth and I
Wish'd creepin Time would rise and vly—
A, half a hundred years an moor
Zunz I a trod theäze earthly vloor !
I zed, the face o' Brue war bright ;
Time smil'd too in thic zummer light.
Wi' Hope bezide en promising
A wordle o' fancies wild ö' whing.
I mine too than one lowering cloud
That zim'd to wrop us like a shroud ;
The death het war o' Doctor Cox—
To thenk o't now the storry shocks !
Vor âll the country vur and near
Shod than vor'n many a horty tear.

* Young eels are called *elvers* in Somersetshire. *Walton*, in his
Angler, says, " Young eels, in the Severn, are called *yelvers*."
In what part of the country through which the Severn passes
they are called yelvers we are not told in Walton's book ; as eels
are called, in Somersetshere, yels, analogy seems to require *yelvers*
for their young ; but I never heard them so called. The elvers
used to be obtained from the salt-water side of the bridge.

The *Doctor* like a duck could zwim ;
No fear o' drownin daver'd him !
The pectur now I zim I zee !
I wish I could het's likeness gee !
His *Son*, my brother *John*, *myzel*,
Or *Evans*, mid the storry tell ;
But thâ be gwon and I, o' âll
O'm left to zâ what did bevâll.
Zo, nif zo be you like, why I
To tell the storry now ool try.

Thic *Evans* had a coward core
And fear'd to venter vrom the shore;
While to an vro, an vur an near,
And now an tan did *Cox* appear
In dalliance with the wâters bland,
Or zwimmin wi' a maëster hand.
We youngsters dree, the youngest I,
To zee the zwimmers âll stood by
Upon the green bonk o' the Brue
Jist whaur a stook let water droo :
A quiet time of joyousness
Zim'd vor a space thic dâ to bless !
A dog' too, faithful to his maëster
War there, and mang'd wi' the disaster—
Vigo, ah well I mine his name !
A Newvoun-lond and very tame !
But Evans only war to blame :
He âllès paddled near the shore
Wi' timid hon and coward core ;

While *Doctor Cox* div'd, zwim'd at ease
Like fishes in the zummer seas ;
Or as the skaiters on the ice
In winin circles wild and nice
Yet in a moment he war gwon,
The wonderment of ivry one :
That is, we *dree* and Evans, âll
That zeed what Blanscue did bevâll.—
Athout one sign, or naise, or cry,
Or shriek, or splash, or groan, or sigh !
Could zitch a zwimmer ever die
In wâter ?—Yet we gaz'd in vain
Upon thic bright and wâter plain :
All smooth and calm—no ripple gave
One token of the zwimmer's grave !
We hir'd en not, we zeed en not !—
The glassy wâter zim'd a blot ?
While Evans, he of coward core,
Still paddled as he did bevore !
At length our fears our silence broke,—
Young as we war, and children âll,
We wish'd to goo an zum one câll ;
But Evans carelissly thus spoke—
" Oh, *Cox* is up the river gone,
Vor sartain ool be back anon ;—
He tâlk'd o' cyder, zed he'd g'up
To Stole's* an drenk a horty cup !"

* Mr. Stole resided near *Newbridge*, about a mile from the spot where the accident occurred ; he was somewhat famous for his cyder.

Conjecture anty as the wine !
And zoon did he het's faleshood vine.

 John Cox took up his father's cloaths—
Poor fellow ! he beginn'd to cry !
Than, Evans vrom the wâter rose ;
" A hunderd vawk'll come bimeby,"
A zed ; whun, short way vrom the shore.
We zeed, what zeed we not avore,
The *head* of Doctor Cox appear—
Het floated in the wâter clear !
Bolt upright war he, and his hair,
That pruv'd he sartainly war there,
Zwimm'd on the wâter !—Evans than,
The stupid'st of a stupid man,
Call'd *Vigo*—pointed to that head—
In *Vigo* dash'd—*Cox was not dead* !
But seiz'd the dog's lag—helt en vast !
One struggle, an het war the last !
Ah ! well do I remember it—
That struggle I sholl ne'er forgit !
Vigo was frightened and withdrew ;
The body zink'd at once vrom view.

 Did *Evans*, gallid *Evans* then,
Câll out, at once, vor father's men ?
(Thâ war at work vor'n very near
A mendin the old Highbridge pier,)
A did'n câll, but 'mus'd our fear—
" A hundred vawk ool zoon be here !"
A zed.—We gid the hue and cry !
And zoon a booät wi' men did vly !

But twar âll auver ! *Cox* war voun
Not at the bottom lyin down,
But up aneen, as jist avore
We zeed en floatin nigh the shore.

But death 'ad done his wust—not âll
Thâ did could life's last spork recall.
　Zo Doctor Cox went out o' life
A vine, a, and as honsom mon,
As zun hath iver shin'd upon ;
A left a family—*a wife*,
　Two *sons*—one *dâter*,
As beautiful as lovely Mâ,
　Of whom a-mâ-bi I mid za
　　Zumthin hereâter :
What thâ veel'd now I sholl not tell—
My hort athin me 'gins to zwell !
Reflection here mid try in vain,
Wither particulars to gain,
Evans zim'd âll like one possest ;
Imagination ! tell the rest !

L'ENVOY.

To âll that sholl theeäze storry read,
The *Truth* must vor it chiefly plead ;
I gee not here a tale o' ort,
Nor snip-snap wit, nor lidden smort.
But ôten, ôten by thic river,
　Have I a pass'd ; yet niver, niver,
Athout a thought o' *Doctor Cox*—

His dog—his death—his floatin locks !
The mooäst whun Brue war deep and clear,
And Lammas dâ an harras near ;—
Whun zummer vleng'd his light abroad,—
The zun in âll his glory rawd ;
How beautiful mid be the dâ
A zumthin âllès zim'd to zâ,
" *Whar whing ! the wâter's deep an' clear,*
But death mid be a lurkin near !"

A DEDICATION.

THENK not, bin I ood be tha fashion,
That I, ZIR, write theäze Dedicâtion ;
I write, I haup I dwon't offend.
Bin I be proud ta câll You FRIEND.
I here ston vooäth, alooän unbidden
To 'muse you wi' my country lidden ;—
Wi' remlet's o' tha Saxon tongue
That to our Gramfers did belong.
Vor âll it is a little thing,
Receave it—Friendship's offering—
Ta pruv, if pruf I need renew,
That I esteem not lightly You.

THE FAREWELL.

A LONGFUL time zunz I this vust begun !
One little tootin moor and I a done.
" One little tootin moor !—Enough,
" Vor once, we've had o' jitchy stuff ;
" Thy lidden to a done 'tis time !
" Jitch words war niver zeed in rhyme !"
Vorgee me vor'm.—Goo little Reed !
Aforn tha vawk an vor me plead :
Thy wild nawtes, mâ-be, thâ ool hire
Zooner than zâter vrom a *lyre.*
Zâ that, *thy mäester's pleas'd ta blaw 'em,*
An haups in time thâ'll come ta knaw 'em ;
An nif zaw be thâ'll please ta hear
A'll gee zum moor another year.
Ive nothin else jist now ta tell :
Goo, little Reed, an than forwel !

FARMER BENNET AN JAN LIDE,

A DIALOGUE.

Farmer Bennet.—Jan! why dwon't ye right my shoes?

Jan Lide.—Bin, maëster 'tis zaw cawld, I can't work wi' tha tacker at âll; I've a brawk it ten times I'm shower ta dâ—da vreaze za hord. Why Hester hanged out a kittle-smock ta drowy, an in dree minits a war a vraur as stiff as a pawker; an I can't avoord ta keep a good vier—I wish I cood—I'd zoon right your shoes and withers too—I'd zoon yarn* zum money, I warnt ye. Can't ye vine zum work vor me, maester, theäze hord times—I'll do any theng ta sar a penny.— I can drash—I can cleave brans—I can make spars— I can thatchy—I can shear ditch, an I can gripy too, bit da vreaze za hord. I can wimmy—I can messy or milky nif ther be need o't. I ood'n mine dreavin plough or any theng.

Farmer Bennet.—I've a got nothing vor ye ta do, Jan; bit Mister Boord banehond ta I jist now that thâ war gwain ta wimmy, ond that thâ wanted zum-body ta help 'em.

* Earn.

Jan Lide.—Aw, I'm glad o't, I'll hirn auver an zee where I can't help 'em ; bit I han't a bin athin tha drashel o' Maester Boord's door vor a longful time, bin I thawt that missis did'n use Hester well ; but I dwon't bear malice, an zaw I'll goo.

Farmer Bennet.—What did Missis Boord zâ or do ta Hester, than ?

Jan Lide.—Why, Hester, a-mâ-be, war zummet ta blame too : vor she war one o'm, d'ye zee, that rawd Skimmerton—thic mâ game that frunted zum o' tha gennel-vawk. Thâ zed 'twar time to a done wi' jitch litter, or jitch stuff, or I dwon knaw what thâ call'd it; bit thâ war a frunted wi' Hester about it : an I zed nif thâ war a frunted wi' Hester, thâ mid be frunted wi' I. This zet missis's back up, an Hester han't a bin a choorin there zunz. Bit 'tis niver-the-near ta bear malice ; and zaw I'll goo auver an zee which wâ tha wine da blaw.

—∘∘:∘:∘∘—

THOMAS CAME

AN

YOUNG MAESTER JIMMY.

Thomas Came.—Aw, Maester Jimmy ! zaw you be a come whim vrom school. I thawt we shood niver zee na moor. We've a mist ye iver zunz thic time, when

we war at zea-wâll, an cut aup tha girt porpus wi' za
many zalmon in hiz belly—zum o'm look'd vit ta eat
as thaw tha wor a bwiled, did'n thâ ?—

Jimmy.—Aw eese, Thomas ; I da mine tha porpus ;
an I da mine tha udder, an tha milk o'n, too.   I be a
come whim, Thomas, an I dwon't thenk I shall goo ta
school again theäze zummer.   I shall be out amangst
ye.   I'll goo wi' ta mawy, an ta hâ-makin, an ta reapy
—I'll come âter, an zet up tha stitches vor ye, Thomas.
An if I da stâ till Milemas, I'll goo ta Matthews fayer
wi'.   Thomas, âve ye had any zenvy theäze year ?—
I zeed a gir'd'l o't amangst tha wheat as I rawd along.
Ave you bin down in ham, Thomas, o' late—is thic
groun, tha ten yacres, haind vor mawin ?

Thomas Came.—Aw, Maester Jimmy ! I da love ta
hire you tâk—da zeem za naatal.   We a had zum zenvy
—an tha ten yacres be a haind—a'll be maw'd in veo
dâs — you'll come an hâ-maky, o'nt ye ?—eese, I knaw
you ool—an I da knaw whool goo a hâ-makin wi', too
—ah, she's a zweet maid— I dwon't wonder at
ye at âll, Maester Jimmy—Lord bless ye, an love ye
booäth.

Jimmy.—Thomas, you a liv'd a long time wi' Father,
an' I dwont like ta chide ye, bit nif you da tâk o' Miss
Cox in thic fashion, I knaw she on't like it, naw moor
sholl I.   Miss Cox, Thomas, Miss Cox ool, a-mâ-be, goo
a hâ-makin wi' I, as she a done avaur now ; bit Sally,
Miss Cox, Thomas, I wish you'd zâ naw moor about er.
—There now, Thomas, dwon't ye zee—why shee's by
tha gate-shord ! I haup she han't a hird what we a bin
a tâkin about.—Be tha thissles skeer'd in tha twenty

yacres, Thomas?—aw, thâ be.   Well, I sholl be glad
when tha ten yacres be a mawed—an when we da make
an end o' hâ-corrin, I'll dance wi' Sally Cox.

Thomas Came.—There, Maester Jimmy! 'tword'n I
that tâk'd o' Sally Cox !

——•o×o×o•——

MARY RAMSEY,

A MONOLOGUE,

To er Scholards.

Commether* *Billy Chubb*, an breng tha hornen book.
Gee me tha vester in tha windor, you *Pal Came !*—
what ! be a sleepid—I'll wâke ye.   Now, *Billy*, there's
a good bway ! Ston still there, an mine what I da zâ to
ye, an whaur I da pwint.—Now ;—cris-cross,† girt â
little â —b—c—d.—That's right *Billy ;* you'll zoon
lorn tha cris-cross-lain—you'll zoon auvergit Bobby
Jiffry—you'll zoon be *a scholard.*—A's a pirty chubby
bway—Lord love'n !

Now, *Pal Came !* you come an vessy wi' yer zister.
—There ! tha forrels o' tha book be a brawk ; why
dwon't ye take moor care o'm ?—Now, read ;—*Het*

---

* Come hither.

† The *cris*, in this compound, and in *cris-cross-lain*, is very
often, indeed most commonly, pronounced *Kirs*.

Came ! why d'ye drean zaw ?—*hum, hum, hum ;*—you da make a naise like a spinnin turn, or a dumbledore—âll in one lidden—*hum, hum, hum,*—You'll niver lorn ta read well thic fashion.—Here, *Pal,* read theäze vesses vor yer zister. There now, *Het,* you mine how yer zister da read, not *hum, hum, hum.*—Eese you ool, ool ye ?—I tell ye, you must, or I'll rub zum rue auver yer hons :—what d'ye thenk o't !—There, be gwon you *Het,* an dwon't ye come anuost yer zister ta vessy wi' er till you a got yer lessin moor parfit, or I'll gee zummet you on't ax me vor. *Pally,* you tell yer Gramfer Palmer that I da zâ *Hetty Came* shood lorn ta knitty ; an a shood buy zum knittin nills and wusterd vor er ; an a shood git er zum nills and dird, vor er to lorn to zawy too.

Now *Miss Whitin,* tha dunces be a gwon, let I hire how pirty you can read.—I âlways zed that Pâson Tuttle's grandâter ood lorn er book well.—Now, *Miss,* what ha ye a got there ?—*Valentine an Orson.*—A pirty storry, bit I be afeard there's naw moril to it.—What be âll tha tuthermy books you a got by yer goodhussey there in tha basket ? Gee's-zee-'em,* nif you please, *Miss Polly.*—Tha *Zeven Champions—Goody Two Shoes —Pawems vor Infant minds.*—Theäzamy here be by vur tha best.—There is a moril ta mooäst o'm ; an thâ be pirty bezides.—Now, *Miss,* please ta read thic— *Tha Notorious Glutton.*——*Pal Came !* turn tha glass ! dwon't ye zee tha zond is âll hirnd out ;—you'll stâ in school tha longer for't nif you dwon't mine it.—Now,

---

* *Let me see them.* This is a singular expression, and is thus to be analysed; *Give us to see them.*

âll o' ye be quiet ta hire *Miss Whitin* read.—There now! what d'ye zâ ta jitch radin as that ?—There, d'ye hire, *Het Came !* she dwon't drean—*hum, hum, hum.*—I shood like ta hire er vessy wi' zum o' ye; bit your bad radin ood spwile her good.

OUT O' BOOKS !

All the childern goo voäth.

SOLILOQUY OF BEN BOND,

THE IDLETON.

(First printed in the Graphic Illustrator.)

BEN BOND was one of those sons of Idleness whom ignorance and want of occupation in a secluded country village too often produce. He was a comely lad, aged sixteen, employed by Farmer Tidball, a querulous and suspicious old man, to look after a large flock of sheep.—The scene of his Soliloquy may be thus described.

A green sunny bank, on which the body may agreeably repose, called the *Sea Wall* ; on the sea side was an extensive common called the *Wath*, and adjoining to it was another called the *Island,* both were occasionally overflowed by the tide. On the other side of the bank were rich enclosed pastures, suitable for fattening the finest cattle. Into these inclosures many of *Ben Bond's* charge were frequently disposed to stray. The season was June, the time mid-day, and the western breezes came over the sea, a short distance from which our scene lay, at once cool, grateful, refreshing, and playful. The rushing *Parret,* with its ever shifting sands, was also heard in the distance. It should be stated, too, that *Larence* is the name usually given in Somersetshire to that imaginary being which presides over the IDLE. Perhaps it may also be useful to state here that the word *Idleton* is more than a provincialism, and should be in our dictionaries.

During the latter part of the Soliloquy Farmer Tidball arrives behind the bank, and hearing poor Ben's discourse with himself, interrupts his musings in the manner described hereafter. It is the history of an occurrence in real life, and at the place mentioned. The writer knew Farmer Tidball personally, and has often heard the story from his wife.

SOLILOQUY

" LARENCE ! why doos'n let I up? Oot let I up?" *Naw, I be slëapid, I can't let thee up eet.*— " Now, Larence ! do let I up. There ! bimeby maester'll come, an a'll beät I athin a ninch o' me life ; do let I up !"— *Naw I wunt.*

" Larence ! I bag o' ee, do ee let I, up! D'ye zee ! tha

shee-ape be âll a breakin droo tha hadge inta tha vive-
an-twenty yacres ; an Former Haggit'll goo ta Lâ wi'n,
an I sholl be kill'd !"—*Naw I wunt—'tis zaw whot :
bezides I hant a had my nap out.* "Larence ! I da zâ,
thee bist a bad un ! Oot thee hire what I da zâ ?
Come now an let I scooce wi'. Lord a massy upon me !
Larence, whys'n thee let I up ?" *Câz I wunt. What !
muss'n I hâ an hour like wither vawk ta ate my bird an
cheese ? I do zâ I wunt ; and zaw 'tis niver-tha-near
to keep on.*

"Maester tawl'd I, nif I wer a good bway, a'd gee I
iz awld wasket ; an I'm shower, nif a da come an vine
I here, an tha shee-ape a brawk inta tha vive-an-twenty
yacres, a'll vleng't awâ vust ! Larence, do ee, do ee
let I up ! Ool ee, do ee !"—*Naw, I tell ee I wunt.*

"There's one o' tha sheep 'pon iz back in tha gripe,
an a can't turn auver ! I mis g'in ta tha groun an
g'out to'n, an git'n out. There's another in tha ditch !
a'll be a buddled ! There's a gird'l o' trouble wi' shee-
ape ! Larence ; cass'n thee let I goo. I'll gee thee a
hâ peny nif oot let me."—*Naw I can't let thee goo eet.*

"Maester'll be shower to come an catch me ! Larence !
doose thee hire ? I da zâ, oot let me up. I zeed Farmer Haggit zoon âter I upt, an a zed, nif a voun one o'
my shee-ape in tha vive-an-twenty yacres, a'd drash I za
long as a cood ston auver me, an wi' a groun ash' too !
There ! Zum o'm be a gwon droo tha vive-an-twenty
yacres inta tha drauve : thâ'll zoon hirn vur anow.
Thâ'll be poun'd. Larence ! I'll gee thee a *penny* nif
oot let I up." *Naw I wunt.*

"Thic not sheep ha got tha shab ! Dame tawl'd I

whun I upt ta-da ta mine tha shab-wâter; I sholl pick it in whun I da goo whim. I vorgot it! Maester war desperd cross, an I war glad ta git out o' tha langth o' iz tongue. I da hate zitch cross vawk! Larence! what, oot niver let I up? There! zum o' tha shee-ape be gwon into *Leek-beds*; an zum o'm be in *Hounlake*; dree or vour o'm be gwon zâ vur as *Slow-wâ*; the ditches be, menny o'm zâ dry 'tis all now rangel common! There! I'll gee thee *dree hâ pence* ta let l goo." *Why, thee hass'n bin here an hoür, an vor what shood I let thee goo? I da zâ, lie still!*

"Larence! why doos'n let I up? There! zim ta I, I da hire thic pirty maid, *Fanny o' Primmer Hill*, a chidin bin I be a lyin here while tha shee-ape be gwain droo thic shord an tuther shord; zum o'm, a-mâ-be, be a drown'd! Larence; doose thee thenk I can bear tha betwitten o' thic pirty maid? She, tha Primrawse o' Primmer-hill; tha Lily o' tha level; tha gawl-cup o' tha mead; tha zweetist honeyzuckle in tha garden; tha yarly vilet; tha rawse o' rawses; tha pirty pollyantice! Whun I seed er last, she zed, " Ben, do ee mind tha shee-ape, an tha yeos an lams, an than zumbody ool mine *you.*" Wi' that she gid me a beautiful spreg o' jessamy, jist a pickt vrom tha poorch,—tha smill war za zweet.

"Larence! I mus goo! I ool goo. You mus let I up. I ont stâ here na longer! Maester'll be shower ta come an drash me. There, Larence! I'll gee *tuther penny*, an that's ivry vard'n I a got. Oot let I goo?" *Naw, I mis ha a penny moor.*

"Larence! do let I up! Creeplin Philip 'll be

shower ta catch me! Thic cockygee! I dwont like en at âll; a's za rough an za zoür. An *Will Popham* too, ta betwite me about tha maid: a câll'd er a rathe-ripe *Lady-buddick.* I dwont mislike tha name at âll, thawf I dwont care vor'n a stra, nor a read mooäte; nor tha tite o' a pin! What da thâ câll (he) Why, tha *upright man,* câs a da ston upright; let'n; an let'n wrassly too: I dwont like zitch *hoss-plâs,* nor *singel-stick* nuther; nor *cock-squailin'*; nor menny wither mâ-games that Will Popham da volly. I'd rather zit in tha poorch, wi' tha jessamy ranglin roun it, and hire Fanny zeng. Oot let I up, Larence?"—*Naw, I tell ee I ont athout a penny moor.*

"*Rawzey Pink,* too, an *Nanny Dubby* axed I about Fanny. What bisniss ad thâ ta up wi't? I dwont like norn 'om? *Girnin Jan* too shawed iz teeth an put in his verdi.—I wish theeäze vawk ood mine ther awn consarns an let I an Fanny alooäne.

"Larence! doose thee meän to let I goo?"—*Eese, nif thee't gee me tuther penny.*—"Why I han't a got a vard'n moor; oot let I up!"—*Not athout tha penny.*—"Now Larence! doo ee, bin I hant naw moor money. I a bin here moor than an hoür; whaur tha yeos an lams an âll tha tuthermy sheep be now I dwon' know.—*Creeplin Philip** ool gee me a lirropin shower anow!

---

* Even remote districts in the country have their satirists, and would-be-wits; and Huntspill, the place alluded to in the Soliloquy, was, about half a century ago, much pestered with them. Scarcely a person of any note escaped a parish libel, and even servants were not excepted. For instance:—

There !—I da thenk I hired zummet or zumbody auver
tha wâll."—

"*Here, d—n thee !* I'll gee tha *tuther penny, an
zummet besides !*" exclaimed *Farmer Tidball,* leaping
down the bank, with a stout sliver of a crab-tree in his
hand.—The sequel may be easily imagined.

> Nanny Dubby, Sally Clink,
> Long Josias an Rawsy Pink,
> ——————————— Girnin Jan,
> Creeplin Philip and the upright man.

Creeplin Philip, (that is "creeplin," because he walked lamely,)
was Farmer Tidball himself; and his servant, William Popham,
was the *upright man.* *Girnin Jan* is Grinning John.

TWO DISSERTATIONS

ON SOME OF THE ANGLO-SAXON PRONOUNS.

BY JAMES JENNINGS.

(From the Graphic Illustrator.)

No. I.—I, IC, ICH, ICHE, UTCHY, ISE, C', CH', CHE
CH'AM, CH'UD, CH'LL.

Until recently few writers on the English Language,
have devoted much attention to the origin of our first
personal pronoun I, concluding perhaps that it would
be sufficient to state that it is derived from the Anglo-
Saxon *ic*. No pains seem to have been taken to explain the connexion which *ic, ich,* and *iche* have with
Ise, c', ch', che', and their combinations in such words
as *ch'am, ch'ud, ch'ill,* &c. Hence we have been led to
believe that such contractions are the vulgar corruptions of an ignorant and, consequently, unlettered people. That the great portion of the early Anglo-Saxons
were an unlettered people, and that the *rural* population were particularly unlettered, and hence for the
most part ignorant, we may readily admit; and even
at the present time, many districts in the west will be
found pretty amply besprinkled with that unlettered
ignorance for which many of our forefathers were dis-

tinguished. But an enquiry into the origin and use of our provincial words will prove, that even our unlettered population have been guided by certain rules in their use of an energetic language. Hence it will be seen on inquiry that many of the words supposed to be *vulgarisms*, and *vulgar* and *capricious* contractions are no more so than many of our own words in daily use; as to the Anglo-Saxon contractions of *ch'am*, *ch'ud*, and *ch'ill*, they will be found equally consistent with our own common contractions of *can't, won't, he'll, you'll,* &c., &c. in our present polished dialect.

Whether, however, our western dialects will be more dignified by an Anglo-Saxon pedigree I do not know; those who delight in tracing descents through a long line of ancestors up to one primitive original ought to be pleased with the literary genealogist, who demonstrates that many of our provincial words and contractions have an origin more remote, and in *their* estimation of course, must be more legitimate than a mere slip from the parent stock, as our personal pronoun, I, unquestionably is.

As to the term "barbarous," Mr. Horace Smith, the author of "*Walter Colyton*," assures me that many of his friends call what he has introduced of the Somerset Dialect in Walter Colyton, "barbarous."—Now, I should like to learn in what its barbarity consists. The plain truth after all is, that those who are unwilling to take the trouble to understand any language, or any dialect of any language, with which they are previously unacquainted, generally consider such new language or such dialect barbarous; and to them it doubtless appears so.

What induces our metropolitan *literati*, those at least who are, or affect to be the *arbitri elegantiarum* among them, to consider the *Scotch* dialect in another light? Simply because such able writers, as *Allan Ramsay, Robert Burns, Sir Walter Scott*, and others, have chosen to employ it for the expression of their thoughts. Let similar able writers employ our *Western Dialect* in a similar way, and I doubt not the result. And why should not our Western dialects be so employed? If *novelty* and *amusement*, to say the least for such writings, be advantageous to our literature, surely novelty and amusement might be conveyed in the dialect of the *West* as well as of the *North*. Besides these advantages, it cannot be improper to observe that occasional visits to the *well-heads* of our language, (and many of these will be found in the West of England) will add to the perfection of our polished idiom itself. *The West may be considered the last strong hold of the Anglo-Saxon in this country.*

I observed, in very early life, that some of my father's servants, who were natives of the *Southern* parts of the county of Somerset, almost invariably employed the word *utchy* for I. Subsequent reflection convinced me that this word, *utchy*, was the Anglo-Saxon *iche*, used as a dissyllable ichè, as the Westphalians, (descendants of the Anglo-Saxons,) down to this day in their Low German (Westphalian) dialect say, "*Ikke*" for "*ich*." How or when this change in the pronunciation of the word, from one to two syllables, took place in in this country it is difficult to determine; but on reference to the works of *Chaucer*, there

is, I think, reason to conclude that *iche* is used sometimes in that poet's works as a dissyllable.

Having discovered that *utchy* was the Anglo-Saxon
iche, there was no difficulty in appropriating *'che, 'c',*
and *ch'* to the same root; hence, as far as concerned
iche in its literal sounds, a good deal seemed unravelled;
but how could we account for *ise*, and *ees*, used so commonly for I in the western parts of *Somersetshire*, as
well as in *Devonshire?* In the first folio edition of the
works of Shakspeare the *ch* is printed, in one instance,
with a mark of elision before it thus, *'ch*, a proof that
the *I* in *iche* was sometimes dropped in a common and
rapid pronunciation; and a proof too, that, we, the
descendants of the Anglo-Saxons, have chosen the initial
letter only of that pronoun, which initial letter the
Anglo-Saxons had in very many instances discarded!

It is singular enough that Shakspeare has the *'ch* for
iche, I, and *ise*, for I, within the distance of a few lines,
in *King Lear*, Act IV. scene 6. But perhaps not
more singular than that, in Somersetshire at the
present time, may be heard for the pronoun I, *utchy* or
ichè, 'ch, and *ise.* To the absence originally of general
literary information, and to the very recent rise of the
study of grammatical analysis, are these anomalies and
irregularities to be attributed.

We see, therefore, that *'ch'ud, ch'am*, and *'ch'ill*, are
simply the Anglo-Saxon *ich*, contracted and combined
with the respective verbs *would, am*, and *will*; that
the *'c'* and *'ch'*, as quoted in the lines given by Miss
Ham, are contracts for the Anglo-Saxon *iche* or *I*, and
nothing else.

It may be also observed, that in more than one modern work containing specimens of the dialect of Scotland and the North of England, and in, I believe, some of Sir Walter Scott's novels, the word *ise* is employed, so that the auxiliary verb *will* or *shall* is designed to be included in that word; and the printing or it thus, *I'se*, indicates that it is so designed to be employed. Now, if this be a *copy* of the *living* dialect of Scotland (which I beg leave respectfully to doubt), it is a " barbarism" which the Somerset dialect does not possess. The *ise* in the west is simply a pronoun and nothing else; it is, however, often accompanied by a contracted verb, as *ise'll* for I will.

In concluding these observations on the first personal pronoun it may be added, that the object of the writer has been to state facts, without the accompaniment of that *learning* which is by some persons deemed so essential in inquiries of this kind. The best learning is that which conveys to us a knowledge of facts. Should any one be disposed to convince himself of the correctness of the *data* here laid before him, by researches among our old authors, as well as from living in the west, there is no doubt as to the result to which he must come. Perhaps, however, it may be useful to quote one or two specimens of our more early Anglo-Saxon, to prove their analogy to the present dialect in Somersetshire.

The first specimen is from *Robert of Gloucester*, who lived in the time of Henry II., that is, towards the latter end of the twelfth century; it is quoted by *Drayton*, in the notes to his *Polyolbion*, song xvii.

> " The meste wo that here *vel* bi King Henry's days,
> In this lond, *icholle* beginne to tell *yuf ich* may."

Vel, for fell, the preterite of to fall, is precisely the sound given to the same word at the present time in Somersetshire. We see that *icholle*, for *I shall*, follows the same rule as the contracts *'ch'ud*, *'ch'am*, and *'ch'ill*. It is very remarkable that *sholl*, for shall, is almost invariably employed in Somersetshire, at the present time. *Yuf* I am disposed to consider a corruption or mistake for *gyf* (give), that is, *if*, the meaning and origin of which have been long ago settled by Horne Tooke in his Purley.

The next specimen is assuredly of a much more modern date; though quoted by *Mr Dibdin*, in his *Metrical History of England*, as from an *old ballad*.

> " *Ch'ill* tell thee what, good fellow,
> Before the vriars went hence,
> A bushel of the best wheate
> Was zold for vourteen pence,
> And vorty egges a penny,
> That were both good and new,
> And this *che* say myself have seene,
> And yet I am no Jew."

With a very few alterations, indeed, these lines would become the *South* Somerset of the present day.

No. II.—ER, EN, A—IT HET—THEEAZE, THEEAZAM, THIZZAM—THIC, THILK—TWORDM—WORDN—ZINO.

There are in *Somersetshire* (besides that particular portion in the *southern* parts of the country in which the Anglo-Saxon *iche* or *utchy* and its contracts prevail) *two* distinct and very different dialects, the boundaries of which are strongly marked by the River *Parret*. To the east and north of that river, and of the town of Bridgewater, a dialect is used which is essentially, (even now) the dialect of all the peasantry of not only that part of Somersetshire, but of Dorsetshire, Wiltshire, Gloucestershire, Hampshire, Surrey, Sussex, and Kent ; and even in the suburban village of *Lewisham*, will be found many striking remains of it. There can be no doubt that this dialect was some centuries ago the language of the inhabitants of all the south and of much of the west portion of our island; but it is in its greatest *purity** and most abundant in the county of Somerset.

---

* Among other innumerable proofs that Somersetshire is one of the strongholds of our old Anglo-Saxon, are the sounds which are there generally given to the vowels A and E. A has, for the most part, the same sound as we give to that letter in the word *father* in our polished dialect: in the words tâll, câll, bâll, and vâll (fall), &c., it is thus pronounced. The E has the sound which we give in our polished dialect to the *a* in pane, cane, &c., both which sounds, it may be observed, are even *now* given to these letters on the Continent, in very many

No sooner, however, do we cross the *Parret* and proceed from Combwich* to *Cannington* (three miles from Bridgewater) than another dialect becomes strikingly apparent. Here we have no more of the *zees*, the *hires*, the *veels*, and the *walks*, and a numerous et cætera, which we find in the eastern portion of the county, in the third person singular of the verbs, but instead we have *he zeeth*, he sees, *he veel'th*, he feels, *he walk'th*, he walks, and so on through the whole range of the similar part of every verb. This is of itself a strong and distinguishing characteristic; but this dialect has many more; one is the very different sounds given to almost every word which is employed, and which thus strongly characterize the persons who use them.†

Another is that *er* for he in the nominative case is most commonly employed; thus for, *he said he would not*, is used *Er zad er ood'n—Er ont goor*, for, *he will not go*, &c.

Again *ise* or *ees*, for I is also common. Many other

places, particularly in Holland and in Germany. The name of Dr. Gall, the founder of the science of phrenology, is pronounced Gâll, as we of the west pronounce tâll, bâll, &c.

* Pronounced *Cummidge*. We here see the disposition in our language to convert *wich* into *idge*; as *Dulwich* and *Greenwich* often pronounced by the vulgar *Dullidge, Greenidge*.

† I cannot pretend to account for this very singular and marked distinction in our western dialects; the fact, however, is so; and it may be added, too, that there can be no doubt both these dialects are the children of our Anglo-Saxon parent.

peculiarities and contractions in this dialect are to a stranger not a little puzzling; and if we prooeed so far westward as the confines of Exmoor, they are, to a plain Englishman, very often unintelligible. *Her* or rather *hare* is most always used instead of the nominative *she*. *Har'th a doo'd it*, she has done it; *Hare zad har'd do't.* She said she would do it. This dialect pervades, not only the western portion of Somersetshire, but the whole of Devonshire. As my observations in these papers apply chiefly to the dialect east of the Parret, it is not necessary to proceed further in our present course; yet *as er* is also occasionally used instead of *he* in that dialect it becomes useful to point out its different application in the two portions of the county. In the eastern part it is used very rarely if ever in the beginning of sentences; but frequently thus: *A did, did er?* He did, did he? *Wordn er gwain?* Was he not going? *Ool er goo?* will he go?

We may here advert to the common corruption, I suppose I must call it, of *a* for *he* used so generally in the west. As *a zed a'd do it* for, he said he would do it. Shakespeare has given this form of the pronoun in the speeches of many of his low characters which, of course, strikingly demonstrates its then very general use among the vulgar; but it is in his works usually printed with a comma thus 'a, to show, probably that it is a corrupt enunciation of he. This comma is, however, very likely an addition by some editor.

Another form of the third personal pronoun employed only in the objective case is found in the west, namely *en* for him, as *a zid en* ·or, rather more commonly, *a zid'n*, he saw him. Many cases however, occur in which *en* is fully heard ; as *gee'l to en*, give it to him. It is remarkable that Congreve, in his comedy of "*Love for Love*," has given to *Ben the Sailor* in that piece many expressions found in the west. " Thof he be my father I an't bound prentice to en." It should be noted here that *he be* is rarely if ever heard in the west, but *he's* or *he is*. *We be, you be*, and *thâ be* are nevertheless very common. *Er*, employed as above, is beyond question aboriginal Saxon ; *en* has been probably adopted as being more euphonious than *him*.*

Het for *it* is still also common amongst the peasantry.

---

* I have not met with *en* for him in any of our more early writers ; and I am therefore disposed to consider it as of comparatively modern introduction, and one among the very few changes in language introduced by the *yeomanry*, a class of persons less disposed to changes of any kind than any other in ·society, arising, doubtless, from their isolated position. It must be admitted, nevertheless, that this change if occasionally adopted in our polished dialect would afford an agreeable variety by no means unmusical. In conversation with a very learned Grecian on this subject, he seemed to consider because the *learned* are constantly, and sometimes very capriciously, introducing *new* words into our language, that such words as *en* might be introduced for similar reasons, namely, mere fancy or caprice ; on this subject I greatly differ from him : our aboriginal Saxon population has never corrupted our language nor destroyed its energetic character half so much as the mere classical scholar. Hence the necessity, in order to a complete knowledge of our mother tongue, that we should study the Anglo-Saxon still found in the provinces.

In early Saxon writers, it was usually written hit, sometimes hyt.

> " Als *hit* in heaven y-doe,
> Evar in yearth beene it also."
> *Metrical Lord's Prayer of* 1160.

Of *theeäze*, used as a demonstrative pronoun, both in the singular and plural, for *this* and *these*, it may be observed, as well as of the pronunciation of many other words in the west, that we have no letters or combination of letters which express exactly the sounds there given to such words. Theeäze is here marked as a dissyllable, but although it is sometimes decidedly two syllables, its sounds are not always thus apparent in Somerset enunciation. What is more remarkable in this world, is its equal application to the singular and the plural. Thus we say *theeäze man* and *theäze men.* But in the plural are also employed other forms of the same pronoun, namely *theeäzam, theeäzamy* and *thizzum.* This last word is, of course, decidedly the Anglo-Saxon ꞅiᵽᵽum. In the west we say therefore *theeäzam here, theeäzamy here,* and *thizzam here* for these, or these here ; and sometimes without the pleonastic and unnecessary *here.*

For the demonstrative *those* of our polished dialect *them,* or *themmy,* and often *them there* or *themmy there* are the usual synonyms ; as, *gee I themmy there shoes ;* that is, give me those shoes. The objective pronoun *me,* is very sparingly employed indeed—I, in general supplying its place as in the preceding sentence : to this *barbarism* in the name of my native dialect, I must plead *guilty*!—if barbarism our metropolitan critics shall be pleased to term it.*

Thic is in the Somersetshire dialect (namely that to which I have particularly directed my attention and which prevails on the *east* side of the Parret) invariably employed for *that*. *Thic house*, that house; *thic man*, that man : in the west of the county it is *thiky*, or *thecky*. Sometimes *thic* has the force and meaning of a personal pronoun, as :

> *Catch and scrabble*
> *Thic that's yable.*—
> Catch and scramble
> He who's able.

Again, *thic that dont like it mid leave it*,—he who does not like it may leave it.

It should be noted that *th* in all the pronouns above mentioned has the obtuse sound as heard in *then*

* By the way I must just retort upon our polished dialect, that it has gone over to the other extreme in avoidance of the I, using *me* in many sentences where I ought most decidedly to be employed. *It was me* § is constantly dinned in our ears for *it was I* : as well as indeed *one* word more, although not a pronoun, this is, the almost constant use in London of the verb *to lay* for the verb *to lie*, and *ketch* for *catch*. If we at head-quarters commit such blunders can we wonder at our provincial detachments falling into similar errors ? none certainly more gross than this !

§ I am aware that some of our lexicographers have attempted a defence of this solecism by deriving it from the French *c'est moi*; but, I think it is from their affected dislike of direct egotism ; and that, whenever they can, they avoid the I in order that they might not be thought at once vulgar and egotistic !

and *this* and not the thin sound as heard in *both, thin,* and many other words of our polished dialect. Chaucer employed the pronoun *thic* very often, but he spells it *thilk;* he does not appear, however, to have always restricted it to the meaning implied in our *that* and to the present Somerset *thic.* *Spenser* has also employed *thilk* in his *Shepherd's Calendar* several times.

> "Seest not *thilk* same hawthorn stud
> How bragly it begins to bud
> And utter his tender head?"
> "Our blonket leveries been all too sad
> For *thilk* same season, when all is yclad
> With pleasance."

I cannot conclude without a few observations on three very remarkable Somersetshire words, namely *twordn, wordn,* and *zino.* They are living evidences of the *contractions* with which that dialect very much abounds.

Twordn means it was not; and is composed of three words, namely *it, wor,* and *not ; wor* is the past tense, or, as it is sometimes called, the preterite of the verb to be, in the third person singular;* and such is the indistinctness with which the sound of the vowel in *were* is commonly expressed in Somersetshire, that *wor, wer,* or *war,* will nearly alike convey it, the sound of the e being rarely if ever long ; *twordn* is therefore

---

* It should be observed here that *was* is rather uncommon among the Somersetshire peasantry—*wor,* or *war,* being there the synonyms ; thus *Spenser* in his " *Shepherd's Calendar.*"
> " The kid,—
> Asked the cause of his great distress,
> And also who and whence that *he wer*

composed, as stated, of three words; but it will be asked what business has the *d* in it? To this it may be replied that *d* and *t* are, as is well known, often converted in our language the one into the other; but by far the most frequently *d* is converted into *t*. Here, however, the *t* is not only converted into *d*, but instead of being placed after *n*, as analogy requires thus, *twornt*, it is placed before it for *euphony* I dare say. Such is the analysis of this singular and, if not euphonious, most certainly expressive word.

Wordn admits of a similar explanation; but this word is composed of two words only, *wor* and *not*; instead of *wornt*, which analogy requires, a *d* is placed before *n* for a similar reason that the *d* is placed before *n* in *twordn*, namely for euphony; *wordn* is decidedly another of the forcible words.

Wordn er gwain?—was he not going, may compete with any language for its energetic brevity.

Zino, has the force and application of an interjection, and has sufficient of the *ore rotundo* to appear a classical dissyllable; its origin is, however, simply the contract of, *as I know*, and it is usually preceeded in Somersetshire by no. Thus, *ool er do it? no, zino! I thawt a oodn.* Will he do it? no, as I know! I thought he would not. These words, *Twordn, Wordn,* and *Zino,* may be thus exemplified:

> You say he was there, and I say that *a wordn;*
> You say that 'twas he, and I tell you that *twordn;*
> You ask, will he go? I reply, not as I know;
> You say *that* he *will,* and *I* must say, *no, Zino!*

CONCLUDING OBSERVATIONS.

I cannot, perhaps, better close this work, than by presenting to the reader the observations of Miss HAM, (a Somersetshire lady of no mean talents), in a letter to me on these dialects.

The lines, of which I desired a copy, contain an exemplification of the use of *utchy* or *ichè*, used contractedly [see UTCHY in the *Glossary*] by the inhabitants of the *South* of Somersetshire, one of the strongholds, as I conceive, of the Anglo-Saxon dialect.

In our polished dialect, the lines quoted by Miss HAM, may be thus rendered—

> Bread and cheese I have had,
> What I had I have eaten,
> More I would [have eaten if] I had [had] it.

If the contradictions be supplied they will stand thus :—

> Bread and cheese *ichè* have a had
> That *ichè* had *ichè* have a eat
> More *ichè* would *ichè* had it.

CLIFTON, *Jan.* 30, 1825.

Sir :

I have certainly great pleasure in complying with your request, although I fear that any com-

munication it is in my power to make, will be of little
use to you in your curious work on the West Country
dialect. The lines you desire are these :

> Bread and cheese 'c' have a had,
> That 'c' had 'c' have a eat,
> More 'ch wou'd 'c' had it.

Sounds which, from association no doubt, carry with
them to my ear the idea of great vulgarity : but which
might have a very different effect on that of an unpre-
judiced hearer, when dignified by an Anglo-Saxon
pedigree. The Scotch dialect, now become *quite
classical* with us, might, perhaps, labour under the
same disadvantage amongst those who hear it spoken
by the vulgar only.

Although I am a native of Somersetshire, I have
resided very little in that county since my childhood,
and, in my occasional visits since, have had little
intercourse with the *aborigines*. I recollect, however,
two or three words, which you might not, perhaps,
have met with. One of them of which I have traditionary knowledge, being, I believe, now quite obsolete.
Pitisanquint was used in reply to an inquiry after
the health of a person, and was, I understand, equivalent to *pretty well*, or *so so*. The word *Lamiger*, which
signifies an invalid, I have no doubt you have met
with. When any one forbodes bad weather, or any
disaster, it is very common to say *Don't ye housenee*.
Here you have the verbal termination, which you
remarked was so common in the West, and which I
cannot help thinking might have been originally used

as a sort of diminutive, and that *to milkee*, signified to milk *a little.*

As my knowledge of these few words is merely oral, I cannot answer for the orthography; I have endeavoured to go as near the sound as possible, and I only wish it were in my power to make some communication more worth your attention. As it is, I have only my best wishes to offer for the success of your truly original work.

I am, Sir, your most obedient,
ELIZABETH HAM.

I have only one or two remarks to add to those of Miss HAM in the preceding letter.

It will be seen, by reference to the exemplifications of the dialect, that occasional *pleonasm* will be found in it, as well as, very often, extraordinary *contraction. I have adone, I have a had,* are examples of the first ; and *'tword'n, g'up, g'under, banehond,* &c. [see BANE-HOND, in the *Glossary*] are examples of the last. *Pitisanquint* appears to me to be simply a contracted and corrupted mode of expressing *Piteous and quaint,* [See PITIS in the *Glossary.*]

Don't ye houseenee is *Do not stay in your houses.* But the implied meaning is, *be active ;* do your best to provide for the bad weather which portends. In Somersetshire, most of the colloquial and idiomatic expressions have more or less relation to agriculture, agricultural occupations, or to the most common concerns of life, hence such expressions have, in process of time, become *figurative*. Thus, *don't ye housenee*, would be readily applied to rouse a person to activity. in order that he may prevent or obviate any approaching or portending evil.

I am still of opinion; indeed I may say, I am quite sure, that the verbal terminations, *sewy*, *knitty*, &c., have no relation to *diminution* in the district East of the Parret.

Upon the whole, it is evident that considerable care and circumspection are necessary in committing to paper the signs of the sounds of a language, of which we have no accredited examples, nor established criterion. In making collections of this work, I have not failed to bear this constantly in mind.

London:
S. & J. BRAWN, Printers, 13, Princes St., Little Queen St.,
Holborn, W.C.

A

Catalogue of Books

PUBLISHED OR SOLD BY

JOHN RUSSELL SMITH,

36, SOHO SQUARE, LONDON, W.

DLARD (George).—The Sutton-Dudleys of England, and the Dudleys of Massachusetts, in New England. 8vo, *pedigrees, &c., cloth.* 15s

An interesting volume to the English genealogist, it contains a good deal of new matter relating to this old English Family and their collateral branches.

AGINCOURT.—A Contribution towards an Authentic List of the Commanders of the English Host in King Henry the Fifth's Expedition. By the Rev. JOSEPH HUNTER, post 8vo. 2s 6d

AKERMAN'S (John Yonge, *Fellow and late Secretary of the Society of Antiquaries*) Archæological Index to Remains of Antiquity of the Celtic, Romano-British, and Anglo-Saxon Periods. 8vo, *illustrated with numerous engravings, comprising upwards of five hundred objects, cloth.* 15s

This work, though intended as an introduction and a guide to the study of our early antiquities, will, it is hoped, also prove of service as a book of reference to the practised Archæologist.

"One of the first wants of an incipient Antiquary is the facility of comparison: and here it is furnished him at one glance. The plates, indeed, form the most valuable part of the book, both by their number and the judicious selection of types and examples which they contain. It is a book which we can, on this account, safely and warmly recommend to all who are interested in the antiquities of their native land."—*Literary Gazette.*

AKERMAN's (J. Y.) Introduction to the Study of Ancient and Modern Coins. Foolscap 8vo, *with numerous wood engravings from the original Coins (an excellent introductory book), cloth.* 6s 6d

CONTENTS :—SECT. 1.—Origin of Coinage—Greek Regal Coins—2. Greek Civic Coins—3. Greek Imperial Coins—4. Origin of Roman Coinage—Consular Coins —5. Roman Imperial Coins—6. Roman British Coins—7. Ancient British Coinage—8. Anglo-Saxon Coinage—9. English Coinage from the Conquest— 10. Scotch Coinage—11. Coinage of Ireland—12. Anglo-Gallic Coins—13. Continental Money in the Middle Ages—14. Various Representatives of Coinage— 15. Forgeries in Ancient and Modern Times—16. Table of Prices of Engli

AKERMAN'S (J. Y.) Remains of Pagan Saxondom, principally from Tumuli in England, drawn from the originals. Described and illustrated. One handsome volume, 4to, *illustrated with 40* COLOURED PLATES, *half morocco.* £2. 2s (original price £3)

The plates are admirably executed by Mr. Basire, and coloured under the direction of the author, which is not the case with a re-issue of the volume now sold bound in cloth. It is a work well worthy the notice of the Archæologist.

AKERMAN'S (J. Y.) Coins of the Romans relating to Britain. Described and Illustrated. *Second edition,* greatly enlarged 8vo, *with plates and woodcuts, cloth.* 10s 6d

The "Prix de Numismatique" was awarded by the French Institute to th author for this work.

"Mr. Akerman's volume contains a notice of every known variety, with copious illustrations, and is published at a very moderate price; it should be consulted, not merely for these particular coins, but also for facts most valuable to all who are interested in Romano-British History."—*Archæol. Journal.*

AKERMAN'S (J. Y.) Ancient Coins of Cities and Princes, Geo graphically Arranged and Described—Hispania, Gallia, Britannia, 8vo, *with engravings of many hundred Coins from actual examples, Cloth.* 7s 6d (original price 18s)

AKERMAN'S (J. Y.) Tradesman's Tokens struck in London and its Vicinity, from 1648 to 1671, described from the originals in the British Museum, &c. 8vo, *with 8 plates of numerous examples, cloth,* 7s 6d (original price 15s.)—LARGE PAPER in 4to, *cloth.* 15s

This work comprises a list of nearly 3000 Tokens, and contains occasional illustrative, topographical, and antiquarian notes on persons, places, streets, old tavern and coffee-house signs, &c., &c., with an introductory account of the causes which led to the adoption of such a currency.

AKERMAN'S (J. Y.) List of Tokens issued by Wiltshire Tradesmen in the Seventeenth Century. 8vo, *plates, sewed.* 1s 6d

AKERMAN'S (J. Y.) Wiltshire Tales, illustrative of the Manners, Customs, and Dialect of that and adjoining Counties. 12mo, *cloth.* 2s 6d

"We will conclude with a simple but hearty recommendation of a little book which is as humourous for the drolleries of the stories as it is interesting as a picture of rustic manners."—*Tallis's Weekly Paper.*

AKERMAN'S (J. Y.) Spring Tide; or, the Angler and his Friends, 12mo, *plates, cloth.* 2s 6d (original price 6s)

These Dialogues incidentally illustrate the Dialect of the West of England.

"Never in our recollection has the contemplative man's recreation been rendered more attractive, nor the delights of a country life set forth with a truer or more discriminating zest than in these pleasant pages."—*Gent.'s Mag.*

ALEXANDER (W., *late Keeper of the Prints in the British Museum*) Journey to Beresford Hall, in Derbyshire, the Seat of Charles Cotton, Esq., the celebrated Author and Angler. Crown 4to, *printed on tinted paper, with a spirited frontispiece, representing Walton and his adopted Son, Cotton, in the Fishing-house, and vignette title page. Cloth.* 5s

Dedicated to the Anglers of Great Britain and the various Walton and Cotton Clubs. *Only 100 printed.*

ALFRED'S (King) Anglo-Saxon Version of the Compendious History of the World by Orosius, with Translation, Notes, and Dissertations, by the Rev. Dr. BOSWORTH, *Professor of Anglo-Saxon at Oxford.* Royal 8vo, *map and facsimiles of the MSS.*, *cloth.* 16s

ALFRED (King).—Memorials of King Alfred, being Essays on the History and Antiquities of England during the Ninth Century—the Age of King Alfred. BY various Authors. Edited and in part written by the Rev. Dr. GILES. Royal 8vo, pp. 400, *coloured plate of K. Alfred's Jewel, seven plates of Anglo-Saxon Coins, and views of Grimbald's Crypt, cloth,* 7s 6d

ALLIES (Jabez, *F.S.A.*) The Ancient British, Roman, and Saxon Antiquities and Folk-Lore of Worcestershire. 8vo, pp. 500, *with 6 plates and 40 woodcuts, Second Edition, cloth.* 7s 6d (original price 14s)

"The good people of Worcestershire are indebted to Mr. Jabez Allies for a very handsome volume illustrative of the history of their native county. His book, which treats *On the Ancient British, Roman, and Saxon Antiquities and Folk lore of Worcestershire*, has now reached a second edition; and as Mr. Allies has embodied in this, not only the additions made by him to the original work, but also several separate publications on points of folk-lore and legendary interest, few counties can boast of a more industriously or carefully compiled history of what may be called its popular antiquities. The work is very handsomely illustrated."—*Notes and Queries.*

ANDERSON (Wm.) Genealogy and Surnames, with some Heraldic and Biographical Notices. 8vo, *woodcuts of Arms and Seals, cloth.* 3s 6d (original price 6s) 1865

ANGLO-SAXON Version of the Life of St. Guthlac, Hermit of Croyland. Printed, for the first time, from a MS. in the Cottonian Library, with a Translation and Notes by CHARLES WYCLIFFE GOODWIN, M.A., Fellow of Catherine Hall, Cambridge. 12mo, *cloth.* 5s

ANGLO-SAXON Version of the Hexameron of St. Basil, and the Anglo-Saxon Remains of St. Basil's Admonitio ad Filium Spiritualem. Now first printed from MSS. in the Bodleian Library, with a Translation and Notes by the Rev. H. W. NORMAN. 8vo, *second edition, enlarged, sewed.* 4s

ANGLO-SAXON.—Narratiunculæ Anglice Conscripta. De pergamenis excribebat notis illustrabat eruditis copiam, faciebat T. OSWALD COCKAYNE, M.A. 8vo. 6s

Containing Alexander the Great's Letter to Aristotle on the situation of India—Of wonderful things in the East—The Passion of St. Margaret the Virgin—Of the Generation of Man, &c.

ANGLO-SAXON.—A Fragment of Ælfric's Anglo-Saxon Grammar, Ælfric's Glossary, and a Poem on the Soul and Body, of the XIIth Century, discovered among the Archives of Worcester Cathedral, by Sir THOMAS PHILLIPPS, Bart. Folio, PRIVATELY PRINTED, sewed. 1s 6d

ARCHÆOLOGIA CAMBRENSIS.—A Record of the Antiquities, Historical, Genealogical, Topographical, and Architectural, of Wales and its Marches. First Series, complete, 4 vols, 8vo, *many plates and woodcuts, cloth.* £2. 2s
Odd Parts may be had to complete Sets.

———— Second Series, 6 vols, 8vo, *cloth.* £3. 3s

———— Third Series, vol 1 to 12. £1. 10s each
Published by the Cambrian Archæological Association.

ARCHÆOLOGICAL INSTITUTE.—Report of the Transactions of the Annual Meeting of the Archæological Institute held at Chichester, July, 1853. 8vo, *many plates and woodcuts, cloth.* 7s 6d
Printed uniformly with the other Annual Congresses of the Institute.

ARCHER FAMILY.—Memorials of Families of the Surname of Archer in various Counties of England, and in Scotland, Ireland, Barbadoes, America, &c. By Capt. J. H. LAWRENCE ARCHER. 4to, *but few copies printed, cloth.* 12s 6d

ATKINSON'S (George, *Serjeant at Law*) Worthies of Westmoreland; or, Biographies of Notable Persons Born in that County since the Reformation. 2 vols, post 8vo, *cloth.* 6s (original price 16s)

AUTOBIOGRAPHY of JOSEPH LISTER (a Nonconformist), of Bradford, Yorkshire, with a contemporary account of the Defence of Bradford and Capture of Leeds, by the Parliamentarians, in 1642. Edited by THOS. WRIGHT, F.S.A. 8vo, *cloth.* 2s

AUTOBIOGRAPHY of THOMAS WRIGHT, of Birkenshaw, in the County of York, 1736-1797. Edited by his Grandson, THOMAS WRIGHT, M.A., F.S.A. Fcp. 8vo, pp. 376, *cloth.* 5s
Particularly interesting about Bradford, Leeds, Halifax, and their neighbourhoods, and a curious picture of manners and persons in the middle of the last century.

AUTOGRAPHICAL Miscellany; a Collection of Autograph Letters, Interesting Documents, &c., executed in facsimile by FREDK. NETHERCLIFT, each facsimile accompanied with a page of letter-press by R. SIMS, of the British Museum. Royal 4to, A HANDSOME VOL, *extra cloth.* £1. 1s (*original price* £1. 16s)
Containing sixty examples of hitherto unpublished Letters and Documents of Blake, Boileau, Buonaparte, Burns, Calvin, Camden, Carrier, Catherine de Medicis, Charles I., Chatterton, Congreve, Crammer, Cromwell, Danton, D'Aubigne, Dryden, Edward VI., Elizabeth, Elizabeth (sister of Louis XVI.), Franklin, Galilei, Glover, Goethe, Goldsmith, Henry VIII., Hyde (Anne), James II., Jonson, Kepler, Kotzebue, Latimer, Loyola, Louis XIV., Louis XVI., Luther, Maintenon, Maria Antoinette, Marlborough, Marmontel, Mary Queen of Scots, Melancthon, Newton, Penn, Pompadour, Pole (Cardinal), Raleigh, Ridley, Robespierre, Rousseau, Rubens, Sand, Schiller, Spenser, Sterne, Tasso, Voltaire, Walpole (Horace), Washington, Wolfe, Wolsey, Wren, and Young.
For the interesting nature of the documents, this collection far excels all the previous ones. With two exceptions (formerly badly executed), they have never been published before.

BAIGENT (F. J., *of Winchester*) History and Antiquities of the Parish Church of Wyke, near Winchester. 8vo, *engravings.* 2s 6d

BANKS' (Sir T. C.) Baronia Anglia Concentrata, or a Concentration of all the Baronies called Baronies in Fee, deriving their Origin from Writ of Summons, and not from any Specific Limited Creation, showing the Descent and Line of Heirship, as well of those Families mentioned by Sir William Dugdale, as of those whom that celebrated Author has omitted to notice; interspersed with Interesting Notices and Explanatory Remarks. Where to is added, the Proofs of Parliamentary Sitting, from the Reign of Edward I. to Queen Anne; also, a *Glossary of Dormant English, Scotch, and Irish Peerage Titles, with reference to presumed existing Heirs.* 2 vols, 4to, *cloth.* 15s (original price £3. 3s)

—————— LARGE PAPER COPY (*very few printed*). 2 vols. £1. 1s

A book of great research, by the well-known author of the "Dormant and Extinct Peerage," and other heraldic and historical works. Those fond of genealogical pursuits ought to secure a copy while it is so cheap. It may be considered a supplement to his former works. Vol. ii. pp. 210-300, contains an Historical Account of the first Settlement of Nova Scotia, and the foundation of the Order of Nova Scotia Baronets, distinguishing those who had seizin of lands there.

BANKS' (W. Stott, *of Wakefield*) Walks in Yorkshire. I. In the North West. II. In the North East. Thick fcap. 8vo, 2 *large maps, cloth.* 5s

—————— N. E. portion separately, comprising Redcar, Saltburn, Whitby, Scarborough, and Filey, and the Moors and Dales between the Tees, &c. Fcap. 8vo, *sewed.* 1s 6d

BARBER (G. D., *commonly called Barber-Beaumont*) Suggestions on the Ancient Britons, in 3 parts. Thick 8vo, *cloth.* 7s 6d (*original price 14s*)

BARKER.—Literary Anecdotes and Contemporary Reminiscences of Professor Porson and others, from the Manuscript Papers of the late E. H. Barker, Esq., of Thetford, Norfolk, with an Original Memoir of the Author. 2 vols, 8vo, *cloth.* 12s 1852

A singular book, full of strange stories and jests.

BARKER (W. Jones) Historical and Topographical Account of Wensleydale, and the Valley of the Yore, in the North Riding of Yorkshire. 8vo, *illustrated with views, seals, arms, &c., cloth.* 4s 6d (original price 8s 6d)

"This modest and unpretending compilation is a pleasant addition to our topographical literature, and gives a good general account of a beautiful part of England comparatively little known. It is handsomely printed with a number of finely executed woodcuts by Mr. Howard Dudley . . . . No guide to the district exists applicable alike to the will-filled and scantly furnished purse—a defect which the auhor has endeavoured to supply by the present volume.

BARNES (Rev. W.) Tiw; or a View of the Roots and Stems of the English as a Teutonic Tongue. Fcap. 8vo, *cloth.* 5s

"I hold that my primary roots are the roots of all the Teutonic languages; and, if my view is the true one, it must ultimately be taken up by the German and other Teutonic grammarians, and applied to their languages."—The Author.

BARNES (Rev. William, *of Came Rectory, Dorchester*) A Philological Grammar, grounded upon English, and formed from a comparison of more than Sixty Languages. Being an Introduction to the Science of Grammars of all Languages, especially English, Latin, and Greek. 8vo (pp. 322), *cloth.* 9s

"Mr. Barnes' work is an excellent specimen of the manner in which the advancing study of Philology may be brought to illustrate and enrich a scientific exposition of English Grammar."—*Edinburgh Guardian.*

" Of the science of Grammar, by induction from the philological facts of many laugnages, Mr. Barnes has, in this volume, supplied a concise and comprehensive manual. Grammarians may differ as to the regularity of the principles on which nations have constructed their forms and usages of speech, but it is generally allowed that some conformity or similarity of practice may be traced, and that an attempt may be made to expound a true science of Grammar. Mr. Barnes has so far grounded his Grammar upon English as to make it an English Grammar, but he has continually referred to comparative philology, and sought to render his work illustrative of general forms, in conformity with principles common, more or less, to the language of all mankind. More than sixty languages have been compared in the course of preparing the volume ; and the general principles laid down will be found useful in the study of various tongues. It is a learned and philosophical treatise."—*Literary Gazette.*

BARNES (Rev. W.) Anglo-Saxon Delectus ; serving as a first Class-Book to the Language. 12mo, *cloth.* 2s 6d

"To those who wish to possess a critical knowledge of their own Native English, some acquaintance with Anglo-Saxon is indispensable ; and we have never seen an introduction better calculated than the present to supply the wants of a beginner in a short space of time. The declensions and conjugations are well stated, and illustrated by references to Greek, the Latin, French, and other languages. A philosophical spirit pervades every part. The Delectus consists of short pieces on various subjects, with extracts from Anglo-Saxon History and the Saxon Chronicle. There is a good Glossary at the end."—*Athenæum*, Oct. 20, 1849.

BARNES (Rev. W.) Notes on Ancient Briton and the Britons. Fcap. 8vo, *cloth.* 3s

" Mr. Barnes has given us the result of his Collections for a Course of Lectures on this subject, and has produced a series of Sketches of the Ancient Britons, their language, laws, and modes of life, and of their social state as compared with that of the Saxons, which will be read with considerable interest."—*Notes and Queries.*

" We are very glad to meet with such pleasant and readable 'Notes' as Mr. Barnes'. They are very unaffected essays, imparting much warmth to the old carcase of British lore, and evincing some real study. He has found out the value of the old Welsh laws, and has made some useful comparisons between them and those of the Saxons with much freshness if not absolute novelty."—*Guardian.*

BARNES' (Rev. W.) Views of Labour and Gold. Fcp. 8vo, *cloth.* 3s

"Mr. Barnes is a reader and a thinker. He has a third and a conspicuous merit—his style is perfectly lucid and simple. If the humblest reader of ordinary intelligence desired to follow out the process by which societies are built up and held together, he has but to betake himself to the study of Mr. Barnes's epitome. The title "Views of Labour and Gold," cannot be said to indicate the scope of the Essays, which open with pictures of primitive life, nad pass on, through an agreeably diversified range of topics, to considerations of the rights, duties, and interests of Labour and Capital, and to the enquiry, What constitutes the utility, wealth, and positive well being of a nation? Subjects of this class are rarely handled with so firm a grasp and such light and *artistic manipulation."—A thenæum.*

" *The opinion of such a Scholar and Clergyman of the Established Church on subjects of political economy cannot fail to be both interesting and instructive*

BARNES' (Rev. W.) Poems, partly of Rural Life, in National English. 12mo, *cloth.* 5s

BARNES' (Rev. W.) Poems of Rural Life in the DORSET DIALECT. Fcap. 8vo, *first collection, fourth edition, cloth.* 5s

———— Second Collection, *second edition*, fcap. 8vo, *cloth.* 5s

———— Third Collection, fcap. 8vo, *cloth.* 4s 6d

BATEMAN (Thos., *of Youlgrave, Derbyshire*) Vestiges of the Antiquities of Derbyshire, and the Sepulchral Usages of its Inhabitants, from the most Remote Ages to the Reformation. 8vo, *with numerous woodcuts of Tumuli and their contents, Crosses, Tombs, &c., cloth.* 15s

BATEMAN'S (Thomas) Ten Years' Diggings in Celtic and Saxon Grave Hills, in the Counties of Derby, Stafford, and York, from 1848 to 1853, with Notices of some former Discoveries hitherto unpublished, and Remarks on the Crania and Pottery from the Mounds. 8vo, *numerous woodcuts, cloth.* 10s 6d

BATTLE ABBEY.—Descriptive Catalogue of the Original Charters, Grants, Donations, etc., constituting the Muniments of Battle Abbey, also the Papers of the Montagus, Sidneys, and Websters, embodying many highly interesting and valuable Records of Lands in Sussex, Kent, and Essex, with Preliminary Memoranda of the Abbey of Battel, and Historical Particulars of the Abbots. 8vo, 234 *pages, cloth.* 1s 6d

BEDFORD'S (Rev. W. K. Riland) The Blazon of Episcopacy, being a complete List of the Archbishops and Bishops of England and Wales, and their Family Arms drawn and described, from the first introduction of Heraldry to the present time. 8vo, 144 *pages, and* 62 *pages of drawings of Arms, cloth.* 15s

This work depicts the arms of a great number of English Families not to be found in other works.

"There has been an amount of industry bestowed upon this curious work which is very creditable to the author, and will be found beneficial to all who care for the subject on which it has been employed."—ATHENÆUM.

BERRY'S (W.) Pedigrees and Arms of the Nobility and Gentry of Hertfordshire. Folio (only 125 printed), *bds.* £1. 10s (*original price £3. 10s*)

BIBLIOGRAPHICAL MISCELLANY, edited by JOHN PETHERAM. 8vo, Nos. 1 to 5 (all published), *with general title.* 1s

CONTENTS.—Particulars of the Voyage of Sir Thomas Button for the Discovery of a North-West Passage, A.D. 1612—Sir Dudley Digges' Of the Circumference of the Earth, or a Treatise of the North-East Passage. 1611-13—Letter of Sir Thomas Button on the North-West Passage, in the State-Paper Office—Bibliographical Notices of Old Music Books, by Dr. Rimbault—Notices of Suppressed Books—Martin Mar Prelate's Rhymes—The Hardwicke Collection of Manuscripts.

BIBLIOTHEQUE Asiatique et Africane, ou Catalogue des Ouvrages relatifs a l'Asie et a l'Afrique qui ont paru jusqu'en 1700, par H. TERNAUX-COMPANS. 8vo, *avec supplement et index, sewed.* 10s 6d

"BIBLIA PAUPERUM." One of the earliest and most curious BLOCK BOOKS, reproduced in facsimile from a copy in the British Museum, by J. Ph. BERJEAU. Royal 4to, *half bound.* £2. 2s

The BIBLIA PAUPERUM, known also by the title of HISTORIÆ VETERIS ET NOVI TESTAMENTI, is a set of woodcuts in which the Old and New Testament are both brought to memory by pictures, and some lines of text in Latin. This name, BIBLIA PAUPERUM, is derived from its use by monks of the poorer orders commonly called PAUPERES CHRISTI.

As a specimen of the earliest woodcuts and of printed block-books, destined to supersede the manuscripts anterior to the valuable invention of Guttenberg, the BIBLIA PAUPERUM is well worthy the attention of the amateur of Fine Arts as well as of the Bibliographer. It consists of 40 engravings, printed on one side only of the leaves, and disposed so as to have the figures opposite to each other.

The engravings were printed by friction, with a substance of a brownish colour instead of printing ink, which was unknown at this early period. To imitate as near as possible the original, the plates in this facsimile are disposed opposite each other, and printed in a brownish colour. Various editions of this Block-Book have been discovered, without any writer being able to say which is the first one. A review of them is given in the printed Introduction of the book.

Besides the rhymed Latin Poetry—of which part was given by Heinecken, and after him by Ottley—the Introduction gives, for the first time, the whole of the Text printed on both sides in the upper compartment, as well as an English Explanation of the subject.

ONLY 250 COPIES HAVE BEEN PRINTED, UNIFORMLY WITH MR. S. LEIGH SOTHERBY'S *Principia Typographica.*

BIGSBY'S (Robert, *M.A., LL.D.*) Historical and Topographical Description of Repton, in the County of Derby, with Incidental View of objects of note in its Vicinity. 4to, a handsome volume, *with* SEVENTY *illustrations on copper, stone, and wood,* cloth. 18s (*original price* £3. 3s)

BLAKE (M.) A Brief Account of the Destructive Fire at Blandford Forum, in Dorsetshire, June 4, 1731. *Reprinted from the edition of 1735, with a plan and 2 views.* 4to, cloth. 2s 6d

BLAVIGNAC (J. D., *Architecte*) Histoire de l'Architecture Sacrée du quatrième au dixième siècle dans les anciens évechés de Geneve, Lausanne, et Sion. One vol, 8vo, 450 *pages,* 37 *plates,* and a 4to Atlas *of* 82 *plates of Architecture, Sculpture, Frescoes, Reliquaries, &c., &c.* £2. 10s

A very remarkable book, and worth the notice of the Architect, the Archæologist, and the Artist.

BOYNE (W., *F.S.A.*) Tokens issued in the Seventeenth Century in England, Wales, and Ireland, by Corporations, Merchants, Tradesmen, &c., described and illustrated. Thick 8vo, 42 *plates,* cloth. £1. 1s (*original price* £2. 2s)

Nearly 9500 Tokens are described in this work, arranged alphabetically under Counties and Towns. To the Numismatist, the Topographer, and Genealogist, it will be found extremely useful.

BOSWORTH (Rev. Joseph, *D.D., Anglo-Saxon Professor in the University of Oxford*) Compendious Anglo-Saxon and English Dictionary. 8vo, *closely printed in treble columns.* 12s

"*This is not a mere abridgment of the large Dictionary, but almost an entirely new work. In this compendious one will be found, at a very moderate price all that is most practical and valuable in the former expensive edition, with a great accession of new words and matter.*"—*Author's Preface.*

BOSWORTH and WARING.—Four Versions of the Holy Gospels, viz., in Gothic, A.D. 360; Anglo-Saxon, 995; Wycliffe, 1389; and Tyndale, 1526, in parallel columns, with Preface and Notes by the Rev. Dr. BOSWORTH, Professor of Anglo-Saxon in the University of Oxford, assisted by GEORGE WARING, M.A., of Cambridge and Oxford. One vol, 8vo, *above* 600 *pages, cloth.* 12s 6d

A very low price has been fixed to ensure an extended sale among students' and higher schools.

—— LARGE PAPER. 4to, *a handsome volume, not many printed. cloth.* £2. 2s

"The texts are printed in four parallel columns, and very great care appears to have been taken in their collation and correction."—ATHENAEUM.

"We heartily welcome this volume, brought out with so much care and ability . . . It does credit to the printers of the University. . . . The work is scholarlike, and is a valuable contribution to the materials for Biblical Criticism. . . We heartily commend it to the study of all who are interested either in the philology of the English language, or in the history and formation of our Authorized Version."—THE CHRISTIAN REMEMBRANCER, *a Quarterly Review.*

"It may almost be a question, whether the present volume phssesses greater interest for the divine or for the philologist. To the latter it must certainly be interesting from the opportunity which it affords him of marking the gradual development of our languages. The four versions of the Gospel, . . . with a learned and instructive preface, and a few necessary notes, form a volume, the value and importance of which need scarcely be insisted upon."—NOTES AND QUERIES.

BLAKEY (Robert) Historical Sketches of the Angling Literature of all Nations, to which is added a Bibliography of English Writers on Angling, by J. R. Smith. Fcap. 8vo, *cloth.* 5s

BOWLES (Rev. W., Lisle) Hermes Britannicus, a Dissertation on the Celtic Deity Teutates, the Mercurius of Cæsar, in further proof and corroboration of the origin and designation of the Great Temple at Abury, in Wiltshire. 8vo, *bds,* 4s (*original price* 8s 6d)

BRIDGER'S (Charles) Index to the Printed Pedigrees of English Families contained in County and Local Histories, the "Herald's Visitations," and in the more important Genealogical Collections. Thick 8vo, *cloth.* 10s 6d

A similar work to Sims's "Index of Pedigrees in the MSS. in the British Museum. What that is for Manuscripts this is for Printed Books. It is the most complete Index of its kind, and contains double the matter of other hasty productions.

BROOKE (Richard, *F.S.A.*) Visits to Fields of Battle in England, of the XVth Century, with some Miscellaneous Tracts and Papers, principally upon Archæological Subjects. Royal 8vo, *plates, cloth.* 15s

The work contains a descriptive account of the scenes of most of the memorable conflicts in the Wars of York and Lancaster, comprising the celebrated battles of Shrewsbury, Blore Heath, Northampton, Wakefield, Mortimer's Cross, Towton, Barnet, Tewkesbury, Bosworth, and Stoke, and genealogical and other particulars of the powerful, warlike, and distinguished personages who were the principal actors in those stirring and eventful times, with plans of some of the fields of Battle, and an Appendix containing the principal Acts of Attainder relative to the Wars of the Roses, and Lists of the Noblemen, *Knights, and other personages attainted by them.*

BROOKE (Richard) A Descriptive Account of Liverpool, as it was during the last Quarter of the XVIIIth Century, 1775—1800. A handsome vol, royal 8vo, *with illustrations, cloth.* 12s 6d (*original price £1. 5s*)

In addition to information relative to the Public Buildings, Statistics, and Commerce of the Town, the work contains some curious and interesting particulars which have never been previously published, respecting the pursuits, habits, and amusements of the inhabitants of Liverpool during that period, with views of its public edifices.

BRUCE (Dr. J. Collingwood, *Author of the "Roman Wall"*) The Bayeux Tapestry Elucidated. 4to, a handsome volume, *illustrated with* 17 COLOURED *plates, representing the entire Tapestry, extra bds.* £1. 1s.

BUCHANAN (W.) Memoirs of Painting, with a Chronological History of the Importation of Pictures by the Great Masters into England since the French Revolution. 2 vols, 8vo, *bds.* 7s 6d (*original price £1. 6s*)

BUNNETT (H. Jones, *M.D.*) Genoa, with Remarks on the Climate, and its influence upon Invalids. 12mo, *cloth.* 4s

BURKE (John) Genealogical and Heraldic History of the Extinct and Dormant Baronetcies of England, Ireland, and Scotland. Medium 8vo, SECOND EDITION, 638 *closely printed pages, in double columns, with about 1000 Arms engraved on wood, fine port. of* JAMES I., *cloth.* 10s (*original price £1. 8s*)

This work engaged the attention of the author for several years, comprises nearly a thousand families, many of them amongst the most ancient and eminent in the kingdom, each carried down to its representative or representatives still existing, with elaborate and minute details of the alliances, achievements, and fortunes, generation after generation, from the earliest to the latest period.

CALTON'S (R. Bell) Annals and Legends of Calais, with Sketches of Emigré Notabilities, and Memoirs of Lady Hamilton. Post 8vo, *with frontispiece and vignette, cloth.* 5s

PRINCIPAL CONTENTS.—History of the Siege by Edward III. in 1346-7, with a roll of the Commanders and their followers present, from a contemporary MS. in the British Museum—The Allotment of Lands and Houses to Edward's Barons—Calais as an English borough—List of the Streets and Householders of the same—Henry VIIIth's Court there—Cardinal Wolsey and his expenses—The English Pale, with the names of Roads, Farmsteads, and Villiages in the English Era—The Sieges of Therouenne and Tournai—The Pier of Calais—Pros and Cons of the place—The Hotel Dessin—Sterne's Chamber—Churches of Notre Dame and St. Nicholas—The Hotel de Ville—Ancient Staple Hall—The Chateau and Murder of the Duke of Gloucester—The Courgain—The Field of the Cloth of Gold—Notice of the Town and Castle of Guisnes, and its surprise by John de Lancaster—The Town and Seigneurio of Ardres—The Sands and Duelling—Villages and Chateau of Sangatte, Coulgon, Mark, Eschalles, and Hammes—Review of the English Occupation of Calais, and its Recapture by the Duke de Guise—The Lower Town and its Lace Trade—Our Commercial Relations with France—Emigré Notabilities—Charles and Harry Tufton, Captain Dormer and Edith Jacquemont, Beau Brummel, Jemmy Urquhart, and his friend Fauntleroy, "Nimrod," Berkeley Craven, Mytton, Duchess of Kingston—A new Memoir of Lady Hamilton, &c. Altogether an interesting volume on England's first Colony.

BURN'S (J. Southerden) The High Commission, Notices of the Court and it. Proceeding. 8vo, cloth, only 100 printed. 3s

BURN's (J., Southerden) History of Parish Registers in England, and Registers of Scotland, Ireland, the Colonies, Episcopal Chapels in and about London, the Geneva Register of the Protestant Refugees, with Biographical Notes, etc. *Second edition, greatly enlarged,* 8vo, *cloth.* 10s 6d

CAMBRIDGE.—Historia Collegii Jesu Cantabrigiensis, a J. Shermanno, olim præs. ejusdem Collegii. Edita J. O. HALLIWELL. 8vo, *cloth.* 2s

CARDWELL (Rev. Dr., *Professor of Ancient History, Oxford*) Lectures on the Coinage of the Greeks and Romans, delivered in the University of Oxford. 8vo, *cloth.* 4s (*original price* 8s 6d)

A very interesting historical volume, and written in a pleasing and popular manner.

CARTWRIGHT.—Memoirs of the Life, Writings, and Mechanical Inventions of Edmund Cartwright, D.D., F.R.S., *Inventor of the Power Loom, &c.* Edited by E. H. STRICKLAND. Post 8vo, *engravings, boards.* 2s 6d (*original price* 10s 6d)

It contains some interesting literary history, Dr. Cartwright numbering among his correspondents, Sir W. Jones, Crabbe, Sir H. Davy, Fulton, Sir S. Raffles, Langhorne, and others. He was no mean Poet, as his legendary tale of "Armine and Elvira" (given in the Appendix) testifies. Sir W. Scott says it contains some excellent poetry, expressed with unusual felicity.

CATALOGUE (*Classified*) of the Library of the Royal Institution of Great Britain, with Indexes of Authors and Subjects, and a List of Historical Pamphlets, chronologically arranged. By BENJ. VINCENT, Librarian. Thick 8vo, pp. 948, *half morocco, marbled edges.* 15s

It will be found a very useful volume to book collectors, and indispensable to public librarians.

CHADWICK (William) The Life and Times of Daniel De Foe, with Remarks, Digressive and Discursive. 8vo, pp. 472, *portrait, cloth* 10s 6d.

"Daniel De Foe devoted his life and energies to the defence of free institutions and good government. He was the Radical of his day. He not only wrote, but suffered for truth and liberty. He was impoverished and persecuted for his labours in this cause ; nay, he was repeatedly imprisoned for his principles, or for his unswerving attachment to them, and for his boldness and honesty in asserting them. He was the vigorous and indefatigable opponent of priestism, of ecclesiastical domination, and of the Popish tendencies of his time. We might not approve of all he wrote against the Catholics, but we should remember that he saw and *felt,* as we cannot, how inherently opposed to true freedom is the Catholic system. Although we live in very different times from those in which De Foe lived, yet his life is full of pregnant lessons for the liberals and friends of religious freedom of our day."—*Bradford Review.*

CHRONICLE of London from 1089 to 1483, written in the 15th Century, and for the first time printed from MSS. in the British Museum, with numerous Contemporary Illustrations of Royal Letters, Poems, descriptive of Public Events and Manners and Customs of the Metropolis. (Edited by SIR HARRIS NICOLAS.) 4to, *facsimile, cloth bds.* 15s

Only 250 copies printed. It forms a Supplement to the Chronicles of Harding, Rastall, Grafton, Hall, and others.

CHATTO (W. A., *Author of " Jackson's History of Wood Engraving"*) Facts and Speculations on the History of Playing Cards in Europe.   8vo, *profusely illustrated with engravings, both plain and coloured, cloth.*   £1. 1s

" The inquiry into the origin and signification of the suits and their marks, and the heraldic, theological, and political emblems pictured from time to time, in their changes, opens a new field of antiquarian interest; and the perseverance with which Mr. Chatto has explored it leaves little to be gained by his successors. The plates with which the volume is enriched add considerably to its value in this point of view. It is not to be denied that, take it altogether, it contains more matter than has ever before been collected in one view upon the same subject. In spite of its faults, it is exceedingly amusing; and the most critical reader cannot fail to be entertained by the variety of curious outlying learning Mr. Chatto has somehow contrived to draw into the investigations."—*Atlas.*

" Indeed, the entire production deserves our warmest approbation."—*Literary Gazette.*

"A perfect fund of antiquarian research, and most interesting even to persons who never play at cards."—*Tait's Magazine.*

" A curious, entertaining, and really learned book."—*Rambler.*

"THE GAME OF THE CHESSE," the First Book printed in England by WILLIAM CAXTON, reproduced in facsimile from a copy in the British Museum, with a few Remarks on Caxton's Typographical Productions, by VINCENT FIGGINS.   4to, pp. 184, *with 23 curious woodcuts, half morocco, uncut.*   £1. 1s—*or, in antique calf, with bevelled boards and carmine edges.*   £1. 8s

Frequently, as we read of the Works of Caxton and the early Englirh Printers, and of their Black Letter Books, very few persons ever had the opportunity of seeing any of these productions, and forming a proper estimate of the ingenuity and skill of those who first practised the " Noble Art of Printing."

THE TYPE HAS BEEN CAREFULLY IMITATED, AND THE WOODCUTS FACSIMILIED BY MISS BYFIELD. The Paper and Watermarks have also been made expressly, as near as possible, like the original; and the book is accompanied by a few remarks of a practical nature, which have been suggested during the progress of the fount, and the necessary study and comparison of Caxton's Works with those of his contemporaries in Germany, by Mr. V. FIGGINS, who spent two years' "labour of love" in cutting the matrixes for the type.

COLLECTION of Letters on Scientific Subjects, illustrative of the Progress of Science in England. Temp. Elizabeth to Charles II. Edited by J. O. HALLIWELL. 8vo, *cloth.* 3s

Comprising letters of Digges, Dee, Tycho Brahe, Lower, Hariott, Lydyatt, Sir W. Petty, Sir C. Cavendish, Brancker, Pell, &c. ; also the Autobiography of Sir Samuel Morland, from a MS. in Lambeth Palace, Nat. Tarpoley's Corrector Analyticus, &c. Cost the subscribers of the Historical Society of Science £1.

COPENHAGEN.—The Traveller's Handbook to Copenhagen and its Environs. By ANGLICANUS. 12mo, *with large map of Sealand, plan of Copenhagen, and views, cloth.* 8s

COSIN's (Mr., *Secretary to the Commissioners of Forfeited Estates*) Names of the Roman Catholics, Non-Jurors, and others, who Refused to Take the Oaths to King George I., together with their Titles, Additions, and Places of Abode, the Parishes and Townships where their Lands lay, the Names of the then Tenants, and the Annual Value of them as returned by themselves. *Reprinted from the Edition of* 1745. 8vo, *cloth.* 5s

A curious book for the Topographer and Genealogist.

CRAIG'S (Rev. J. Duncan) A Hand-Book to the modern Provençal Language, spoken in the South of France, Piedmont, &c., comprising a Grammar, Dialogues, Legends, Vocabularies, &c., useful for English Tourists and others. Royal 12mo, *cloth.* 3s 6d
This little book is a welcome addition to our literature of comparative philology in this country, as we have hitherto had no grammar of the sweet lyrical tongue of Southern France.

CRESWELL'S (Rev. S. F.) Collections towards the History of Printing in Nottinghamshire. Small 4to, *sewed.* 2s

DALE (Bryan, *M.A.*) Annals of Coggeshall, otherwise Sunnedon, in the County of Essex. Post 8vo, *plates, cloth.* 7s 6d

D'ALTON (John, *Barrister-of-Law, of Dublin*) Illustrations, Historical and Genealogical, of the most Ancient FAMILIES OF IRELAND (500), Members of which held Commissions in King James's Service in the War of the Revolution, wherein their respective Origins, Achievements, Forfeitures, and ultimate Destinies are set forth. 2 thick vols, 8vo, pp. 1400, *cloth.* £1. 1s

DANISH.—English-Danish Dialogues and Progressive Exercises. By E. F. ANCKER. 12mo, *cloth.* 5s 1851—Key to Ditto. 5s

DAVIES (Robt., F.S.A., *Town Clerk of York*) Extracts from the Municipal Records of the City of York during the Reigns of Edward IV., Edward V., and Richard III., with Notes, illustrative and explanatory, and an Appendix, containing some Account of the Celebration of the Corpus Christi Festival at York, in the Fifteenth and Sixteenth Centuries. 8vo, *cloth.* 4s (*original price* 10s 6d)

DAVIES (Robt.) The Fawkes's of York in the 16th Century, including Notices of Guy Fawkes, the Gunpowder Plot Conspirator. Post 8vo. 1s 6d

DE GAULLE (Chas.) The Celts of the Nineteenth Century, an Appeal to the Living Representatives of the Celtic Race. Translated, with Notes, by J. D. MASON. 8vo, *sewed.* 2s

DEVLIN (J. Dacres) Helps to Hereford History, Civil and Legendary, in an Ancient Account of the Ancient Cordwainer's Company of the City, the Mordiford Dragon, and other Subjects. 12mo (*a curious volume*), *cloth.* 3s 6d
"A series of very clever papers,"—*Spectator.*
"A little work full of Antiquarian information, presented in a pleasing and popular form."—*Nonconformist*

DRUCE Family.—A Genealogical Account of the Family of Druce, of Goring, in the County of Oxford, 1735. 4to, only 50 copies PRIVATELY PRINTED, *bds.* 7s 6d

EDMONDS (Richard, *late of Penzance*) The Land's End District: its Antiquities, Natural History, Natural Phenomena, and Scenery; also a Brief Memoir of Richard Trevithick, C.E. 8vo, *maps, plates, and woodcuts, cloth.* 7s 6d

ELLIS' (W. S.) Notices of the Families of Ellis. Part I. 8vo. 2s

ELLIS (W. Smith) A Plea for the Antiquity of Heraldry, with an Attempt to Expound its Theory and Elucidate its History. 8vo, *sewed.* 1s

ELLIS' (W. S.) Hurtspierpoint (in Sussex), its Lords and Families. 8vo, *plates.* 1s 6d

ELLIOTT.—Life, Poetry, and Letters of Ebenezer Elliott, the Corn-Law Rhymer (of Sheffield). Edited by his Son-in-Law, JOHN WATKINS. Post 8vo, *cloth, (an interesting volume).* 3s (*original price 7s 6d*)

ENGLAND as seen by Foreigners in the Days of Elizabeth and James the First, comprising Translations of the Journals of the two Dukes of Wirtemberg in 1592 and 1610, both illustrative of Shakespeare. With Extracts from the Travels of Foreign Princes and others. With Copious Notes, an Introduction, and ETCHINGS. By WILLIAM BRENCHLEY RYE, *Assistant Keeper of the Department of Printed Books, British Museum.* Thick foolscap 4to, *elegantly printed by Whittingham, extra cloth.* 15s

"This curious volume has been the labours of a scholar's love, and will be read with ease by all. The idea of assembling the testimonies of foreign visitors, and showing us how we appeared to others in the days of Bess, by way of contrast and comparison to the aspect we present in the days of Victoria, was one which involved much arduous research. Mr. Rye had had no predecessor. . . . . He has not only added an introduction to the works he assembles and translates, but has enriched them with some hundred pages of notes on all kinds of subjects, exhibiting a wide and minute research."—*Fortnightly Review.* (G. H. LEWES.)

"It contains a good deal of curious and amusing matter."—*Saturday Review.*

"Mr. Rye's work claims the credit of a valuable body of historical annotation."—*Athenæum.*

"The book is one of the most entertaining of the class we have seen for a long while. It contains a complete and lively reflex of English life and manners at the most fascinating period of our history."—*London Review.*

"A book replete both with information and amusement, furnishing a series of very curious pictures of England in the Olden Time."—*Notes and Queries.*

"It is difficult to convey a just impression of Mr. Rye's volume in a short criticism, because the really interesting feature of it is the quaintness, and, to modern eyes, the simplicity of most of the narratives, which cannot be reproduced with full effect except in quotations, for which we have no space."—*Pall Mall Gazette.*

"A handsome, well-printed, entertaining book—entertaining and something more, and comes very welcome to the time. . . . It is in such accidental notices that the chief interest and the not slight value of collections such as this consists: and when they are as well edited, they have a use on the shelves after their freshness is past: they help our familiarity with our history."—*Reader.*

EVANS (John, F.S.A., *Secretary to the Numismatic Society*) Coins of the Ancient Britons. Arranged and Described. Thick 8vo, *many plates, engraved by F. W. Fairholt, F.S.A., and cuts, cloth, a handsome volume.* £1. 1s

The "Prix de Numismatique" has been awarded by the French Academie des Inscriptions et Belles Lettres, to the author, for this book.

FOSBROKE (T. Dudley, *F.S.A.*) The Tourist's Grammar, or Rules relating to the Scenery and Antiquities incident to Travellers. Including an Epitome of Gilpin's Principles of the Picturesque. Post 8vo. *bds.* 2s (original price 7s)

FINLAYSON (James) Surnames and Sirenames, the Origin and History of certain Family and Historical Names, and Remarks on the Ancient Right of the Crown to Sanction and Veto the Assumption of Names, and an Historical Account of the Names of Buggey and Bugg. 8vo. 1s 6d (*original price* 3s 6d)

FRENEAU (Philip) Poems on Various Subjects, but chiefly illustrative of the Events and Actors in the American War of Independence, *reprinted from the rare edition printed at Philadelphia in 1786, with a Preface.* Thick fcap. 8vo, *elegantly printed, cloth.* 6s

Freneau enjoyed the friendship of Adams, Franklin, Jefferson, Madison, and Munroe, and the last three were his constant correspondents while they lived. His Patriotic Songs and Ballads, which were superior to any metrical compositions then written in America, were everywhere sung with enthusiasm. See Griswold's " Poets and Poetry of America," and Duyckinck's " Cyclop. of American Literature."

GILBERT (Walter B.) The Accounts of the Corpus Christi Fraternity, and Papers relating to the Antiquities of Maidstone. 12mo, *cloth, gilt leaves.* 3s 6d

GILES (Rev. Dr.) The Writings of the Christians of the Second Century, namely, Athenagoras, Tatian, Theophilus, Hermias, Papias, Aristides, Quadratus, etc., collected and first translated, complete. 8vo, *cloth.* 7s 6d

Designed as a continuation of Abp. Wake's *Apostolical Epistles,* which are those of the first-century.

GILES (Rev. Dr.) Heathen Records to the Jewish Scripture History, containing all the Extracts from the Greek and Latin Writers in which the Jews and Christians are named, collected together and translated into English, with the original Text in juxtaposition. 8vo, *cloth.* 7s 6d

GILES (Rev. Dr.) Codex Apochryphus Novi Testamenti, the Uncanonical Gospels and other Writings referring to the First Ages of Christianity, in the original Languages of Arabic, Greek, and Latin, collected together from the editions of Fabricius, Thilo and others. 2 vols, 8vo, *cloth.* 14s

GILES (Rev. Dr.) History of the Parish and Town of Bampton, in Oxfordshire, with the District and Hamlets belonging to it. 8vo, *plates, second edition, cloth.* 7s 6d

GILES (Rev. Dr.) History of Witney and its Neighbouring Parishes, Oxon. 8vo, *plates, cloth.* 6s

GILES (Rev. Dr.) Passages from the Poets, chronologically arranged. Thick 12mo, nearly 700 pages, *cloth,* 7s 6d

It contains choice passages from more than 400 English Poets, in chronological order. It will be found a useful volume to candidates at competitive examinations in English Literature.

GREENHOW (Robt., *Librarian to the Dept. of State, U.S.A.*) History of Oregon and California, and the other Territories on the North-West Coast of America, accompanied by a Geographical View and Map, and a number of Proofs and Illustrations of the History. 8vo, *large map, cloth.* 7s 6d (*original price* 18s)

GILES (Rev. Dr.) Excerpta ex Scriptoribus Classicis de Britannia. A Complete Collection of those passages in the Classic Writers (124 in number), which make mention of the British Isles, Chronologically Arranged, from Ante-Christi 560 to Anno Dom. 1333. 8vo, *cloth.* 3s (*original price* 7s 6d)
An Introduction to every History of Great Britain.

GRENVILLE (Henry) Chronological Synopsis of the Four Gospels on a new plan, with Notes. 8vo, *cloth.* 1s 6d
Designed to show that on a minute critical analysis, the writings of the four Evangelists contain no contradictions within themselves, and that such passages that have appeared to many critics to raise doubt as to the consistency of these Records of our Lord's Ministry, really afford, when explained, the most satisfactory proofs that there was no COLLUSION between the several writers, and that they may therefore be thoroughly relied on as "INDEPENDENT" witnesses of the Truth of what they record.

HADFIELD (James, *Architect*) Ecclesiastical Architecture of the County of Essex, from the Norman Era to the Sixteenth Century, with Plans, Elevations, Sections, Details, &c., from a Series of Measured Drawings, and Architectural and Chronological Descriptions. Royal 4to, 80 *plates, leather back, cloth sides,* £1. 11s 6d

HAIGH'S (Daniel Henry, D.D.) The Conquest of Britain by the Saxons. A Harmony of the History of the Britons, the Works of Gildas, the "Brut," and the Saxon Chronicle, with reference to the Events of the Fifth and Sixth Centuries. 8vo, *plates of Runic Inscriptions, cloth.* 15s

HAIGH'S (Daniel Henry, D.D.) The Anglo-Saxon Sagas, an Examination of their value as aids to History, serving as a Sequel to "The Conquest of Britain by the Saxons." 8vo, *cloth.* 8s 6d
It analyses and throws new historical evidence on the origin of the Poems of Beowulf, the Lament of Deor, the Saga of Waldhere, Scyld Scefing, the fight at Finnesham, the Story of Horn, the Lay of Hildebrand, &c.

HAKEWILL (H.) Roman Remains discovered in the Parishes of North Leigh and Stonesfield, Oxfordshire. 8vo, *map, and 2 plates.* 2s 6d

HALLIWELL'S (James Orchard, F.R.S., &c.) Dictionary of Archaic and Provincial Words, Obsolete Phrases, Proverbs, and Ancient Customs, from the Reign of Edward I. 2 vols, 8vo, containing upwards of 1,000 pages, *closely printed in double columns, cloth, a new and cheaper edition.* 15s
It contains above 50,000 words (embodying all the known scattered glossaries of the English language), forming a complete key for the reader of our old Poets, Dramatists, Theologians, and other authors, whose works abound with allusions, of which explanations are not to be found in ordinary Dictionaries and books of reference. Most of the principal Archaisms are illustrated by examples selected from early inedited MSS. and rare books, and by far the greater portion will be found to be original authorities.

HALLIWELL (J. O.) the Nursery Rhymes of England, collected chiefly from Oral Tradition. The SIXTH EDITION, enlarged, with many Designs by W. B. SCOTT, Director of the School of Design, *Newcastle-on-Tyne.* 12mo, *cloth, gilt leaves.* 4s 6d
The largest collection ever formed of these old ditties.

HALLIWELL'S (J. O.) Popular Rhymes and Nursery Tales, with Historical Elucidations. 12mo, *cloth.* 4s 6d

This very interesting volume on the traditional literature of England is divided into Nursery Antiquities, Fireside Nursery Stories, Game Rhymes, Alphabet Rhymes, Riddle Rhymes, Nature Songs, Proverb Rhymes, Places, and Families, Superstition Rhymes, Custom Rhymes, and Nursery Songs, a large number are here printed for the first time. It may be consinered a sequel to the preceding article.

HALLIWELL'S (J. O.) Early History of Freemasonry in England. Illustrated by an English Poem of the XIVth Century, with Notes. Post 8vo, *second edition, with a facsimile of the original MS. in the British Museum, cloth.* 2s 6d

"The interest which the curious poem, of which this publication is chiefly composed, has excited, is proved by the fact of its having been translated into German, and of its having reached a second edition, which is not common with such publications. Mr. Halliwell has carefully revised the new edition, and increased its utility by the addition of a complete and correct Glossary."—LITE- RARY GAZETTE.

HALLIWELL'S (J. O.) The Manuscript Rarities of the University of Cambridge. 8vo, *bds.* 3s (*original price,* 10s 6d)

A companion to Hartshorne's "Book Rarities" of the same university.

HALLIWELL'S (J. O.) A Dictionary of Old English Plays, existing either in print or in manuscript, from the earliest times to the close of the 17th century, including also Notices of Latin Plays written by English Authors during the same period, with particulars of their Authors, Plots, Characters, &c. 8vo, *cloth.* 12s

Twenty-five copies have been printed on THICK PAPER, price £1. 1s.

HALLIWELL'S (J. O.) Rambles in Western Cornwall, by the Footsteps of the Giants ; with Notes on the Celtic Remains of the Land's End District and the Isles of Scilly. Fcp. 4to, *elegantly printed by Whittingham, cloth.* 7s 6d

HALLIWELL (J. O.) Notes of Family Excursions in North Wales, taken chiefly from Rhyl, Abergele, Llandudno, and Bangor. Fcp. 4to, *with engravings, elegantly printed by Whittingham, cloth.* 5s

HALLIWELL'S (J. O.) Roundabout Notes, chiefly upon the Ancient Circles of Stones in the Isle of Man. Fcp. 4to, *only* 100 *printed.* 2s

HALLIWELL'S (J. O.) Introduction to the Evidences of Christi- anity. Fcp. 8vo, 2ND EDITION, *cloth.* 1s 6d (*original price* 3s 6d)

The only book which contains in a popular form the Ancient Heathen unconscious testimonies to the truth of Christianity.

HARROD (Henry, F.S.A.) Gleanings among the Castles and Con- vents of Norfolk. 8vo, *many plates and woodcuts, cloth.* 17s 6d. —LARGE PAPER, £1. 3s 6d.

"This volume is creditable to Mr. Harrod in every way, alike to his industry, aste, and his judgment. It is the result of ten years' labour. . . . . The volume is so full of interesting matter that we hardly know where to begin our extracts or more detailed notices."—GENTLEMAN'S MAGAZINE, November, 1857.

HOLLOWAY'S (W., of Rye) History and Antiquities of the Ancient Port and Town of Rye, in Sussex, compiled from the Original Documents. Thick 8vo (*only* 200 *printed*) cloth. £1. 1s

HOLLOWAY'S (W.) History of Romney Marsh, in Kent, from the time of the Romans to 1833, with a Dissertation on the Original Site of the Ancient Anderida. 8vo, *with maps and plates, cloth.* 12s

HARTLIB.—A Biographical Memoir of Samuel Hartlib, Milton's familiar Friend, with Bibliographical Notices of Works published by him, and a reprint of his Pamphlet entitled "An Invention of Engines of Motion." By Henry Dircks, C.E., author of the Life of the Marquis of Worcester, &c. Post 8vo, *cloth.* 3s 6d

To have been the familiar friend of Milton, the correspondent of Boyle and Evelyn, Pepys and Wren, and to have had the honour of suggesting to Milton his tract on Education and of receiving his high praise in his own lofty and sonorous language, is honour enough to make Hartlib's name and life worthy of a special work.

HAWKINS (J. S., *F.S.A.*) History of the Origin and Establishment of Gothic Architecture, and an Inquiry into the mode of Painting upon and Staining Glass, as practised in the Ecclesiastical Structures of the Middle Ages. Royal 8vo, 1813, 11 *plates, bds.* 4s (original price 12s)

HERBERT'S (The Hon. Algernon) *Cyclops Christianus*, or an Argument to disprove the supposed Antiquity of the Stonehenge and other Megalithic Erections in England and Brittany. 8vo, *cloth.* 4s (*original price* 6s)

HORNE (R. H., *Author of "Orion," etc.*) Ballad Romances. 12mo, pp. 248, *cloth.* 3s (*original price* 6s 6d)

Containing the Noble Heart, a Bohemian Legend ; the Monk of Swineshead Abbey, a Ballad Chronicle of the Death of King John ; The Three Knights of Camelott, a Fairy Tale ; The Ballad of Delora, or the Passion of Andrea Como : Bedd Gelert, a Welsh Legend ; Ben Capstan, a Ballad of the Night Watch ; the Elfe of the Woodlands, a Child's Story.

"Pure fancy of the most abundant and picturesque description. Mr. Horne should write us more fairy tales ; we know none to equal him since the days of Drayton and Herrick.—Examiner.

"The opening poem in this volume is a fine one, it is entitled the 'Noble Heart,' and not only in title but in treatment well imitates the style of Beaumont and Fletcher."—Athenæum.

HUME (Rev. A., LL.D., F.S.A., &c., *of Liverpool*) Ancient Meols, or some Account of the Antiquities found near Dove Point, on the Sea Coast of Cheshire, including a Comparison of them with Relics of the same kind respectively procured elsewhere. 8vo, *full of engravings, cloth.* £1. 1s

HUNTER (Rev. Joseph, *F.S.A.*) The Pilgrim Fathers—Collections concerning the Church or Congregation of Protestant Separatists formed at Scrooby, in North Nottinghamshire, in the time of James I., the Founders of New Plymouth, the Parent Colony of New England. 8vo, *with View of the Archiepiscopal Palace at Scrooby inserted, cloth.* 8s

This work contains some very important particulars of these personages, and their connections previously to their leaving England and Holland, which were entirely unknown to former writers, and have only recently been discovered *through* the indefatigable exertions of the author. Prefixed to the volume, are some beautiful Prefatory Stanzas by Richard Monckton Milnes, Esq., M.P. (now Lord Houghton.)

HUSSEY (Rev. Arthur) Notes on the Churches in the Counties of Kent, Sussex, and Surrey mentioned in Domesday Book, and those of more recent date ; with some Account of the Sepulchral Memorials and other Antiquities. Thick 8vo, *fine plates, cloth.* 12s (*original price* 18s)

HUTTON (W., *of Derby*) Description of Blackpool, in Lancashire. 8vo, *3rd edition.* 1s 6d

IRVING (Joseph, *of Dumbarton*) History of Dumbartonshire, with Genealogical Notices of the Principal Families in the County ; the whole based on Authentic Records, Public and Private. Thick 4to, pp. 636, *maps, plates, and portraits, cloth.* £3.

JOHNES (Arthur J.) Philological Proofs of the Original Unity and Recent Origin of the Human Race, derived from a Comparison of the Languages of Europe, Asia, Africa, and America. 8vo, *cloth.* 6s (*original price* 12s 6d)

Printed at the suggestion of Dr. Prichard, to whose works it will be found a useful supplement.

JONES' (Morris Charles) Valle Crucis Abbey, its Origin and Foundation Charter. 8vo. 1s

JORDAN (Rev. J., *the Vicar*) Parochial History of Enstone, in the County of Oxford.   Post 8vo, *a closely printed volume of nearly* 500 *pages, cloth.* 7s

JUNIUS—The Authorship of the Letters of Junius Elucidated, including a Biographical Memoir of Lieut.-Col. Barré, M.P.   By John Britton, F.S.A., &c.   Royal 8vo, *with Portraits of Lord Shelburne, John Dunning, and Barré, from Sir Joshua Reynolds's picture, cloth.* 6s—LARGE PAPER, in 4to, *cloth.* 9s

An exceedingly interesting book, giving many particulars of the American War and the state of parties during that period.

KELKE (Rev. W. Hastings) Notices of Sepulchral Monuments in English Churches from the Norman Conquest to the Nineteenth Century. 8vo, *many woodcuts.* 2s (*original price* 3s 6d)

KELLY (William, *of Leicester*) Notices illustrative of the Drama, and other Popular Amusements, chiefly in the Sixteenth and Seventeenth Centuries, incidentally illustrating Shakespeare and his Contemporaries, Extracted from the Chamberlain's Accounts and other Manuscripts of the Borough of Leicester, with an Introduction and Notes by William Kelly. Post 8vo, *plates, cloth.* 9s

——— Large Paper Copies, in 4to, only 25 printed (*only 4 copies remain*), *half morocco, Roxburghe style.* £1. 5s

KENRICK (Rev. John) Roman Sepulchral Inscriptions, their Relation to Archæology, Language, and Religion.   Post 8vo, *cloth.* 3s 6d

KING (Richard John) The Forest of Dartmoor and its Borders in Devonshire, an Historical Sketch. Foolscap 8vo, *cloth.* 3s

KERRY (Rev. Chas.) History and Antiquities of the Hundred of Bray, in Berkshire. 8vo, *cloth.* 7s 6d

—— The same, *with* 10 *folding pedigrees, cloth.* 10s 6d

KNOCKER'S (Edw., *Town Clerk of Dover*) Account of the Grand Court of Shepway, holden on Bredonstone Hill, at Dover, for the Installation of Viscount Palmerston as Constable of Dover and Warden of the Cinque Ports, in 1861. With Notes on the Origin and Antiquity of the Cinque Ports, Two Ancient Towns, and their Members. Foolscap 4to, *engravings, elegantly printed by Whittingham, cloth.* 15s

KYNANCE COVE ; or, The Cornish Smugglers, a Tale of the Last Century. By W. B. FORFAR, *Author of " Pentowan," " Pengersick Castle,"* etc., etc. Fcap. 8vo, *boards.* 2s

LAMBARDE'S (William, *Lawyer and Antiquary*) A Perambulation of Kent, containing the Description, Hystorie, and Customs of that Shire. Written in 1576. Thick 8vo, *cloth.* 5s (*original price* 12s)
The first county history published, and one of the most amusing and *naïve* old books that can be imagined.

LANARKSHIRE—The Upper Ward of Lanarkshire Described and Delineated. The Archæological and Historical Section by G. VERE IRVING, F.S.A., Scot ; the Statistical and Topographical Section by ALEX. MURRAY. 3 vols, 8vo, *many engravings, cloth.* £3. 3s.

—— LARGE PAPER, 3 vols, 4to, *half morocco.* £5. 5s

LANGLEY'S (L.) Introduction to Anglo-Saxon Reading ; comprising Ælfric's Homily on the Birthday of St. Gregory, with a Copious Glossary, &c. 12mo, *cloth.* 2s 6d
Ælfric's Homily is remarkable for beauty of composition, and interesting as setting forth Augustine's mission to the "Land of the Angles."

LAPPENBERG'S (Dr. J. M.) History of England under the Norman Kings, with an Epitome of the Early History of Normandy. Translated, with Additions, by BENJ. THORPE. 8vo, *cloth.* 15s

LATHBURY (Rev. Thomas) History of the Nonjurors : their Controversies and Writings, with Remarks on some of the Rubrics in the Book of Common Prayer. Thick 8vo, *cloth.* 6s (*original price* 14s)

LATHBURY'S (Rev. T.) History of the Convocation of the Church of England from the Earliest Period to the Year 1742. *Second edition, with considerable additions.* Thick 8vo, *cloth.* 5s (*original price* 12s)

LAWRENCE (Sir James, *Knight of Malta*) On the Nobility of the British Gentry, or the Political Ranks and Dignities of the British Empire compared with those on the Continent. Post *8vo.* 1s 6d
Useful for foreigners in Great Britain, and to Britons abroad, particularly of those who desire to be presented at Foreign Courts, to accept Foreign Military *Service,* to be invested with Foreign title, to be admitted into foreign orders,

LETTERS of the **KINGS** of **ENGLAND**—Now first collected from the Originals in Royal Archives, and from other Authentic Sources, Private as well as Public. Edited, with Historical Introduction and Notes, by J. O. HALLIWELL. *Two handsome volumes,* post 8vo, *with portraits of Henry VIII. and Charles I., cloth.* 8s *(original price £1. 1s)*

These volumes form a good companion to Ellis's Original Letters.

The collection comprises, for the first time, the love-letters of Henry VIII. to Anne Boleyn, in a complete form, which may be regarded, perhaps, as the most singular documents of the kind that have descended to our times ; the series of letters of Edward VI. will be found very interesting specimens of composition ; some of the letters of James I., hitherto unpublished, throw light on the Murder of Overbury, and prove beyond a doubt the King was implicated in it in some extraordinary and unpleasant way ; but his Letters to the Duke of Buckingham are of the most singular nature ; only imagine a letter from a Sovereign to his Prime Minister commencing thus : "My own sweet and dear child, blessing, blessing, blessing on thy heart-roots and all thine." Prince Charles and the Duke of Buckingham's Journey into Spain has never been before so fully illustrated as it is by the documents given in this work, which also includes the very curious letters from the Duke and Duchess of Buckingham to James I.

LIBER ALBUS : the White Book of the City of London. Compiled A.D. 1419, by JOHN CARPENTER, *Common Clerk ;* RICHARD WHITTINGTON, *Mayor.* Translated from the Original Latin and Anglo-Norman, by H. T. Riley, M.A. 4to, pp. 672 *(original price 18s), the few remaining copies offered, in cloth, at 9s—Half morocco (Roxburghe style), 10s 6d—Whole bound in vellum, carmine edges, 12s—Whole morocco, carmine edges, 13s 6d*

Extensively devoted to details which must of necessity interest those who care to know something more about their forefathers than the mere fact that they have existed. Many of them—until recently consigned to oblivion ever since the passing away of the remote generations to which they belonged—intimately connected with the social condition, usages, and manners of the people who—uncouth, unlearned, ill-housed, ill-fed, and comfortless though they were, still formed England's most important, most wealthy, and most influential community throughout the chequered and troublous times of the 13th and 14th centuries. During this period, in fact, there is hardly a phase or feature of English national life upon which, in a greater or less degree, from these pages of the "Liber Albus," some light is not reflected.

LIBRARY OF OLD AUTHORS.

Elegantly and uniformly printed in foolscap 8vo, in cloth. Of some there are LARGE PAPER *copies for the connoisseur of choice books.*

THE Vision and Creed of **PIERS PLOUGHMAN**. Edited by THOMAS WRIGHT ; a new edition, revised, with additions to the Notes and Glossary. 2 vols. 10s   1856

"'The Vision of Piers Ploughman' is one of the most precious and interesting monuments of the English Language and Literature, and also of the social and political condition of the country during the fourteenth century. . . . Its author is not certainly known, but its time of composition can, by internal evidence, be fixed at about the year 1362. On this and on all matters bearing upon the origin and object of the poem, Mr. Wright's historical introduction gives ample information. . . . . In the thirteen years that have passed since the first edition of the present text was published by the late Mr. Pickering, our old literature and history has been more studied, and we trust that a large circle of readers will be prepared to welcome this cheaper and

THE Dramatic and Poetical Works of JOHN MARSTON. Now first
collected, and edited by J. O. HALLIWELL, F.R.S., &c. 3 vols.
15s   1856

"The edition deserves well of the public; it is carefully printed, and the
annotations, although neither numerous nor extensive, supply ample explanations upon a variety of interesting points. If Mr. Halliwell had done no more
than collect these plays, he would have conferred a boon upon all lovers of
our old dramatic poetry."—*Literary Gazette.*

REMARKABLE Providences of the Earlier Days of American Co-
lonisation. By INCREASE MATHER, of *Boston*, N.E. With Introductory Preface by George Offor. *Portrait.* 5s   1856

A very singular collection of remarkable sea deliverances, accidents, remarkable phenomena, witchcraft, apparitions, &c., &c., connected with inhabitants
of New England, &c., &c. A very amusing volume, conveying a faithful portrait of the state of society, when the doctrine of a peculiar providence and
personal intercourse between this world and that which is unseen was fully
believed.

THE Table Talk of JOHN SELDEN. With a Biographical Preface and
Notes by S. W. SINGER. *Third edition, portrait.* 5s   1860

———— LARGE PAPER. Post 8vo, *cloth.* 7s 6d   1860

"Nothing can be more interesting than this little book, containing a lively
picture of the opinions and conversations of one of the most eminent scholars
and most distinguished patriots England has produced. There are few volumes
of its size so pregnant with sense, combined with the most profound earning:
it is impossible to open it without finding some important fact or discussion,
something practically useful and applicable to the business of life. Coleridge
says, 'There is more weighty bullion sense in this book than I ever found in
the same number of pages in any uninspired writer.' . . . . . Its merits
had not escaped the notice of Dr. Johnson, though in politics opposed to much
it inculcates, for in reply to an observation of Boswell, in praise of the French
Ana, he said, 'A few of them are good, but we have one book of the kind better
than any of them—Selden's Table Talk.' "—*Mr. Singer's Preface.*

THE Poetical Works of WILLIAM DRUMMOND, of Hawthornden.
Now first published entire. Edited by W. B. TURNBULL. *Fine
portrait.* 5s   1856

"The sonnets of Drummond," says Mr. Hallam, "are polished and elegant,
free from conceit and bad taste, and in pure unblemished English."

ENCHIRIDION, containing Institutions—Divine, Contemplative,
Practical, Moral, Ethical, Œconomical, and Political. By
FRANCIS QUARLES. *Portrait.* 3s   1856

"Had this little book been written at Athens or Rome, its author would have
been classed with the wise men of his country."—*Headley.*

THE Works in Prose and Verse of Sir THOMAS OVERBURY. Now
first collected. Edited, with Life and Notes, by E. F. RIMBAULT.
Portrait after Pass. 5s   1856

HYMNS and Songs of the Church. By GEORGE WITHER. Edited,
with Introduction, by EDWARD FARR. Also the Musical Notes,
composed by Orlando Gibbons. *With portrait after Hole.* 5s
                                                            1856

*"Mr. Farr has added a very interesting biographical introduction, and we hope
to find that the public will put their seal of approbation to the present edition
of an author who may fairly take his place on the same shelf with George Herbert."—Gent's Mag., Oct., 1856.*

HALLELUJAH; or, Britain's Second Remembrancer, in Praiseful and Penitential Hymns, Spiritual Songs, and Moral Odes. By GEORGE WITHER. With Introduction by EDWARD FARR. *Portrait.* 6s 1857

Hitherto this interesting volume has only been known to the public by extracts in various publications. So few copies of the original are known to exist, that the copy from which this reprint has been taken cost twenty-one guineas.

MISCELLANIES. By JOHN AUBREY, F.R.S., the *Wiltshire Antiquary*. FOURTH EDITION. With some Additions and an Index. *Portrait and cuts.* 4s 1857

CONTENTS :—Day Fatality, Fatalities of Families and Places, Portents, Omens, Dreams, Apparitions, Voices, Impulses, Knockings, Invisible Blows, Prophecies, Miracles, Magic, Transportation by an Invisible Power, Visions in a Crystal, Converse with Angels, Corpse Candles, Oracles, Ectasy, Second Sight, &c. ; with an Appendix, containing his Introduction to the Survey of North Wiltshire.

THE Iliads of HOMER, Prince of Poets, never before in any language truly translated, with a Comment on some of his chief Places. Done according to the Greek by GEORGF CHAPMAN, with Introduction and Notes by the Rev. RICHARD HOOPER. 2 vols, sq. fcap. 8vo. SECOND AND REVISED EDITION, *with portrait of Chapman, and frontispiece.* 12s 1865

"The translation of Homer, published by George Chapman, is one of the greatest treasures the English language can boast."—*Godwin.*

"With Chapman, Pope had frequently consultations, and perhaps never translated any passage till he read his version."—*Dr. Johnson.*

"He covers his defects with a daring, fiery spirit, that animates his translation, which is something like what one might imagine Homer himself to have writ before he arrived at years of discretion."—*Pope.*

"Chapman's translation, with all its defects, is often exceedingly Homeric, which Pope himself seldom obtained."—*Hallam.*

"Chapman writes and feels as a Poet—as Homer might have written had he lived in England in the reign of Queen Elizabeth."—*Coleridge.*

"I have just finished Chapman's Homer. Did you ever read it ?—it has the most-continuous power of interesting you all along. . . . The earnestness and passion which he has put into every part of these poems would be incredible to a reader of mere modern translation."—*Charles Lamb.*

HOMER'S ODYSSEY. Translated according to the Greek by GEORGE CHAPMAN. With Introduction and Notes by REV. RICHARD HOOPER. 2 vols, square fcp. 8vo, *with facsimile of the rare original frontispiece.* 12s. 1857

HOMER'S Battle of the Frogs and Mice ; HESIOD'S Works and Days ; MUSÆUS'S Hero and Leander ; JUVENAL'S Fifth Satire. Translated by GEORGE CHAPMAN. Edited by Rev. RICHARD HOOPER. Square fcp. 8vo, *frontispiece after Pass.* 6s. 1858

"The editor of these five rare volumes has done an incalculable service to English Literature by taking George Chapmanis folios out of the dust of time-honoured libraries, by collating them with loving care and patience, and, through the agency of his enterprising publisher, bringing Chapman entire and complete within the reach of those who can best appreciate and least afford to purchase the early editions."—*Athenæum.*

POETICAL Works of ROBERT SOUTHWELL, Canon of Loretto, now first completely edited by W. B. Turnbull. 4s   1856

" His piety is simple and sincere—a spirit of unaffected gentleness and kindliness pervades his poems—and he is equally distinguished by weight of thought and sweetness of expression."—*Saturday Review.*

THE Dramatic Works of JOHN WEBSTER. Edited, with Notes, etc., by WILLIAM HAZLITT. 4 vols. £1.   1857

———— LARGE PAPER, 4 vols, post 8vo, *cloth.* £1. 10s

This is the most complete edition, containing two more plays than in Dyce's edition.

THE Dramatic Works of JOHN LILLY (the Euphuist). Now first collected, with Life and Notes by F. W. FAIRHOLT. 2 vols. 10s.   1858

———— LARGE PAPER, 2 vols, post 8vo, *cloth.* 15s

THE Poetical Works of RICHARD CRASHAW, Author of "Steps to the Temple," "Sacred Poems, with other Delights of the Muses," and "Poemata," now first collected. Edited by W. B. TURNBULL. 5s. 1858

" He seems to have resembled Herbert in the turn of mind, but possessed more fancy and genius."—ELLIS.

LA MORT d'ARTHUR. The History of King Arthur and the Knights of the Round Table. Compiled by Sir THOMAS MALORY, Knight. Edited from the Edition of 1634, with Introduction and Notes, by THOMAS WRIGHT, M.A., F.S.A. 3 vols, SECOND AND REVISED EDITION. 15s.   1866

———— LARGE PAPER, 3 vols, post 8vo, *cloth.* £1. 2s 6d

ANECDOTES and Characters of Books and Men. Collected from the Conversation of Mr. Pope and other eminent Persons of his Time. By the Rev. JOSEPH SPENCE. With Notes, Life, etc., by S. W. SINGER. The second edition, *portrait.* 6s.   1858

———— LARGE PAPER, post 8vo, *cloth.* 7s 6d.   1858

" The ' Anecdotes ' of kind-hearted Mr. Spence, the friend of Pope, is one of the best books of *ana* in the English language."—*Critic.*

Dr. COTTON MATHER'S Wonders of the Invisible World, being an account of the Trials of several Witches lately executed in New England, and of the several remarkable curiosities therein occurring. To which are added Dr. INCREASE MATHER'S Further Account of the Tryals, and Cases of Conscience concerning Witchcrafts, and Evil Spirits Personating Men. *Reprinted from the rare original editions of 1693, with an Introductory Preface. Portrait.* 5s.   1862

THE Dramatic and Poetical Works of THOMAS SACKVILLE, Lord Buckhurst, and Earl of Dorset. With Introduction and Life by the Hon. and Rev. R. W. SACKVILLE WEST. *Fine portrait from a picture at Buckhurst, now first engraved.* 4s.   1859

REMAINS of the EARLY POPULAR POETRY OF ENGLAND, collected and edited by W. CAREW HAZLITT. 4 vols, with many curious

LUCASTA.—The Poems of RICHARD LOVELACE, now first edited and the Text carefully revised, with Life and Notes by W. CAREW HAZLITT, *with 4 plates.* 5s.　　1864

—————— LARGE PAPER. Post 8vo, *cloth.* 7s 6d

THE WHOLE OF THE WORKS OF ROGER ASCHAM, now first collected and revised, with Life of the Author. By the Rev. Dr. GILES, formerly Fellow of C. C. C., Oxford. 4 vols. £1.　　1866

—————— LARGE PAPER, 4 vols, post 8vo, *cloth.* £1. 10s.

Ascham is a great name in our national literature. He was one of the first founders of a true English style in prose composition, and of the most respectable and useful of our scholars.—*Retrospective Review.*

———————

LONG (Henry Lawes) On the March of Hannibal from the Rhone to the Alps. 8vo, *map.* 2s 6d

LOWER'S (Mark Antony, *M.A., F.S.A.*) Patronymica Britannica, a Dictionary of Family Names. Royal 8vo, 500 *pages, with illustrations, cloth.* £1. 5s

This work is the result of a study of British Family Names, extending over more than twenty years. The favourable reception which the Author's "English Surnames" obtained in the sale of Three Editions, and the many hundreds of communications to which that work gave rise, have convinced him that the subject is one in which considerable interest is felt. He has therefore been induced to devote a large amount of attention to the origin, meaning, and history of our family designations; a subject which, when investigated in the light of ancient records and of modern philology, proves highly illustrative of many habits and customs of our ancestors, and forms a very curious branch of Archæology.—*Preface.*

LOWER'S (M. A.) Curiosities of Heraldry, with Illustrations from Old English Writers. *With illuminated Title-page, and numerous engravings from designs by the Author.* 8vo, *cloth.* 14s

"The present volume is truly a worthy sequel (to the 'SURNAMES') in the same curious and antiquarian line, blending with remarkable facts and intelligence, such a fund of anecdote and illustration, that the reader is almost surprised to find that he has learned so much while he appeared to be pursuing mere amusement. The text is so pleasing that we scarcely dream of its sterling value; and it seems as if, in unison with the woodcuts, which so cleverly explain its points and adorn its various topics, the whole design were intended for a relaxation from study, rather than an ample exposition of an extraordinary and universal custom, which produced the most important effect upon the minds and habits of mankind."—*Literary Gazette.*

"Mr. Lower's work is both curious and instructive, while the manner of its treatment is so inviting and popular, that the subject to which it refers, which many have hitherto had too good reason to consider meagre and unprofitable, assumes, under the hands of the writer, the novelty of fiction with the importance of historical truth."—*Athenæum.*

LOWER'S (M. A.) Contributions to Literature, Historical, Antiquarian, and Metrical. Post 8vo, *woodcuts, cloth.* 7s 6d

Contents: 1. Local Nomenclature—2. The Battle of Hastings, an Historical Essay—3. The Lord Dacre, his mournful end, a Ballad—4. Historical and Archæological Memoir on the Iron Works of the South of England, *with numerous illustrations*—5. Winchelsea's Deliverance, or the Stout Abbot of Battayle, in Three Fyttes—6. The South Downs, a Sketch, Historical, Anecdotical, and Descriptive—7. On the Yew Trees in Churchyards—8. A Lyttel Geste of a Greate Eele, a pleasaunt Ballad—9. A Discourse of Genealogy—10. An Antiquarian Pilgrimage in Normandy, with woodcuts—11. Miscellanea, &c., &c.

LOWER'S (M. A.) Chronicle of Battel Abbey, in Sussex, originally compiled in Latin by a Monk of the Establishment, and now first translated, with Notes and an Abstract of the Subsequent History of the Abbey. 8vo, *with illustrations, cloth.* 9s

This volume, among other matters of local and general interest, embraces —New Facts relative to the Norman Invasion—The Foundation of the Monastery—The Names and Rentals of the Original Townsmen of Battel—Memoirs of several Abbots, and Notices of their Disputes with the Bishops of Chichester, respecting Jurisdiction—The Abbey's Possessions—A Speech of Thomas a Becket, then Chancellor of England, in favour of Abbot Walter de Luci—Several Miracles—Anecdotes of the Norman Kings—and an Historical Sketch of the Abbey, from 1176 to the present time by the Translator.

LOWER'S (M. A.) Memorials of the Town of Seaford, Sussex. 8vo, *plates.* 3s 6d

LOWER'S (M. A.) Bodiam (in Sussex), and its Lords. 8vo, *engravings.* 1s

LOWER'S (M. A.) Worthies of Sussex, Biographical Sketches of the most eminent Natives or Inhabitants of the County, from the Earliest Period to the Present Time, with Incidental Notices illustrative of Sussex History. Royal 4to, *many engravings, cloth.* £1. 16s

LOWER'S (M. A.) Sussex Martyrs, their Examinations and Cruel Burnings in the Time of Queen Mary, comprising the interesting Personal Narrative of Richard Woodman, extracted from "Foxe's Monuments." With Notes. 12mo, *sewed.* 1s

LOWER'S (M. A.) The Stranger at Rouen, a Guide for Englishmen. 12mo, *plates.* 1s

LUKIS (Rev. W. C.) Account of Church Bells, with some Notices of Wiltshire Bells and Bell-Founders, containing a copious List of Founders, a comparative Scale of Tenor Bells and Inscriptions from nearly 500 Parishes in various parts of the Kingdom. 8vo, 13 *plates, cloth.* 3s 6d (*original price 6s*)

MADDEN (Fred. W., *of the Medal Room, British Museum*) Hand-Book to Roman Coins. Fcap. 8vo, *plates of rare examples, cloth.* 5s

A very useful and trustworthy guide to Roman Coins.

MANTELL (Dr. Gideon A.) Day's Ramble in and about the Ancient Town of Lewes, Sussex. 12mo, *engravings, cloth.* 2s

MARTIN MAR-PRELATE CONTROVERSY.

AN EPISTLE to the Terrible Priests of the Convocation House. By Martin Mar-Prelate. 1588. With Introduction and Notes by J. Petherham. Post 8vo. 2s

COOPER (*Bishop of Winchester***)** An Admonition to the People of England against Martin Mar-Prelate, 1589, with Introduction. Post 8vo, pp. 216. 3s 6d

PAP with a Hatchet, being a Reply to Martin Mar-Prelate, 1589, with Introduction and Notes. Post 8vo. 2s

HAY any Worke for Cooper? Being a Reply to the Admonition to the People of England. By Martin Mar-Prelate, 1589, with Introduction and Notes. Post 8vo. 2s 6d

AN ALMOND for a Parrot, being a Reply to Martin Mar-Prelate, 1589, with Introduction. Post 8vo. 2s 6d

PLAINE PERCEVALL the Peace-Maker of England, being a Reply to Martin Mar-Prelate, with Introduction. Post 8vo. 2s

---

MATON'S (Dr. W. G.) Natural History of Wiltshire, as comprehended within Ten Miles round Salisbury. 8vo. *Privately printed.* 2s

MAYNARD'S (James) Parish of Waltham Abbey, in Essex, its History and Antiquities. Post 8vo, *engravings, cloth.* 2s 6d

MENZIES (Mrs. Louisa J.) Legendary Tales of the Ancient Britons, rehearsed from the Early Chronicles. Fcap. 8vo, *cloth.* 3s
Contents: 1. Esyllt and Sabrina—2. Lear and his three Daughters—3. Cynedda and Morgan—4. The Brothers Beli and Bran—5. Ellidure the Compassionate—6. Alban of Verulam—7. Vortigern—8. Cadwallon and the Final Struggle of the Britons.

MICHAEL ANGELO considered as a Philosophic Poet, with translations by John Edward Taylor. Post 8vo. Second edition. *Cloth.* 2s 6d (*original price* 5s)

MILTON'S Early Reading, and the *prima stamina* of his "Paradise Lost," together with Extracts from a Poet of the XVIth Century (*Joshua Sylvester*). By Charles Dunster, *M.A.* 12mo, *cloth.* 2s 6d (*original price* 5s)

MILTON; a Sheaf of Gleanings after his Biographers and Annotators. By the Rev. Joseph Hunter. Post 8vo. 2s 6d

MOORE (Thomas) Notes from the Letters of Thomas Moore to his Music Publisher, James Power (*the publication of which was suppressed in London*), with an Introduction by Thomas Crofton Croker, *F.S.A.* Post 8vo, *cloth.* 3s 6d
The impressions on the mind of a reader of these Letters of Moore in Lord Lord Russell's edition will be not only incomplete, but erroneous, without the information to be derived from this very interesting volume.

MORLAND.—Account of the Life, Writings, and Inventions of Sir Samuel Morland, Master of Mechanics to Charles II. By J. O. Halliwell. 8vo, *sewed.* 1s

MUNFORD (Rev. Geo., *Vicar of East Winch, Norfolk*) Analysis of Domesday Book for the County of Norfolk. 8vo, *with pedigrees and arms, cloth.* 10s 6d
"Many extracts have been made at various times for the illustration of local descriptions, from the great national (but almost unintelligible) record known as Domesday Book: but Mr. Munford has done more in the case of his own county, for he supplies a complete epitome of the part of the survey relating to Norfolk, giving not only the topographical and statistical facts, but also a great deal that is instructive as to the manners and condition of the people, the state of the churches and other public edifices, the mode of cultivation and land tenure, together with a variety of points of interest to the ecclesiologist and antiquary."—Bury Post.

NARES' (Archdeacon) A Glossary, or Collection of Words, Phrases, Customs, Proverbs, &c., illustrating the Works of English Authors, particularly Shakespeare and his Contemporaries. A New Edition, with considerable Additions, both of Words and Examples. By JAMES O. HALLIWELL, *F.R.S.*, and THOMAS WRIGHT, *M.A., F.S.A.* 2 thick vols, 8vo, *cloth.* £1. 1s

The Glossary of Archdeacon Nares is by far the best and most useful work we possess for explaining and illustrating the obsolete language and the customs and manners of the 16th and 17th Centuries, and it is quite indispensable for the readers of the literature of the Elizabethan period. The additional words and examples are distinguished from those in the original text by a † prefixed to each. The work contains between FIVE and SIX THOUSAND additional examples, the result of original research, not merely supplementary to Nares, but to all other compilations of the kind.

NASH'S (D. W., *Member of the Royal Society of Literature*) Taliesin, or, the Bards and Druids of Britain. A Translation of the Remains of the earliest Welsh Bards, and an examination of the Bardic Mysteries. 8vo, *cloth.* 14s

NASH'S (D. W.) The Pharaoh of the Exodus. An Examination of the Modern Systems of Egyptian Chronology. 8vo, *with frontispiece of the Egyptian Calendar, from the ceiling of the Ramasseum, at Thebes, cloth.* 12s

NAVAL ARCHITECTURE, Elements of Naval Architecture, being a Translation of the Third Part of Clairbois's "Traite Elementaire de la Construction des Vaisseaux." By J. N. STRANGE, Commander, R.N. 8vo, *with five large folding plates, cloth.* 5s

———— Lectures on Naval Architecture, being the Substance of those delivered at the United Service Institution. By E. GARDINER FISHBOURNE, Commander, R. N. 8vo, *plates, cloth.* 5s 6d

Both these works are published in illustration of the "Wave System."

NETHERCLIFF'S (F. G.) Hand-Book to Autographs, being a Ready Guide to the Handwriting of Distinguished Men and Women of Every Nation, designed for the Use of Literary Men, Autograph Collectors, and others. Containing 700 Specimens, with a Biographical Index by R. Sims, of the British Museum. 8vo, *cloth extra, gilt edges.* 10s 6d (original price 15s)

———— The Same. PRINTED ONLY ON ONE SIDE. 8vo, *cloth extra.* £1. 1s

The specimens contain two or three lines each besides the signature, so that to the historian such a work will reccomend itself as enabling him to test the genuineness of the document he consults, whilst the judgment of the autograph collector may be similarly assisted, and his pecuniary resources economized by a judicious use of the Manual. To the bookworm, whose name is Legion, we would merely observe, that daily experience teaches us the great value and interest attached to books containing Marginal Notes and Memoranda, when traced to be from the pens of eminent persons.

NEWTON (William) A Display of Heraldry. 8vo, *many hundred engravings of Shields, illustrating the Arms of English Families, cloth.* 14s

NEWTON (William) London in the Olden Time, being a Topographical and Historical Memoir of London, Westminster and Southwark ; accompanying a Pictorial Map of the City and Suburbs, as they existed in the reign of Henry VIII., before the Dissolution of the Monasteries ; compiled from Authentic Documents. Folio, *with the coloured map, 4 feet 6 inches by 3 feet 3 inches, mounted on linen, and folded into the volume, leather back, cloth sides,* £1. 1s (*original price* £1. 11s 6d)

NORFOLK'S (E. E.) Gleanings in Graveyards : a Collection of Curious Epitaphs. *Third Edition, revised and enlarged,* fcap. 8vo, *cloth.*   3s

NUMISMATIC Chronicle and Journal of the Numismatic Society. New Series, Edited by W. S. W. Vaux, John Evans, and F. W. Madden.   Nos. 1 to 24, Published Quarterly.   5s *per Number.*

This is the only repertory of Numismatic intelligence ever published in England.   It contains papers on coins and medals, of all ages and countries, by the first Numismatists of the day, both English and Foreign.

Odd parts may be had to complete a few of this and the former series in 20 vols.

OLD BALLADS.—Catalogue of a unique Collection of 400 Ancient English Broadside Ballads, printed entirely in the 𝔅𝔩𝔞𝔠𝔨 𝔩𝔢𝔱𝔱𝔢𝔯, lately on sale by J. Russell Smith. With Notes of their Tunes, and Imprints.   Post 8vo, *a handsome volume, printed by Whittingham, in the old style, half bound.*   5s

———— A Copy on thick paper, *without the prices to each, and a different title-page, only 10 copies so printed.*   10s 6d

PARISH'S (Sir Woodbine, *many years Charge d'Affairs at Buenos Ayres*) Buenos Ayres, and the Provinces of the Rio de la Plata, from their Discovery and Conquest by the Spaniards to the Establishment of their Political Independence ; with some Account of their Present State, Appendix of Historical Documents, Natural History, &c.   Thick 8vo, *Second Edition, plates and woodcuts, also a valuable map by Arrowsmith, cloth.*   10s 6d (original price 14s)

" Among the contributions to the geography of the South American Continent, the work of our Vice-President, Sir Woodbine Parish, holds a very important place.   Professing to be a second edition of a former book, it is, in reality, almost a new work, from the great quantity of fresh matter it contains on the geography, statistics, natural history, and geology of this portion of the world." —*President of the Royal Geographical Society's Address.*

PATERSON'S (Jas.) Histories of the Counties of Ayr and Wigton. Post 8vo, vol 1. Kyle, in two parts, *cloth.*   £1. 1s

———— Vol II, Carrick, post 8vo, *cloth.*   12s

Particularly full of information about the Family History of the district.

PEDLER (E. H., *of Liskeard*) The Anglo-Saxon Episcopate of Cornwall, with some Account of the Bishops of Crediton. 8vo, *cloth.*   3s 6d (original price 7s 6d)

PETTIGREW (Thos. Jos.) On Superstitions connected with the History and Practice of Medicine and Surgery. 8vo, *frontispiece, cloth.* 4s (*original price* 8s)

PETTIGREW (Thos. Jos.) Inquiries into the Particulars connected with Death of Amy Robsart (Lady Dudley), at Cumnor Place, Berks, Sept. 8, 1560; being a refutation of the Calumnies charged against Sir Robert Dudley, Anthony Forster, and others. 8vo, 2s

PILGRIMAGES to St. Mary of Walsingham and St. Thomas of Canterbury. By DESIDERIUS ERASMUS. Newly Translated. With the Colloquy of Rash Vows, by the same Author, and his Characters of Archbishop Warham and Dean Colet, with Notes by J. GOUGH NICHOLS. Post 8vo, *engravings, cloth.* 3s 6d (*original price* 6s)

PIOZZI, Love Letters of Mrs. Piozzi (formerly Mrs. Thrale, the friend of Dr. Johnson), written when she was eighty, to the handsome actor, William Augustus Conway, aged Twenty-seven. 8vo, *sewed.* 2s

"——— written at three, four, and five o'clock (in the morning) by an octogenary pen; a heart (as Mrs. Lee says) twenty-six years old, and as H. L. P. feels it to be, *all your own.*"—*Letter V.*, 3rd *Feb.*, 1820.

"This is one of the most extraordinary collections of love epistles we have chanced to meet with, and the well-known literary reputation of the lady—the Mrs. Thrale, of Dr. Johnson and Miss Burney celebrity—considerably enhances their interest. The letters themselves it is not easy to characterise; nor shall we venture to decide whether they more bespeak the drivelling of dotage, or the folly of love; in either case they present human nature to us under a new aspect, and furnish one of those riddles which nothing yet dreamt of in our philosophy can satisfactorily solve."—*Polytechnic Review.*

POPE.—Facts and Conjectures on the Descent and Family Connections of Pope, the Poet. By the REV. JOSEPH HUNTER. Post 8vo. 2s

POPE.—Additional Facts concerning the Maternal Ancestry of Pope, in a Letter to Mr. Hunter. BY ROBERT DAVIES, F.S.A. Post 8vo. 2s

POPULAR Treatises on Science, written during the Middle Ages, in Anglo-Saxon, Anglo-Norman, and English, edited by Thomas Wright, M.A. 8vo, cloth. 3s

CONTENTS :—An Anglo-Saxon Treatise on Astronomy of the Tenth Century, now first published from a MS. in the British Museum, with a translation ; Livre des Creatures, by Phillippe de Thaun, now first printed, with a translation (extremely valuable to Philologists, as being the earliest specimens of Anglo-Norman remaining, and explanatory of all the symbolical signs in early sculpture and painting); the Bestiary of Phillippe de Thaun, with a translation ; Fragments on Popular Science from the Early English Metrical Lives of the Saints (the earliest piece of the kind in the English Language).

POSTE (Rev. Beale) Celtic Inscriptions on Gaulish and British Coins, intended to supply materials for the Early History of Great Britain, with a Glossary of Archaic Celtic Words, and an *Atlas* of Coins. 8vo, *many engravings, cloth.* 10s 6d

POSTE (Beale) Vindication of the " Celtic Inscriptions on Gaulish and British Coins." 8vo, *plates, and cuts, cloth.* 1s

POSTE (Rev. Beale, M.A.) Britannic Researches ; or, New Facts and Rectifications of Ancient British History. 8vo (pp. 448), *with engravings, cloth.* 15s

"The author of this volume may justly claim credit for considerable learning, great industry, and, above all, strong faith in the interest and importance of his subject. . . . On various points he has given us additional information, and afforded us new views. for which we are bound to thank him. The body of the book is followed by a very complete index, so as to render reference to any part of it easy : this was the more necessary, on account of the multifariousness of the topics treated, the variety of persons mentioned, and the many works quoted."—*Athenaeum*, Oct. 8, 1853.

"The Rev. Beale Poste has long been known to antiquaries as one of the best read of all those who have elucidated the earliest annals of this country. He is a practical man, has investigated for himself monuments and manuscripts, and we have in the above-named volume the fruits of many years' patient study. The objects which will occupy the attention of the reader are—1. The political position of the principal British powers *before* the Roman conquest—under the Roman dominion, and struggling unsuccessfully against the Anglo-Saxon race; 2. The Geography of Ancient Britain ; 3. An investigation of the Ancient British Historians, Gildas and Nennius, and the more obscure British chroniclers ; 4. The ancient stone monuments of the Celtic period ; and, lastly, some curious and interesting notices of the early British Church. Mr. Poste has not touched on subjects which have received much attention from others, save in cases where he had something new to offer, and the volume must be regarded therefore, as an entirely new collection of discoveries and deductions tending to throw light on the darkest, as well as the earliest, portion of our national history."—*Atlas.*

POSTE (Rev. Beale) Britannia Antiqua, or Ancient Britain brought within the Limits of Authentic History. 8vo, pp. 386, *map, cloth.* 14s

A Sequel to the foregoing work.

PUBLICATIONS OF THE ANGLIA CHRISTIANA SOCIETY.

GIRALDUS Cambrensis, De Instructione Principum, with a Preface, Chronological Abstract and Marginal Notes (in English), by the Rev. J. S. Brewer. 8vo, *boards.* 5s   1846

Now first printed from the Manuscript in the Cottonian Library, particularly illustrating the Reign of Henry II. Among our earlier chroniclers, there is not a more lively writer than Giraldus de Barri.

CHRONICON Monasterii de Bello, with a Preface, Chronological Abstract, and Marginal Notes (in English), by the Editor. 8vo, *boards.* 5s   1846

A very curious History of Battle Abbey, in Sussex, by one of the Monks. Printed from a MS. in the Cottonian Library.

LIBER ELIENSIS, ad fidem Codicum Variorum. Vol 1 (all printed), with English Preface and Notes, by the Rev. D. Stewart, of the College, Ely. 8vo, *boards.* 5s   1848

An important chronicle of the early transactions connected with the Monastery of Ely, supposed to have been compiled by Richard the Monk, between 1108 and 1131.

The above three volumes are all the Society printed. They are well worthy of being placed on the same shelf with the Camden, Caxton, Surtees, and Chetham Societies' publications. From the limited number of members of the Society, the books are little known. J. R. Smith having become the proprietor of the few remaining copies, recommends an early purchase.

PROVINCIAL DIALECTS OF ENGLAND:

A DICTIONARY of Archaic and Provincial Words, Obsolete Phrases, &c., by J. O. HALLIWELL, F.R.S., &c.   2 vols, 8vo, 1000 pp., in double columns, FIFTH EDITION, *cloth.*   15s

GLOSSARY of Provincial and Local Words Used in England.   By F. GROSE, F.S.A., with which is now incorporated the Supplement.   By SAMUEL PEGGE, F.S.A.   Post 8vo, *cloth.*   4s 6d

BROCKETT'S (J. Trotter) Glossary of North Country Words, with their Etymology and Affinity to other Languages and Occasional Notices of Local Customs and Popular Superstitions.   THIRD EDITION, corrected and enlarged by W. E. BROCKETT.   2 vols, in 1, post 8vo, *cloth.*   10s 6d (*original price* 21s)

SPECIMENS of Cornish Provincial Dialect, collected and arranged by Uncle Jan Treenodle, with some Introductory Remarks and a Glossary by an Antiquarian Friend; also a Selection of Songs and other Pieces connected with Cornwall.   Post 8vo, *with a curious portrait of Dolly Pentreath, cloth.*   4s

CORNISH Dialect and Poems, viz.—

   1 Treagle of Dozmary Pool, and Original Cornish Ballads.
   2 Cornish Thalia: Original Comic Poems illustrative of the Dialect.
   3 A Companion to the Cornish Thalia.   By H. J. DANIELL.
   4 Mirth for "One and all."   By H. J. DANIELL.
   5 Humourous Cornish Legends.   By H. J. DANIELL.
   6 A Budget of Cornish Poems, by various Authors.
   7 Dolly Pentreath, and other Humorous Cornish Tales.
   8 The Great Mine Conference, and other Pieces.
   9 Rustic Poems.   By GEORGE HAMLYN, *the "Dartmoor Bloomfield."*
  10 Mary Anne's Experiences: her Wedding and Trip up the Tamar.   By H. J. DANIELL.
  11 Mary Anne's Career, and Cousin Jack's Adventures.   By H. J. DANIELL.
  12 A New Budget of Cornish Poems.   By H. J. DANIELL.
  13 Mirth for Long Evenings.   By H. J. DANIELL.
  14 Bobby Poldree and his Wife Sally at the Great Exhibition tion.   By H. J. DANIELL.   All 12mo, *Sixpence* each.

A GLOSSARY of the Words and Phrases of Cumberland.   By WILLIAM DICKINSON, F.L.S.   12mo, *cloth,*   2s

JOHN NOAKES and MARY STYLES, a Poem, exhibiting some of *the most* striking lingual localisms peculiar to Essex, with a *Glossary.*   By CHARLES CLARK, Esq., of Great Totham Hall, *Essex.*   Post 8vo, *cloth.*   2s.

NATHAN HOGG'S Letters and Poems in the Devonshire Dialect. *The fifth Edition, with additions.* Post 8vo. *Coloured wrapper.* 1s.

"These letters, which have achieved considerable popularity, evince an extensive acquaintance with the vernacular of the county and its idioms and phrases, while the continuous flow of wit and humour throughout cannot fail to operate forcibly upon the risible faculties of the reader. In the Witch story Nathan has excelled himself, and it is to be hoped we have not seen his last effort in this branch of local English literature. The superstitions of Jan Vaggis and Jan Plant are most graphically and amusingly portrayed, and the various incidents whereby the influence of the 'Evil Eye' is sought to be counteracted, are at once ludicrous and irresistible."—*Plymouth Mail.*

NATHAN HOGG'S New Series of Poems in the Devonshire Dialect, including the Witch Story of Mucksy Lane, and the Kenton Ghost. *Dedicated by Permission to his Highness Prince Louis Lucien Bonaparte.* Post 8vo, 4th *edition enlarged, coloured wrapper.* 1s

A GLOSSARY of Words used in Teesdale, in the County of Durham. Post 8vo, *cloth.* 2s 6d (*original price,* 6s)

"Contains about two thousand words . . . It is believed the first and only collection of words and phrases peculiar to this district, and we hail it therefore as a valuable contribution to the history of language and literature . . . . the author has evidently brought to bear an extensive personal acquaintance with the common language."—*Darlington Times.*

POEMS of Rural Life in the Dorset Dialect. By the Rev. WILLIAM BARNES, of Came Rectory, Dorchester. *First Collection.* Fcp. 8vo, FOURTH EDITION, *cloth.* 5s.

——— Second Collection. Fcap. 8vo. SECOND EDITION, *cloth.* 5s.

——— Third Collection. Fcap. 8vo, *cloth.* 4s 6d.

"The author is a genuine poet, and it is delightful to catch the pure breath of song in verses which assert themselves only as the modest vehicle of rare words and Saxon inflections. We have no intention of setting up the Dorset patois against the more extended provincialism of Scotland, still less of comparing the Dorsetshire poet with the Scotch; yet we feel sure that these poems would have delighted the heart of Burns, that many of them are not unworthy of him, and that (at any rate) his best productions cannot express a more cordial sympathy with external nature, or a more loving interest in human joys and sorrows."—*Literary Gazette.*

GRAMMAR and Glossary of the Dorset Dialect. By the Rev. W. BARNES. 8vo. 2s 6d.

DIALECT of South Lancashire, or Tim Bobbin's Tummas and Meary, revised and Corrected, with his Rhymes, and an enlarged Glossary of Words and Phrases chiefly used by the Rural Population of the Manufacturing Districts of South Lancashire. By SAMUEL BAMFORD. 12mo, *second edition, cloth.* 3s 6d.

LEICESTERSHIRE Words, Phrases, and Proverbs. By A. B. EVANS, D.D., *Head Master of Market Bosworth Grammar School.* 12mo, *cloth.* 5s.

A GLOSSARY of the Provincialisms of the County of Sussex. By W. DURRANT COOPER, F.S.A. Post 8vo, *second edition, enlarged, cloth.* 3s 6d

A GLOSSARY of Northamptonshire Words and Phrases, with Examples of their Colloquial Use, with illustrations from various Authors, to which are added the Customs of the County. By Miss A. E. BAKER. 2 vols, post 8vo, *cloth.* 16s (*original price* £1. 4s)

"We are under great obligations to the lady, sister to the local historian of Northamptonshire, who has occupied her time in producing this very capital Glossary of Northamptonshire provincialisms."—*Examiner.*

"The provincial dialects of England contain and preserve the elements and rudiments of our compound tongue. In Miss Baker's admirable 'Northamptonshire Glossary,' we have rather a repertory of archaisms than vulgarisms. But it is much more than a vocabulary; it preserves not only dialectical peculiarities, but odd and disappearing customs; and there is hardly a page in it which does not throw light on some obscurity in our writers, or recall old habits and practices."—*Christian Remembrancer, Quarterly Review.*

WESTMORELAND and Cumberland.—Dialogues, Poems, Songs, and Ballads, by various Writers, in the Westmoreland and Cumberland Dialects, now first collected, to which is added a Copious Glossary of Words peculiar to those Counties. Post 8vo, (pp. 408), *cloth.* 9s.

A GLOSSARY of Provincial Words in use in Wiltshire, showing their Derivation in numerous instances, from the Language of the Anglo-Saxons. By JOHN YONGE AKERMAN, Esq., F.S.A. 12mo, *cloth.* 3s

THE DIALECT of Leeds and its Neighbourhood, illustrated by Conversations and Tales of Common Life, etc., to which are added a Copious Glossary, Notices of the various Antiquities, Manners, and Customs, and General Folk-lore of the District. Thick 12mo, pp. 458, *cloth.* 6s

This is undoubtedly the best work hitherto published on the dialects of Yorkshire in general, and of Leeds in particular. The author, we believe one of our fellow townsmen—for his introductory remarks are dated 'Leeds, March, 1861'—has used not only great industry, but much keen observation, and has produced a book which will everywhere be received as a valuable addition to the archæological literature of England.—*Leeds Intelligencer.*

A LIST of Provincial Words in Use in Wakefield, Yorkshire, with Explanations, including a few descriptions and localities. By W. S. BANKS. 12mo. 1s 6d

THE Yorkshire Dialect, exemplified in various Dialogues, Tales, and Songs, applicable to the County, with a Glossary. Post 8vo. 1s.

A GLOSSARY of Yorkshire Words and Phrases, collected in Whitby and its Neighbourhood, with examples of their colloquial use and allusions to local Customs and Traditions. By an INHABITANT. 12mo, *cloth.* 3s 6d

A GLOSSARY, with some Pieces of Verse of the Old Dialect of the English Colony in the Baronies of Forth and Bargy, Co. Wexford, Ireland. Formerly collected by JACOB POOLE, of Growton, now edited with Notes and Introduction by the REV. W. BARNES, Author of the Dorset Poems and Glossary. Fcap.

PUBLICATIONS OF THE CAXTON SOCIETY.

**OF CHRONICLES AND OTHER WRITINGS ILLUSTRATIVE OF THE HISTORY
AND MISCELLANEOUS LITERATURE OF THE MIDDLE AGES.**

*Uniformly printed in 8vo. with English Prefaces and Notes.   Of
several of the Volumes only 100 copies have been
printed, and only three sets can be completed.*

CHRONICON Henrici de Silgrave.   Now first printed from the
Cotton MS.   By C. Hook.   5s 6d

GAIMAR (Geoffrey) Anglo-Norman Metrical Chronicle of the Anglo
Saxon Kings.   Printed for the first time entire, with Appendix,
containing the Lay of Havelok the Dane, the Legend of Er-
nulph, and Life of Hereward the Saxon.   Edited by T. Wright,
Esq., F.S.A.   Pp. 284 (*only to be had in a set*)

The only complete edition; that in the Monumenta Historica Britannica,
printed by the Record Commission, is incomplete.

LA REVOLTE du Comte de Warwick contre le Roi Edouard IV.,
now first printed from a MS. at Ghent, to which is added a
French letter, concerning Lady Jane Grey and Queen Mary,
from a MS. at Bruges.   Edited by Dr. Giles.   3s 6d

WALTERI Abbatis Dervensis Epistolæ, now first printed from a
MS. in St. John's College, Cambridge.   By C. Messiter.
4s 6d

BENEDICTI Abbatis Petriburgensis de Vita et Miraculis St. Tho-
mae Cantaur, now first printed from MS. at Paris and Lambeth.   By Dr. Giles.   10s.

GALFRIDI le Baker de Swinbroke, Chronicon Angeliae temp. Edward II. et III., now first printed.   By Dr. Giles.   10s

EPISTOLÆ Herberti de Losinga, primi Episcopi Norwicensis, et
Oberti de Clara, et Elmeri Prioris Cantuariensis, now first
printed.   By Col. Anstruther.   8s

ANECDOTA Bedae Lanfranci, et aliorum (inedited Tracts, Letters,
Poems, &c., Bede, Lanfranc, Tatwin, etc.)   By Dr. Giles.   10s

RADULPHI Nigri Chronica Duo, now first printed from MSS. in
the British Museum,   By Lieut. Col. Anstruther.   8s

MEMORIAL of Bishop Waynflete, Founder of St. Mary Magdalene
College, Oxford.   By Dr. Peter Heylyn.   Now first edited from
the original MS.   By J. R. Bloxam, D.D., Fellow of the same
College.   5s 6d

ROBERT GROSSETETE (Bishop of Lincoln) " Chasteau d'Amour,"
to which is added, " La Vie de Sainte Marie Egyptienne," and
an English Version (of the 13th Century) of the " Chasteau
d'Amour," now first edited.   By M. Cooke.   6s 6d

GALFREDI Monumentis Historia Britonum, nunc primum in
Anglia novem codd. MSS. collatis.   Editit J. A. Giles.   10s

ALANI Prioris Cantuariensis postea Abbatis Tewkesberiensis, Scripta quae extant. Edita J. A. GILES. 6s 6d

CHRONICON Angliæ Petriburgense Iterum post Sparkium cum cod. MSS. contulit. J. A. GILES. 6s 6d

VITA Quorandum Anglo-Saxonum, Original Lives of Anglo-Saxons and others who lived before the Conquest (*in Latin*). Edited by Dr. GILES. 10s

SCRIPTORES Rerum Gestarum Wilhelmi Conquestoris. In Unum collecti. Ab J. A. GILES. 10s.

CONTINENS:—1. Brevis relatio de Willelmo nobilissimo Comite Normannorum. 2. Protestatio Willelmi primi de primatu Cantuariensis Ecclesiæ. 3. Widonis Ambrianensis Carmen de Hastingensi. 4. Charta Willelmi Bastardi. 5. Epistola Will. conquestoris ad Gregorium papam. 6. Excerpta de vita Willelmi Conquestoris. 7. De Morte Will. Conq. 8. Hymnus de Morte Will. Conq. 9. De Morte Lanfranci. 10. Gesta Will. Ducis Normannorum. 11. Excerptum ex cantatorio S. Huberti. 12. Annalis Historia brevis sive Chronica Monasterii S. Stephani Cadomensis. 13. Carmen de Morte Lanfranci. 14. Charta a rege Will. concessa Anglo-Saxonice scripta. 15. Du Roi Guillaume d'Angleterre par Chretien de Troyes. 16. Le Dit de Guillaume d'Angleterre.

QUEEN DAGMAR'S Cross, *facsimile in gold and colours* of the Enamelled Jewel in the Old Northern Museum, Copenhagen, with Introductory Remarks by Prof. GEORGE STEPHENS, F.S.A. 8vo, *sewed.* 3s

RAINE (Rev. James) History and Antiquities of North Durham, as subdivided into the Shires of Norham, Island, and Bedlington, which from the Saxon period until 1844 constituted part of the County of Durham, but are now united to Northumberland. BOTH PARTS *complete*, folio, *fine plates* (wanting 3 plates in the first part) *bds.* £1. 5s

———— Part II. (*wanting by many Subscribers*) *quite complete.* 18s. LARGE PAPER. £1. 1s

RAINE'S (Rev. Jas.) Saint Cuthbert, with an Account of the State in which his remains were found upon the opening of his Tomb in Durham Cathedral, 1827. 4to, *plates and woodcuts, bds.* (*a very interesting vol*). 10s 6d. (Original price, £1. 11s 6d)

"From the four corners of the earth they come,
To kiss this shrine—this mortal-breathing saint."

RAINE'S (Rev. Jas.) Catterick Church, Yorkshire, a correct copy of the contract for its building in 1412. Illustrated with Remarks and Notes. *With thirteen plates of views, elevations, and details,* by A. SALVIN, *Architect.* 4to, *cloth.* 6s.—Or LARGE PAPER, *cloth.* 9s

RAINE (Rev. James) Historical Account of the Episcopal Castle or Palace of Auckland. Royal 4to, *fine views, portraits, and seals,* *cloth.* 10s 6d (*original price,* £1. 1s)

RAINE (Rev. John, *Vicar of Blyth*) The History and Antiquities of the Parish of Blyth, in the Counties of Nottingham and York, comprising Accounts of the Monastery, Hospitals, Chapels, and Ancient Tournament Field, of the Parish of the Castle and Manor of Tickill, and of the Family Possessions of De Buili, the First and Norman Lord thereof, together with Biographical Notices of Roger Mowbray, Philip of Olcotes, Bishop Sanderson, John Cromwell, and others, with Appendix of Documents, &c. *4to plates and pedigrees, cloth.* 15s (*original price, £1. 6s*)

—— LARGE PAPER, royal 4to. £1. 5s

These copies have an additional view of the Remains of Scrooby Palace, not issued with the early copies.

RECORDE.—The Connection of Wales with the Early Science of England, illustrated in the Memoirs of Dr. Robert Recorde, the first Writer on Arithmetic, Geometry, Astronomy, &c., in the English Language. By J. O. HALLIWELL. *8vo, sewed.* 1s

REDFERN'S (Francis, *of Uttoxeter*), the History of Uttoxeter, in Staffordshire, with Notices of Places in the Neighbourhood. Post 8vo, *many engravings, cloth,* 7s 6d

THE RELIQUARY; a Depository for Precious Relics, Legendary, Biographical, and Historical, illustrative of the Habits, Customs, and Pursuits of our Forefathers. Edited by LLEWELLYN JEWITT, F.S.A. 8vo, Nos. 1 to 26, *illustrated with engravings, published quarterly.* 2s 6d per No.

RELIQUIÆ ANTIQUÆ; Scraps from Ancient Manuscrips, illustraing chiefly Early English Literature and the English Language. Edited by Wright and Halliwell. 8vo, Vol II., in Nos. 12s

Many subscribers want the second volume. A number of odd parts of both vols to complete copies.

RETROSPECTIVE REVIEW (New Series) consisting of Criticisms upon, Analysis of, and Extracts from, curious, useful, valuable, and scarce Old Books. 8vo, Vols I. and II., *all printed, cloth.* 10s 6d (*original price, £1. 1s*). 1853—54

These two volumes form a good companion to the old series of the *Retrospective*, in 16 vols; the articles are of the same length and character.

REYNOLDS' (Sir Joshua) Notes and Observations on Pictures chiefly of the Venetian School, being Extracts from his Italian Sketch Books; also the Rev. W. Mason's Observations on Sir Joshua's Method of Colouring, with some unpublished Letters, of Dr. Johnson, Malone, and others; with an Appendix, containing a Transcript of Sir Joshua's Account Book, showing the Paintings he executed, and the Prices he was paid for them. Edited by William Cotton, Esq. 8vo, *cloth.* 5s

"The scraps of the Critical Journal, kept by Reynolds at Rome, Florence, and Venice, will be esteemed by high-class *virtuosi.*"—*Leader.*

RIMBAULT (E. F., *LL.D., F.S.A.,* &c.)—A Little Book of Songs and Ballads, gathered from Ancient Music Books, MS. and Printed. *Elegantly printed* in post 8vo., pp. 240, *hf. morocco.* 6s

"Dr. Rimbault has been at some pains to collect the words of the songs which used to delight the rustics of former times."—*Atlas.*

RIMBAULT (Dr. E. F.) Bibliotheca Madrigaliana.—A Bibliographical Account of the Musical and Poetical Works published in England during the Sixteenth and Seventeenth Centuries, under the Titles of Madrigals, Ballets, Ayres, Canzonets, &c., &c. 8vo, *cloth.* 5s

It records a class of books left undescribed by Ames, Herbert, and Dibdin, and furnishes a most valuable Catalogue of Lyrical Poetry of the age to which it refers.

ROBERTS' (George, *of Lyme Regis*)—Life, Progresses, and Rebellion of James, Duke of Monmouth, &c., to his Capture and Execution, with a full account of the "Bloody Assize," under Judge Jefferies, and Copious Biographical Notices.   2 vols, post 8vo, *plates and cuts, cloth,* 7s 6d (*original price,* £1. 4s.)

Two very interesting volumes, particularly so to those connected with the West of England.   Quoted for facts by Lord Macaulay.

ROBERTS' (George) The Social History of the People of the Southern Counties of England in Past Centuries, illustrated in regard to their Habits, Municipal Bye-laws, Civil Progress, &c.   Thick 8vo, *cloth.*   7s 6d (*original price,* 16s)

An interesting volume on old English manners and customs, mode of travelling, punishments, witchcraft, gipsies, pirates, stage-players, pilgrimages, prices of labour and provisions, the clothing trade of the West of England, &c., &c., compiled chiefly from original materials, as the archives of Lyme-Regis and Weymouth, family papers, church registers, &c.   Dedicated to Lord Macaulay.

ROBIN HOOD.—The Great Hero of the Ancient Minstrelsy of England, "Robin Hood," his Period, real Character, &c., investigated, and perhaps ascertained.   By the Rev. JOSEPH HUNTER. Post 8vo.   2s 6d.

ROBINSON (J. B., *of Derby*)—Derbyshire Gatherings; a Fund of Delight for the Antiquary, the Historian, the Topographer, and Biographer, and General Reader.   *A handsome 4to, with engravings, extra cloth, gilt edges.*   £1. 5s

ROMAN COINS.—Records of Roman History, from Cnæus Pompeius to Tiberius Constantinus, as exhibited on the Roman Coins, Collected by Francis Hobler, formerly Secretary to the Numismatic Society of London.   2 vols, royal 4to, *frontispiece and numerous engravings, in cloth.*   £1. 1s (*original price* £2. 2s, only 250 printed).

"A work calculated not only to interest the professed numismatist, but also to instruct the classical student and the historian.   The unpublished Coins are rather numerous, especially when we consider how many works have been printed on the Roman series, and how much it has been studied. . . . . The value of the work is much enhanced by the illustrations, executed by Mr. Fairholt, with the peculiar spirit and fidelity which indicate his experienced hand."—*C. Roach Smith's Collectanea Antiqua.*

SACRED MUSIC.—By the Rev. W. Sloane Evans, M.A.   Royal 8vo, *third edition, sewed.*   1s 6d (*original price,* 6s)

SALVERTE'S (Eusebius) History of the Names of Men, Nations, and Places, in their Connection with the Progress of Civilization. Translated by the Rev. L. H. Mordaque, M.A., Oxon. 2 vols, 8vo, *cloth.* £1. 4s

"Notre nom propre c'est nous-memes."
"Nomina si nescis perlit cognitio rerum."

"Full of learning, well written, and well translated."—*Daily News.*

"These two volumes are filled with a minute and philosophical enquiry into the origin of names of all sorts among all nations, and show profound scholarship and patient skill in wide and elaborate research. Much of the work is, necessarily, too profound for general readers—particularly the appendices to the second volume—but the larger part of the enquiry is so curious and interesting that any ordinary reader will fully appreciate and profit by the researches."—*Birmingham Journal.*

SANDYS' (W., F.S.A.)—Christmastide, its History, Festivities, and Carols (*with their music*). In a handsome vol. 8vo, *illustrated with 20 engravings after the designs of F. Stephanoff, extra cloth, gilt edges.* 5s (*original price* 14s)

"Its title vouches that *Chrismastide* is germane to the time. Mr. Sandys has brought together, in an octavo of some 300 pages, a great deal of often interesting information beyond the stale gossip about "Christmas in the olden time," and the threadbare make-believes of jollity and geniality which furnish forth most books on the subject. His carols, too, which include some in old French and Provençal, are selected from numerous sources, and comprise many of the less known and more worth knowing. His materials are presented with good feeling and mastery of his theme. On the whole the volume deserves, and should anticipate, a welcome."—*Spectator.*

SANDYS (W.) and S. A. FORSTER.—History of the Violin and other Instruments played on with a Bow, from the Earliest Times to the Present, also an Account of the Principal Makers, English and Foreign. Thick 8vo, pp. 408, *with many engravings, cloth.* 14s

SANDY'S (Charles, *of Canterbury*) Consuetudes Kanciæ. A History of Gavelkind, and other remarkable Customs, in the County of Kent. 8vo, *illustrated with facsimiles, a very handsome volume, cloth.* 15s.

SANDYS (Charles) Critical Dissertation on Professor Willis's "Architectural History of Canterbury Cathedral." 8vo. 2s 6d

"Written in no quarrelsome or captious spirit; the highest compliment is paid to Professor Willis where it is due. But the author has made out a clear case, in some very important instances, of inaccuracies that have led the learned Professor into the construction of serious errors thoughout. It may be considered as an indispensable companion to his volume, containing a great deal of extra information of a very curious kind."—*Art-Union.*

SAULL (W. D.) On the Connection between Astronomical and Geological Phenomena, addressed to the Geologists of Europe and America. 8vo, *diagrams, sewed.* 2s

SCRASE FAMILY.—Genealogical Memoir of the Family of Scrase, of Sussex. By M. A. LOWER. 8vo. 1s 6d

SHAKESPERIANA.

A LIFE OF SHAKESPEARE, including many particulars respecting the Poet and his Family, never before published. By J. O. HALLIWELL, F.R.S., etc. 8vo, *illustrated with 75 engravings on wood, most of which are of new objects from drawings by Fairholt, cloth.* 15s.   1848

This work contains upwards of forty documents respecting Shakespeare and his family, *never before published*, besides numerous others, indirectly illustrating the Poet's biography. All the anecdotes and traditions concerning Shakespeare are here, for the first time, collected, and much new light is thrown on his personal history, by papers exhibiting him as selling Malt, Stone, &c. Of the seventy-six engravings which illustrate the volume, *more than fifty have never before been engraved.*

It is the only life of Shakespeare to be bought separately from his works.

NEW ILLUSTRATIONS of the Life, Studies, and Writings of Shakespeare. By the Rev. JOSEPH HUNTER. 2 vols, 8vo, *cloth.* 7s 6d (*original price £1. 1s*).   1845

Supplementary to all editions of the works of the Poet.

Part 2, price 8s., and Parts 3, 4, and 5 together, price 8s., may be had to complete copies.

SHAKESPEARE'S Versification, and its Apparent Irregularities Explained by Examples from Early and Late English Writers. By W. SIDNEY WALKER, Edited by WM. NANSOM LETTSOM. *Foolscap* 8vo, *cloth.* 6s.   1854

"The reader of Shakespeare would do well to make himself acquainted with this excellent little book previous to entering upon the study of the poet."—*Mr. Singer, in the Preface to his New Edition of Shakespeare.*

A CRITICAL Examination of the Text of Shakespeare ; together with Notes on his Plays and Poems, by the late W. SIDNEY WALKER. Edited by W. Nanson Lettsom. 3 vols, foolscap 8vo, *cloth.* 18s.   1860

"Very often we find ourselves differing from Mr. Walker on readings and interpretations, but we seldom differ from him without respect for his scholarship and care. His are not the wild guesses at truth which neither gods nor men have stomach to endure, but the suggestions of a trained intelligence and a chastened taste. Future editors and commentators will be bound to consult these volumes, and consider their suggestions."—*Athenæum.*

"A valuable addition to our Philological Literature, the most valuable part being the remarks on contemporary literature, the mass of learning by which the exact meaning and condition of a word is sought to be established."—*Literary Gazette.*

"Mr. Walker's Works undoubtedly form altogether the most valuable body of verbal criticism that has yet appeared from an individual."—*Mr. Dyce's Preface to Vol. 1. of his Shakespeare, 1864.*

NARES' (Archd.) Glossary, or Collection of Words, Phrases, Customs, Proverbs, etc., illustrating the Works of English Authors, particularly Shakespeare and his Contemporaries. A new edition, with Considerable Additions both of Words and Examples. By James O. Halliwell, F.R.S., and Thomas Wright, M.A., F.S.A. 2 thick vols, 8vo, *cloth.* £1. 1s.   1867

The Glossary of Archdeacon Nares is by far the best and most useful Work we possess for explaining and illustrating the obsolete language, and the customs and manners of the Sixteenth and Seventeenth Centuries, and it is quite indespensable for the readers of the literature of the Elizabethan period. The additional words and examples are distinguished from those of the original text by a † prefixed to each. The work contains between *five and six thousand additional examples,* the result of original research, not merely supplementary

A LETTER to Dr. Farmer (in reply to Ritson), relative to his Edition of Shakespeare, published in 1790.   By EDMUND MALONE. 8vo, *sewed.* 1s   1792

COMPARATIVE Review of the Opinions of James Boaden in 1795 and in 1796, relative to the Shakespeare MSS. 8vo, 2s   1796

ESSAY on the Genius of Shakespeare, with Critical Remarks on the Characters of Romeo, Hamlet, Juliet, and Ophelia, by H. M. GRAVES. Post 8vo, *cloth.* 2s 6d (*original price* 5s 6d)   1826

HISTORICAL Account of the Monumental Bust of Shakespeare, in the Chancel of Stratford-upon-Avon Church, by ABR. WIVELL. 8vo, 2 *plates.* 1s 6d   1827

VORTIGERN, an Historical Play, represented at Drury Lane, April 2, 1796, as a supposed newly discovered Drama of Shakespeare, by WILLIAM HENRY IRELAND. *New Edition, with an original Preface.* 8vo, *facsimile.* 1s 6d (*original price* 3s 6d)   1832
   The Preface is both interesting and curious, from the additional information it gives respecting the Shakespeare Forgeries, containing also the substance of the author's " Confessions."

SHAKESPEARE's Will, copied from the Original in the Prerogative Court, preserving the Interlineations and Facsimiles of the three Autographs of the Poet, with a few Preliminary Observations, by J. O. HALLIWELL. 4to. 1s   1838

TRADITIONARY Anecdotes of Shakespeare, collected in Warwickshire in 1693. 8vo, *sewed.* 1s   1838

OBSERVATIONS on an Autograph of Shakespeare, and the Orthography of his Name, by Sir FRED. MADDEN. 8vo, *sewed.* 1s 1838

SHAKESPEARE's Autobiographical Poems, being his Sonnets clearly developed, with his Character, drawn chiefly from his Works, by C. A. BROWN. Post 8vo, *cloth.* 4s 6d   1838

SHAKESPERIANA, a Catalogue of the Early Editions of Shakespeare's Plays, and of the Commentaries and other Publications illustrative of his works.   By J. O. HALLIWELL. 8vo, *cloth.* 3s
     1841
   " Indispensable to everybody who wishes to carry on any inquiries connected with Shakespeare, or who may have a fancy for Shakesperian Bibliography."— *Spectator.*

REASONS for a New Edition of Shakespeare's Works, by J. PAYNE COLLIER. 8vo. 1s   1842

ACCOUNT of the only known Manuscript of Shakespeare's Plays, comprising some important variations and corrections in the " Merry Wives of Windsor," obtained from a Playhouse Copy of that Play recently discovered.   By J. O. HALLIWELL. 8vo. 1s   1843

" WHO was 'Jack Wilson,' the Singer of Shakespeare's Stage ?" An Attempt to prove the identity of this person with John Wilson, Doctor of Music in the University of Oxford, A.D. 1844. By E. F. RIMBAULT, LL.D. 8vo. 1s

CRITICISM applied to Shakespeare. By C. BADHAM. Post 8vo. 1s
1846

CROKER (Crofton).—Remarks on an Article inserted in the Papers of the Shakespeare Society. Small 8vo, *sewed*, 1s. 1849

THE Tempest as a Lyrical Drama. By MORRIS BARNETT. 8vo. 1s
1850

A FEW Remarks on the Emendation, "Who Smothers her with Painting," in the Play of Cymbeline, discovered by Mr. Collier, in a Corrected Copy of the Second Edition of Shakespeare, by J. O. HALLIWELL, &c. 8vo. 1s 1852

CURIOSITIES of Modern Shakespeare Criticism. By J. O. HALLIWELL. 8vo, *with the first facsimile of the Dulwich Letter, sewed.* 1s 1853

A FEW Notes on Shakespeare, with Occasional Remarks on the Emendations of the Manuscript-Corrector in Mr. Collier's copy of the folio, 1632, by the REV. ALEXANDER DYCE. 8vo, *cloth.* 5s 1853

"Mr. Dyce's Notes are peculiarly delightful, from the stores of illustration with which his extensive reading, not only among our writers, but among those of other countries, especially of the Italian poets, has enabled him to enrich them. All that he has recorded is valuable. We read this little volume with pleasure, and closed it with regret."—*Literary Gazette.*

A FEW Words in Reply to the Rev. A. Dyce's "Few Notes on Shakespeare," by the Rev. JOSEPH HUNTER. 8vo. 1s 1853

THE Grimaldi Shakespeare.—Notes and Emendations on the Plays of Shakespeare, from a recently discovered annotated copy by the late Joe Grimaldi, Esq., Comedian. 8vo, *woodcuts.* 1s
1853

A humourous squib on Collier's Shakespeare Emendations.

THE Moor of Venice, Cinthio's Tale, and Shakespeare's Tragedy. By JOHN EDWARD TAYLOR. Post 8vo. 1s 1855

CURSORY Notes on Various Passages in the Text of Beaumont and Fletcher, as edited by the Rev. Alexander Dyce, and on his "Few Notes on Shakespeare," by the Rev. JOHN MITFORD. 8vo, *sewed.* 2s 6d 1856

BACON and Shakespeare, an Inquiry touching Players, Playhouses, and Play-writers, in the Reign of Q. Elizabeth; to which is appended an Abstract of a Manuscript Autobiography of Tobie Matthews, by W. H. SMITH. Foolscap 8vo, *cloth.* 2s 6d 1857

"Lord Palmerston was tolerably well up in the chief Latin and English Classics; but he entertained one of the most extraordinary paradoxes touching the greatest of them that was ever broached by a man of his intellectual calibre. He maintained that the Plays of Shakespeare were really written by Bacon, who passed them off under the name of an actor, for fear of compromising his professional prospects and philosophic gravity. Only last year, when this subject was discussed at Broadlands, Lord Palmerston suddenly left the room, and speedily returned with a small volume of dramatic criticisms (*Mr. Smith's book*) in which the same theory was supported by supposed analogies of thought and expression. 'There,' said he, 'read that, and you will come over to my

HAMLET.—An Attempt to Ascertain whether the Queen were an Accessory before the Fact, in the Murder of her First Husband. 8vo, *sewed.* 2s   1856
"This pamphlet well deserves the perusal of every student of Hamlet."— *Notes and Queries.*

SHAKESPEARE's Story-Teller, Introductory Leaves, or Outline Sketches, with Choice Extracts in the Words of the Poet himself, with an Analysis of the Characters, by George Stephens, *Professor of the English Language and Literature in the University of Copenhagen.* 8vo, Nos. 1 to 6. 6d each.   1856

PERICLES, Prince of Tyre, a Novel, by Geo. Wilkins, printed in 1608, and founded upon Shakespeare's Play, edited by PROFESSOR MOMMSEN, with Preface and Account of some original Shakespeare editions extant in Germany and Switzerland, and Introduction by J. P. COLLIER. 8vo, *sewed.* 5s   1857

LLOYD (W. Watkiss) Essays on the Life and Plays of Shakespeare, contributed to the Edition by S. W. Singer, 1856. Thick post 8vo, *half calf gilt, marbled edges.* 9s   1858
Only 50 copies privately printed.

THE Sonnets of Shakespeare, *rearranged* and divided into Four Parts, with an Introduction and Explanatory Notes. Post 8vo, *cloth.* 3s 6d   1859

STRICTURES on Mr. Collier's New Edition of Shakespeare, published in 1858, by the Rev. ALEXANDER DYCE. 8vo, *cloth.* 5s (*original price* 7s 6d)   1859

THE Shakespeare Fabrications, or the MS. Notes of the Perkins folio, shown to be of recent origin; with Appendix on the Authorship of the Ireland Forgeries, by C. MANSFIELD INGLEBY, LL.D. Foolscap 8vo, *with a facsimile, shewing the* pseudo *old writing and the pencilled words, cloth.* 3s   1859

STRICTURES on Mr. Hamilton's Inquiry into the Genuineness of the MS. Corrections in J. Payne Collier's Annotated Shakespeare. Folio, 1632. By SCRUTATOR. 8vo, *sewed.* 1s   1860

SHAKESPEARE and the Bible, shewing how much the great Dramatist was indebted to Holy Writ for his Profound Knowledge of Human Nature. By the Rev. T. R. EATON. Fcap. 8vo, *cloth.* 2s 6d   1860

THE Footsteps of Shakespeare, or a Ramble with the Early Dramatists, containing New and Interesting Information respecting Shakespeare, Lyly, Marlowe, Green, and others. Post 8vo, *cloth.* 5s 6d   1861

SHAKESPEARE, his Friends and Contemporaries. By G. M. Tweddell. Second Edition, 8vo, Parts I to III. 6d each.   1861—3

THE Shakespeare Cyclopædia, or a Classified and Elucidated Summary of Shakespeare's Knowledge of the Works and Phenomena of Nature. By J. H. Fennell, 8vo, Part I., *sewed.* 1s   1862

A BRIEF Hand Book of the Records belonging to the Borough of Stratford-on-Avon; with Notes of a few of the Shakespearian Documents. Square post 8vo, *cloth (only 50 printed)*. 7s 6d
1862

SHAKESPEARE No Deerstealer; or, a Short Account of Fulbroke Park, near Stratford-on-Avon. By C. Holte Bracebride. 8vo, *privately printed.* 1s 6d
1862

WHELER's Historical Account of the Birthplace of Shakespeare, reprinted from the edition of 1824, with a few prefatory remarks by J. O. Halliwell. 8vo, *front.* 1s 6d
1863

BRIEF Hand List of the Collections respecting the Life and Works of Shakespeare, and the History and Antiquities of Stratford-upon-Avon, formed by the late Robert Bell Wheler, and presented by his sister to that Town, to be preserved for ever in the Shakespeare Library and Museum. Small square 8vo. 7s 6d
Chiswick Press, 1863

Only 100 copies printed at the expense of Mr. Halliwell, not for sale.

SHAKESPEARE'S Coriolanus. Edited, with Notes and Preface, by F. A. LEO, with a quarto facsimile of the Tragedy of Coriolanus, from the folio of 1623, photolithographed by A. BURCHARD, and with Extracts from North's Plutarch. 4to, *elegantly printed, extra cloth.* 15s
1864

SHAKSPERE and Jonson.—Dramatic *versus* Wit-Combats—Auxiliary Forces—Beaumont and Fletcher, Marston, Decker, Chapman, and Webster. Post 8vo. 4s.
1864

REPRINTS of Scarce Pieces of Shakespearian Criticism, No. 1, "Remarks on Hamlet, 1736." Fcap. 8vo. 1s 6d
1864

THREE Notelets on Shakespeare—I. Shakespeare in Germany; II. The Folk-lore of Shakespeare; III. Was Shakespeare a Soldier? By WILLIAM J. THOMS, F.S.A. Post 8vo, *cloth.* 4s 6d　1865

"On this subject of Shakespeare in Germany, Mr. W. J. Thoms has reprinted a paper read some years ago before the Society of Antiquaries, together with two other 'Notelets' on the Poet—'The Folk Lore of Shakespeare,' from the ATHENÆUM, and 'Was Shakespeare a Soldier?' from NOTES AND QUERIES. Not the least of Mr. Thoms's many services to English literature is the invention of that admirable word *folk-lore,* which appeared for the first time in these columns only a few years ago, and has already become a domestic term in every corner of the world. His illustration of Shakespeare's knowledge of this little world of fairy dreams and legends is a perfect bit of criticism. He answers the query as to Shakespeare's having seen martial service in the affirmative; and therein we think his argument sound, his conclusion right. These 'Notelets' were very well worthy of being collected into a book."—*Athenæum.*

SHAKESPEARE's Editors and Commentators. By the Rev. W. R. ARROWSMITH, Incumbent of Old St. Pancras. 8vo, *sewed.* 1s 6d
1865

NEW Readings in Shakspere, or Proposed Emendations of the Text. By ROBERT CARTWRIGHT, M.D. 8vo, *sewed.* 2s　1866

THE SHAKESPEARE EXPOSITOR: being Notes, and Emendations on his Works. By THOMAS KEIGHTLEY. Thick fcap. 8vo,

SHAKESPEARE's Jest Book.—A Hundred Mery Talys, from the only perfect copy known. Edited, with Introduction and Notes, by Dr. HERMAN OESTERLEY. Fcap. 8vo, *nicely printed by Whittingham, half morocco.*   4s 6d

The only perfect copy known of the "Hundred Mery Talys" was lately discovered in the Royal Library at Gottingen. This is a verbatim reprint, supplying all the chasms and lost tales in former editions, with copious Notes by the editor, pointing out the origin of the various tales, and authors who have used them.

———

SHARPE's (Samuel, *author of the History of Ancient Egypt, &c.*)—The Egyptian Antiquities in the British Museum described. Post 8vo, *with many woodcuts, cloth.*   5s.   1862

"We strongly counsel every one who desires to obtain a true knowledge of the Egyptian Department of the Museum to lose no time in obtaining this cheap and excellent volume."—*Daily News.*

"Mr. Sharpe here presents the student of Egyptian antiquity and art with a very useful book. . . . . To the accomplished student this book will be useful as a reminder of many things already known to him; to the tyro it may serve as a guide and *aide-memoire:* to the mere visitor to the Galleries in the British Museum, this will be a handy guide book, in which an immediate answer may be sought and found for the oft-repeated questions before these wondrous remains—of what are their natures? what their meanings? what their purposes?"—*Athenæum.*

SHARPE (Samuel) Egyptian Mythology and Egyptian Christianity, with their Influence on the Opinions of Modern Christendom. Post 8vo, *with* 100 *engravings, cloth.*   3s.

SHARPE (Samuel) History of Egypt, from the Earliest Times till the Conquest by the Arabs, A.D. 620.   2 vols, 8vo, third edition (*excepting the engravings, the same as the fourth*), *elegantly printed, cloth.*   4s 6d (*original price* 16s)

SHARPE (Samuel) Critical Notes on the Authorized English Version of the New Testament, being a Companion to the Author's "New Testament, translated from Griesbach's Text." Fcap. 8vo, SECOND EDITION, *cloth.*   2s 6d

SHEPHERD (Charles).—Historical Account of the Island of Saint Vincent, in the West Indies, with large Appendix on Population, Meteorology, Produce of Estates, Revenue, Carib Grants, etc. 8vo, *plates, cloth.*   3s (*original price* 12s)

SINDING (Professor, *of Copenhagen*) History of Scandinavia, from the early times of the Northmen, the Seakings, and Vikings, to the present day.   First English Edition, thoroughly revised and augmented. 8vo, pp. 490, *large map and portrait of Q. Margaret, cloth.*   6s

SKELTON (John, *Poet Laureate to Henry VIII*) Poetical Works, the Bowge of Court, Colin Clout, Why come ye not to Court? (his celebrated Satire on Wolsey), Phillip Sparrow, Elinour Rumming, etc., with Notes and Life.   By the Rev. A. DYCE. 2 vols, 8vo, *cloth.*   16s (*original price* £1. 12s)

" The power, the strangeness, the volubility of his language, the audacity of his satire, and the perfect originality of his manner, made Skelton one of the most extraordinary writers of any age or country."—*Southey.*

SIMS (Richard, *of the Dept. of MSS. in the British Museum*) A Manual for the Genealogist, Topographer, Antiquary, and Legal Professor, consisting of Descriptions of Public Records, Parochial and other Registers, Wills, County and Family Histories, Heraldic Collections in Public Libraries, &c. 8vo, SECOND EDITION, pp. 540, *cloth.* 15s

This work will be found indispensable by those engaged in the study of Family History and Heraldry, and by the compiler of County and Local History, the Antiquary and the Lawyer. In it the Public and other Records, most likely to afford information to genealogical inquirers, are fully described, and their places of present deposit indicated. Such Records are—The Domesday Books—Monastic Records—Cartæ Antiquæ—Liber Niger—Liber Rubeus—Testa de Nevil—Placita in various Courts—Charter Rolls—Close Rolls—Coronation Rolls—Coroners' Rolls—Escheat Rolls—Fine Rolls—French, Gascon, and Norman Rolls—Hundred Rolls—Liberate Rolls—Memoranda Rolls—Oblata and other Rolls—Inquisitions Post Mortem—Inquisitions ad quod Damnum—Fines and Recoveries—Sign Manuals and Signet Bills—Privy Seals—Forfeitures, Pardons, and Attainders—Parliamentary Records—County Palatine Records—Scotch, Irish, and Welsh Records—also Wills—Parochial and other Registers—Registers of Universities and Public Schools—Heraldic Collections—Records of Clergymen, Lawyers, Surgeons, Soldiers, Sailors, &c., &c.

The whole accompanied by valuable Lists of Printed Works and Manuscripts in various Libraries, namely:—at the British Museum—The Bodleian, Ashmolean, and other Libraries at Oxford—The Public Library, and that of Caius College, Cambridge—The Colleges of Arms in London and Dublin—The Libraries of Lincoln's Inn, and of the Middle and Inner Temple—at Chetham College, Manchester; and in other repositories too numerous to mention.

The more important of these Lists are those of Monastic Cartularies—Extracts from Plea and other Rolls—Escheats—Inquisitions, &c.—Tenants in Capite—Recusants—Subsidies—Crown Lands—Wills—Parochial and other Registers—Heralds' Visitations—Royal and Noble Genealogies—Peerages, Baronetages, Knightages—Pedigrees of Gentry—County and Family Histories—Monumental Inscriptions—Coats of Arms—American Genealogies—Lists of Gentry—Members of Parliament—Freeholds—Officers of State—Justices of Peace—Mayors, Sheriffs, &c.—Collegians, Church Dignitaries—Lawyers—The Medical Profession—Soldiers—Sailors, etc.

To these is added an "Appendix," containing an Account of the Public Record Offices and Libraries mentioned in the work, the mode of obtaining admission, hours of attendance, fees for searching, copying, &c. Table of the Regnal Years of English Sovereigns; Tables of Dates used in Ancient Records, &c.

SIMS (Richard) Handbook to the Library of the British Museum, containing a brief History of its Formation, and of the various Collections of which it is composed, Descriptions of the Catalogues in present use, Classed Lists of the Manuscripts, etc., and a variety of Information indispensable for Literary Men, with some Account of the principal Public Libraries in London. Sm. 8vo (pp. 438) *with map and plan, cloth.* 2s 6d

It will be found a very useful work to every literary person or public institution in all parts of the world.

"A little Handbook of the Library has been published, which I think will be most useful to the public."—*Lord Seymour's Reply in the H. of Commons, July, 1854.*

"I am much pleased with your book, and find in it abundance of information which I wanted."—*Letter from Albert Way, Esq., F.S.A., Editor of the "Promptorum Parvulorum," &c.*

"I take this opportunity of telling you how much I like your nice little 'Handbook to the Library of the British Museum,' which I sincerely hope may have the success which it deserves."—*Letter from Thos. Wright, Esq., F.S.A., Author of the 'Biographia Britannica Literaria,' &c.*

"Mr. Sims's 'Handbook to the Library of the British Museum' is a very comprehensive and instructive volume. . . . . . I venture to predict for it

SLOANE—EVANS (W. S.) Grammar of British Heraldry, cons ting of Blazon and Marshalling with an Introduction on the Rise and Progress of Symbols and Ensigns. 8vo, SECOND EDITION, *many plates, cloth.* 5s (*original price* 13s)

SMITH'S (Henry Ecroyd) Reliquiae Isurianae, the Remains of the Roman Isurium, now Aldborough near Boroughbridge, York, shire, illustrated and described. Royal 4to, with 37 *plates, cloth.* £1. 5s

The most highly illustrated work ever published on a Roman Station in England.

SMITH'S (Charles Roach, F.S.A.) History and Antiquities of Rich-borough, and Lymme, in Kent, Small 4to, *with many engravings on wood and copper, by F. W. Fairholt, cloth.* £1. 1s

"No antiquarian volume could display a trio of names more zealous, successful, and intelligent, on the subject of Romano-British remains, than the three here represented—Roach Smith, the ardent explorer; Fairholt, the excellent illustrator, and Rolfe, the indefatigable collector.—*Literary Gazette.*

SMITH (W., *jun., of Morley*) Rambles about Morley (West Riding of Yorkshire) with Descriptive and Historic Sketches, also an Account of the Rise and Progress of the Woollen Manufacture in this Place. Royal 12mo, *map and numerous engravings, cloth.* 5s

SMITH'S (Toulmin) Memorials of Old Birmingham, Men and Names, Founders, Freeholders, and Indwellers, from the 13th to the 16th Century, with particulars as to the earliest Church of the Reformation built and endowed in England, from original and unpublished documents. Royal 8vo, *plates, cloth.* 4s 6d

SMITH (John Russell) Bibliothecana Cantiana.—A Bibliographical Account of what has been published on the History, Topography, Antiquities, Customs, and Family Genealogy of the County of Kent, with Biographical Notes. 8vo (pp. 370) *with two plates of facsimiles of autographs of 33 eminent Kentish Writers.* 5s (original price 14s)

SMITH (J. R.) A Bibliographical Catalogue of English Writers on Angling and Ichthyology. Post 8vo. 1s 6d

SMITH (J. R.) A Bibliographical List of all the Works which have been published towards illustrating the Provincial Dialects of England. Post 8vo. 1s

"Very serviceable to such as prosecute the study of our provincial dialects, or are collecting works on that curious subject. . . . We very cordially recommend it to notice."—*Metropolitan.*

SPEDDING (James, *Editor of Lord Bacon*) Publishers and Authors. Post 8vo, *cloth.* 2s

Mr. Spedding wishes to expose the present mystery (?) of publishing, he thinks from a number of cases that we publishers do not act on the square. However, there are two sides to the question; but his book will be useful to the uninitiated.

STEPHENS' (Professor George, *of Copenhagen*) the Old Northern Runic Monuments of Scandinavia and England, now first Collected and Deciphered. Folio, Part 1, pp. 362, *with about* 150 *engravings.* £2. 10s

The Author promises the second and concluding Part next year.

STEPHENS' (Professor) The Ruthwell Cross (near Annan, Dumfries-shire) with its Runic Verses, by Cædmon, and Cædmon's Cross-Lay, "The Holy Rood, a Dream," from a Transcript of the 10th Century, with Translations, Notes, &c. Folio, *with two plates, sewed.* 10s

This will be included in the forthcoming second part of Professor Stephens's work, this portion is published separately to meet the wishes of a number of Archæologists.

STIRRY'S (Thos.) A Rot amongst the Bishops, or a Terible *Tempest* in the *Sea* of Canterbury, set forth in lively emblems, to please the Judicious Reader. (*A Satire on Abp. Laud*), *four very curious woodcut emblems, cloth.* 3s

A facsimile of the very rare original edition, which sold at Bindley's sale for £13.

SURREY HILLS.—A Guide to the Caterham Railway and its Vicinity. Post 8vo, *2nd and revised edition, with a map, sewed.* 6d

Thousands of tourists and pleasure-seekers go hundreds of miles for beautiful scenery without perhaps finding a country of more varied and interesting character than that to be met with in the Caterham Valley, and within twenty miles of the metropolis.

SURTEES (Rev. Scott. F., *of Sprotburgh, Yorkshire*) Waifs and Strays of North Humber History. Post 8vo, 3 *plates, cloth.* 3s 6d

SURTEES (Rev. Scott F.) Julius Cæsar, Did he Cross the Channel (into Kent)? Post 8vo, *cloth.* 1s 6d

" In giving an answer in the negative to the above question, we ask for a fair and dispassionate hearing, and in order to avoid circumlocution pass at once our Rubicon, and propound as capable of all proof the following historical heresy, viz., that Caesar never set foot at Boulogne or Calais, never crossed the Channel, or set eyes on Deal or Dover, but that he sailed from the mouths of the Rhine or Scheldt, and landed in Norfolk on both his expeditions."—AUTHOR.

TESTAMENT (The New) translated from Griesbach's Text, by SAMUEL SHARPE, Author of the History of Egypt, &c. 5th edition. 12mo, pp. 412, *cloth.* 1s 6d

The aim of the translator has been to give the meaning and idiom of the Greek as far as possible in English words. The book is printed in paragraphs (the verses of the authorised version are numbered in the margins) the speeches by inverted commas, and the quotations from the "Old Testament" in italics, those passages which seem to be poetry in a smaller type. *It is entirely free from any motive to enforce doctrinal points.* Five large impressions of the volume sufficiently test its value.

We cordially recommend this edition of the New Testament to our readers and contributors.—*British Controversialist.*

Upon the whole, we must admit that his is the most correct English Version in existence, either of the whole or of any portion of the New Testament.—*The Ecclesiastic*, and repeated by the *English Churchman.*

TESTAMENT (Old).—The Hebrew Scriptures, translated by SAMUEL SHARPE, being a revision of the authorized English Old Testament. 3 vols, fcap. 8vo, *cloth, red edges.* 7s 6d

"In the following Revision of the Authorized Version of the Old Testament, the aim of the Translator has been to shew in the Text, by greater exactness, those peculiarities which others have been content to point out in Notes and Commentaries. He has translated from Van der Hooght's edition of the Hebrew Bible, printed in Amsterdam in 1705; except when, in a few cases, he has followed some of the various readings so industriously collected by Dr. Kennicott."—*Preface.* A Prospectus may be had.

TANSWELL'S (John, *of the Inner Temple*) the History and Antiquities of Lambeth. 8vo, *with numerous illustrations, cloth.* 4s 6d (*original price* 7s 6d)

THOMPSON (James) Handbook of Leicester. 12mo, *Second Edit., woodcuts, bds.* 2s

THOMPSON (Ebenezer) A Vindication of the Hymn "Te Deum Laudamus," from the Corruptions of a Thousand Years, with Ancient Versions in Anglo Saxon, High German, Norman French, &c., and an English Paraphrase of the XVth Century, now first printed. Fcap. 8vo, *cloth.* 3s

A book well worth the notice of the Ecclesiastical Antiquary and the Philologist.

THOMPSON (Ebenezer) on the Archaic Mode of expressing Numbers in English, Anglo-Saxon, Friesic, etc. 8vo (*an ingenious and learned pamphlet, interesting to the Philologist*). 1s

TIERNEY'S (Rev. Canon) History and Antiquities of the Castle and Town of Arundel, including the Biography of its Earls. 2 vols, royal 8vo, *fine plates, cloth,* 14s (*original price,* £2. 10s.)

TITIAN.—Notices of the Life and Works of Titian the Painter. By Sir Abraham Hume. Royal 8vo, *portrait, cloth.* 6s.

TONSTALL (Cuthbert, *Bishop of Durham*) Sermon preached on Palm Sunday, 1539, before Henry VIII.; *reprinted verbatim from the rare edition by Berthelet, in* 1539. 12mo. 1s 6d.

An exceedingly interesting Sermon, at the commencement of the Reformation; Strype in his "Memorials," has made large extracts from it.

TORRENT of PORTUGAL; an English Metrical Romance. Now first published, from an unique MS. of the XVth Century, preserved in the Chetham Library at Manchester. Edited by J. O. Halliwell, &c. Post 8vo, *cloth, uniform with Ritson, Weber, and Ellis's publications, cloth.* 5s.

"This is a valuable and interesting addition to our list of early English metrical romances, and an indispensable companion to the collections of Ritson, Weber, and Ellis,"—*Literary Gazette.*

TOPOGRAPHER (The) and Genealogist. Edited by J. G. Nichols. 3 vols, 8vo, *cloth.* £1. 5s (pub £3. 3s)

This extremely valuable work forms a sequel to the "Collectanea Topographica Genealogica," and the intrinsic value and originality of the materials comprised therein, will entitle it not only to preservation, but to frequent reference.

TOWNEND's (William) The Descendants of the Stuarts. An Unchronicled Page in England's History. 8vo, *portraits and folding pedigrees,* SECOND EDITION, WITH ADDITIONS, *half morocco,* 5s (original price 10s)

This volume contains a most minute, precise, and valuable history of the Descendants of the Stuart Family. Neither of our Historians from Hume to Macaulay give even the more prominent facts in connection with many branches of the House of Stuart.

"This is a really interesting contribution to what we may term the private records of history. . . . . What Mr. Townend has done is full of curious information. His Genealogical tables shew all the ramifications which spring out of the matrimonial alliances of the descendants of the Stuarts, and very curious *possibilities* some of these indicate. . . . . We promise our readers that this volume contains much that is worthy of perusal and recollection, as well as much that is suggestive."—*Globe.*

TOXOPHILUS; the School of Shooting (the first English Treatise on *Archery*. By ROGER ASCHAM, reprinted from the Rev. Dr. Giles's Edition of Ascham's Whole Works. Fcap. 8vo, *cloth*. 3s

TROLLOPE (Rev. W.) History of the Royal Foundation of Christ's Hospital, Plan of Education, Internal Economy of the Institution, and Memoirs of Eminent Blues. 4to, *plates, cloth*. 8s 6d (*original price £3. 3s*)

TUCKETT (John) Pedigrees and Arms of Devonshire Families, as recorded in the Herald's Visitation of 1620, with Additions from the Harleian MSS. and the Printed Collections of West-cote and Pole. 4to, Parts I. to XII. Each 5s

TURNER'S (Sir Gregory Page) Topographical Memorandums for the County of Oxford. 8vo, *bds*. 2s

TWEDDELL (G. M.) The Bards and Authors of Cleveland and South Durham. By G. M. TWEDDELL. 8vo, Parts I. to VI. 6d each.

TWO LEAVES of King Waldere and King Gudhere, a hitherto unknown Old English Epic of the 8th Century belonging to the Saga Cycle of King Theodoric and his Men. Now first published with a Modern English Reading, Notes, and Glossary by GEORGE STEPHENS, *English Professor in the University of Copenhagen.* Royal 8vo, *with four Photographic Facsimiles of the MS. of the 9th Century, recently discovered at Copenhagen.* 15s—*Without Facsimiles.* 7s 6d

VASEY (George) A Monograph of the Genus Bos.—The Natural History of Bulls, Bisons, and Buffaloes, exhibiting all the known Species (with an Introduction containing an Account of Experiments on Rumination from the French of M. FLOURENS). 8vo, *with 72 engravings on wood by the Author, cloth.* 6s (*original price 10s 6d*)

Written in a scientific and popular manner, and printed and illustrated uniformly with the works of Bell, Yarrell, Forbes, Johnston, &c. Dedicated to the late Mr. Yarrell, who took great interest in the progress of the work. Mr. Vasey engraved many of the beautiful woodcuts in Mr. Yarrell's works.

VASEY'S (George) Illustrations of Eating, displaying the Omnivorous Character of Man, and exhibiting the Natives of various Countries at Feeding-time. Fcap. 8vo, *with woodcuts by the Author.* 2s

VERNON'S (E. J., *B.A., Oxon*) Guide to the Anglo-Saxon Tongue, on the Basis of Professor Rask's Grammar; to which are added Reading Lessons in Verse and Prose, with Notes, for the Use of Learners. 12mo, *cloth.* 5s

"Mr. Vernon has, we think, acted wisely in taking Rask for his model; but let no one suppose from the title that the book is merely a compilation from the work of that philologist. The accidence is abridged from Rask, with constant revision, correction, and modification; but the syntax, a most important portion of the book, is original, and is compiled with great care and skill; and the latter half of the volume consists of a well-chosen selection of extracts from Anglo-Saxon writers, in prose and in verse, for the practice of the student, who will find great assistance in reading them from the grammatical notes with which they are accompanied, and from the glossary which follows them... This volume, well studied, will enable anyone to read with ease the generality of Anglo-Saxon writers; and its cheapness places it within the reach of every class. It has our hearty recommendation."—*Literary Gazette.*

VICARS' (John) England's Worthies, under whom all the Civil and Bloody Warres, since Anno 1642 to Anno 1647, are related. Royal 12mo, *reprinted in the old style (similar to Lady Willoughby's Diary), with copies of the 18 rare portraits after Hollar, etc.,* half morocco. 5s

WACE (Master, *the Anglo-Norman Poet*) His Chronicle of the Norman Conquest, from the Roman de Rou. Translated into English Prose, with Notes and Illustrations, by EDGAR TAYLOR, F.S.A. 8vo, *many engravings from the Bayeux Tapestry, Norman Architecture, Illuminations, etc., cloth.* 15s *(original price £1. 8s)*

Only 250 copies printed, and very few remain unsold; the remaining copies are now in J. R. Smith's hands, and are offered at the above low price in consequence of the death of Mr. Pickering; hitherto no copies have been sold under the published price.

WACKERBARTH (F..D.) Music and the Anglo-Saxons, being some Account of the Anglo-Saxon Orchestra, with Remarks on the Church Music of the 19th Century. 8vo, 2 *plates, sewed.* 4s

WARNE (Charles, *F.S.A.*) The Celtic Tumuli of Dorset ; an Account of Personal and other Researches in the Sepulchral Mounds of the Durotriges. Folio, *plates and woodcuts, cloth.* £1. 10s

WAYLEN (James, *of Devizes*) History and Antiquities of the Town of Marlborough, and more generally of the entire Hundred of Selkley, in Wiltshire. Thick 8vo, *woodcuts, cloth.* 14s

This volume describes a portion of Wilts not included by Sir R. C. Hoare and other topographers.

WEST (Mrs.) A Memoir of Mrs. John West, of Chettle, Dorset. By the Rev. JOHN WEST, A.M. A new edition, with Brief Memoir of the Writer. 12mo, *cloth.* 2s 6d

The fourth edition of an interesting volume of Religious Biography. The Rev. John West was the first missionary to the Indians of Prince Rupert's Land, the first wooden church at Red River was partly built by his own hands.

WESLEY—Narrative of a Remarkable Transaction in the Early Life of John Wesley. Now first printed from a MS. in the British Museum. SECOND EDITION ; to which is added a Review of the Work by the late Rev. Joseph Hunter, F.S.A. 8vo, *sewed.* 2s

A very curious love affair between J. W. and his housekeeper; it gives a curious insight into the early economy of the Methodists. It is entirely unknown to all Wesley's biographers.

WILLIAMS (John, *Archdeacon of Cardigan*) Essays, Philological, Philosophical, Ethnological, and Archæological, connected with the Prehistorical Records of the Civilised Nations of Ancient Europe, especially of that Race which first occupied Great Britain. Thick 8vo, with 7 *plates, cloth.* 16s

WINDSOR.—Annals of Windsor, being a History of the Castle and Town, with some Account of Eton and Places Adjacent. By R. R. TIGHE and J. E. DAVIS, Esqs. In 2 thick vols, roy. 8vo, *illustrated with many engravings, coloured and plain, extra cloth.* £1. 5s *(original price £4. 4s)*

WILLMOTT (Robert Aris, *some time Incumbent of Bear Wood, Berks*) A Journal of Summer Time in the Country. Fourth Edition; to which is added an Introductory Memoir by his Sister. Foolscap 8vo, *elegantly printed by Whittingham, extra cloth.* 5s

This 'Journal of Summer Time' is a genial gossip of literary matters under the various days of the month from May to August. It is full of anecdote, and full of interest; and is a sort of literary natural history, like that of Selbourne by good Gilbert White. The observations, the reading, the meditations of a well-trained, well-filled mind, give this volume its charm, and make it one which even the best-informed reader may wile away an hour with in recalling his own wanderings in the literary fields. The great glory of this book is that it is thoroughly natural. It does not aim at fine writing or sensational stories, but jots down from day to day such memoranda as a well-stored mind, familiar with the great treasures of our literature, would give forth in the quiet of a country parsonage, when summer smiled over the fields and woods, and a garden gave forth its pleasant sights and sounds.—*Birmingham Journal.*

WORSAAE'S (J. J. A., *of Copenhagen*) Primeval Antiquities of Denmark, translated and applied to the illustration of similar remains in England, by W. J. Thoms, F.S.A. 8vo, *many engravings, cloth.* 4s 6d (original price 10s 6d)

WRIGHT'S (Thomas, *M.A., F.S.A., Member of the Inststute of France*) Essay on Archæological Subjects, and on various Questions connected with the History of Art, Science, and Literature in the Middle Ages. 2 vols, post 8vo, *printed by Whittingham, illustrated with* 120 *engravings, cloth.* 16s

Contents:—1. On the Remains of a Primitive People in the South-East corner of Yorkshire. 2. On some ancient Barrows, or Tumuli, opened in East Yorkshire. 3. On some curious forms of Sepulchral Interment found in East Yorkshire. 4. Treago, and the large Tumulus at St. Weonard's. 5. On the Ethnology of South Britain at the period of the Extinction of the Roman Government in the Island. 6. On the Origin of the Welsh. 7. On the Anglo-Saxon Antiquities, with a particular reference to the Fausset Collection. 8. On the True Character of the Biographer Asser. 9. Anglo-Saxon Architecture, illustrated from illuminated Manuscripts. 10. On the Literary History of Geoffrey of Monmouth's History of the Britons, and of the Romantic Cycle of King Arthur. 11. On Saints' Lives and Miracles. 12. On Antiquarian Excavations and Researches in the Middle Ages. 13. On the Ancient Map of the World preserved in Hereford Cathedral, as illustrative of the History of Geography in the Middle Ages. 14. On the History of the English Language. 15. On the Abacus, or Mediæval System of Arithmetic. 16. On the Antiquity of Dates expressed in Arabic Numerals. 17. Remarks on an Ivory Casket of the beginning of the Fourteenth Century. 18. On the Carvings on the Stalls in Cathedral and Collegiate Churches. 19. Illustrations of some Questions relating to Architectural Antiquities—(*a*) Mediæval Architecture illustrated from Illuminated Manuscripts: (*b*) A Word more on Mediæval Bridge Builders: (*c*) On the Remains of proscribed Races in Mediæval and Modern Society, as explaining certain peculiarities in Old Churches. 20. On the Origin of Rhymes in Mediæval Poetry, and its bearing on the Authencity of the Early Welsh Poems. 21. On the History of the Drama in the Middle Ages. 22. On the Literature of the Troubadours. 23. On the History of Comic Literature during the Middle Ages. 24. On the Satirical Literature of the Reformation.

"Mr. Wright is a man who thinks for himself, and one who has evidently a title to do so. Some of the opinions published in these Essays are, he tells us, the result of his own observations or reflections, and are contrary to what have long been those of our own antiquaries and historians."—*Spectator.*

"*Two volumes exceedingly valuable* and important to all who are interested *in the Archæology of the Middle Ages*; no mere compilations, but replete with *fine reasoning,* new theories, and useful information, put in an intelligible *manner on* subjects that have been hitherto but imperfectly understood."—

WRIGHT (Thomas) Essays on the Literature, Popular Superstitions, and History of England in the Middle Ages. 2 vols, post 8vo, *elegantly printed, cloth.* 16s

CONTENTS:—Essay 1. Anglo-Saxon Poetry—2. Anglo-Norman Poetry—3. Chansons de Geste, or historical romances of the Middle Ages—4. Proverbs and Popular Sayings—5. Anglo-Latin Poets of the Twelfth Century—6. Abelard and the Scholastic Philosophy—7. Dr. Grimm's German Mythology—8. National Fairy Mythology of England—9. Popular Superstitions of Modern Greece, and their connection with the English—10. Friar Rush and the Frolicsome Elves—11. Dunlop's History of Fiction—12. History and Transmission of Popular Stories—13. Poetry of History—14. Adventures of Hereward the Saxon—15. Story of Eustace the Monk—16. History of Fulke Fitzwarine—17. Popular Cycle or Robin Hood Ballads—18. Conquest of Ireland by the Anglo-Normans—19. Old English Political Songs—20. Dunbar, the Scottish Poet.

WRIGHT (Thomas) Biographia Britannica Literaria, or Biography of Literary Characters of Great Britain and Ireland. ANGLO-SAXON PERIOD. Thick 8vo, *cloth.* 6s (*original price* 12s)

—— The Anglo-Norman Period. Thick 8vo, *cloth,* 6s (*original price* 12s)

Published under the superintendence of the Council of the Royal Society of Literature.

There is no work in the English Language which gives the reader such a comprehensive and connected History of the Literature of these periods.

WRIGHT (Thomas) Wanderings of an Antiquary, chiefly upon the Traces of the Romans in Britain, *many illustrations*, post 8vo, *cloth.* 4s 6d (original price 8s 6d)

WRIGHT'S (Thomas) Saint Patrick's Purgatory, an Essay on the Legends of Hell, Purgatory, and Paradise, current during the Middle Ages. Post 8vo, *cloth.* 6s

"It must be observed that this is not a mere account of St. Patrick's Purgatory, but a complete history of the legends and superstitions relating to the subject, from the earliest times, rescued from old MSS. as well as from old printed books. Moreover, it embraces a singular chapter of literary history omitted by Warton and all former writers with whom we are acquainted : and we think we may add, that it forms the best introduction to Dante that has yet been published."—*Literary Gazette.*

"This appears to be a curious and even amusing book on the singular subject of Purgatory, in which the idle and fearful dreams of superstition are shown to be first narrated as tales, and then applied as means of deducing the moral character of the age in which they prevailed."—*Spectator.*

WRIGHT'S (Thomas) Anecdota Literaria, a Collection of Short Poems in English, Latin, and French, illustrative of the Literature and History of England in the XIIIth Century, and more especially of the Condition and Manners of the Different Classes of Society. 8vo, *cloth, only 250 copies printed.* 5s

WROXETER. The Roman City of Uriconium at Wroxeter, Salop; illustrative of the History and Social Life of our Romano-British forefathers. By J. Corbet Anderson. *A handsome volume, post 8vo, with numerous cuts drawn on wood from the actual objects by the author, extra cloth.* 12s 6d

YORKSHIRE.—The History of the Township of Meltham, near Huddersfield, by the late Rev. JOSEPH HUGHES, edited with addition by C. H. Post 8vo, *cloth.* 7s 6d

Several other books relating to Yorkshire, are interspersed through this Cata-

ADDENDA.

TWAMLEY'S (C.) Historical and Descriptive Account of Dudley Castle in Staffordshire. Post 8vo, *cloth.* 4s

SCOTT (Henry, *Minister of Anstruther Wester*). *Fasti-Ecclesiæ Scoticanæ*; the Sucession of Ministers to the Parish Churches of Scotland, from the Reformation, A.D. 1560, to the present time. Part I. Synod of Lothian and Tweedale. 4to, pp. 400, *cl.* £1. 10s
To be completed in 3 parts—the second is now in the Printer's hands.

"The design of the present work is to present a comprehensive account of the Succession of Ministers of the Church of Scotland, since the period of the Reformation. An attempt is made to give some additional interest by furnishing incidental notices of their lives, writings, and families, which may prove useful to the Biographer, the Genealogist, and the Historian.

"The sources from which the work has been compiled are the various records of Kirk Sessions, Presbyteries, Synods, and General Assemblies, together with the Books of Assignations, Presentations to Benefices, and the Commissariat Registers of Confirmed Testaments. From these authentic sources the information here collected will, it is believed, be found as accurate as the utmost care can render it. Having been commenced at an early period of life, this work has been prosecuted during all the time that could be spared from professional engagements for a period of nearly fifty years.

"Some idea of the labour and continuous research involved in preparing the work may be formed, when the Author states, that he has visited all the Presbyteries in the Church, and about seven hundred and sixty different Parishes, for the purpose of examining the existing records. In this way he has had an opportunity of searching eight hundred and sixty volumes of Presbytery, and one hundred volumes of Synod Records, besides those of the General Assembly, along with the early Registers of Assignations and Presentations to Benefices, and about four hundred and thirty volumes of the Testament Registers in the different Commissariats."—*Extract from Preface.*

RECORDS of the Convention of the Royal Burghs of Scotland, with extracts from other Records relating to the affairs of the Burghs of Scotland, 1295-1597, edited by J. D. Marwick. 4to, pp. 600, *cloth, only* 150 *printed for sale.* £1. 10s

PASSAGES from the Autobiography of a "Man of Kent," together with a few rough Pen and Ink Sketches by the same hand of some of the people he has met, the changes he has seen, and the places he has visited, 1817-1865. Thick post 8vo. *Cloth.* 5s

KENRICK (Rev. John, *Curator of Antiquities in the Museum at York, author of "Ancient Egypt under the Pharaohs," "History of Phœnicia,"* &c.) Papers on subjects of Archæology and History communicated to the Yorkshire Philosophical Society. 8vo, *cloth.* 3s 6d. (Original price 9s.)

Contents.

The Rise, Extension, and Suppression of the Order of Knights Templar in Yorkshire.
Historical Traditions of Pontefract Castle, including an Enquiry into the Place and manner of Richard the Second's Death.
Relation of Coins to History, illustrated from Roman Coins found at Methal, in Yorkshire.
The Causes of the Destruction of Classical Literature.
The History of the Recovery of Classical Literature.
The Reign of Trajan, illustrated by a monument of his reign found at York.
Roman Wax Tablets found in Transylvania.
New Year's Day in Ancient Rome.

HISTORY of the Hebrew Nation and its Literature. By SAMUEL SHARPE, author of the History of Ancient Egypt, &c. Post 8vo, *cloth.* 5s

TEXTS from the Holy Bible explained by the Help of Ancient Monuments. By SAMUEL SHARPE, Author of the History of Egypt and other works. Post 8vo, *with* 160 *drawings on wood, chiefly by* JOSEPH BONOMI, *Curator of Soane's Museum.* Post 8vo, *cloth.* 3s 6d (pub at 5s)

ON THE Chronology of the Bible. By SAMUEL SHARPE, Author of the "History of Egypt," &c. Fcp. 8vo, *cloth.* 1s 6d

ANALECTA Anglo-Saxonica: a Selection in Prose and Verse, from Anglo-Saxon Authors of various Ages; with a Glossary. Designed chiefly as a first book for students. By BENJAMIN THORPE, F.S.A. A New Edition with corrections and improvements. Post 8vo, *cloth.* 7s 6d

ENGLISH Retraced, or Remarks on the "Breeches" Bible (the Genevan Version) and the English of the present day. Post 8vo, *cloth.* 2s (pub at 5s)

An ingenious and instructive volume, the result of a good deal of reading.

A GLOSSARY of the Cotswold (Gloucestershire) Dialect, illustrated by examples from Ancient Authors. By the late Rev. RICHARD WEBSTER HUNTLEY, A.M., of Boxwell Court, Gloucestershire. Crown 8vo, *cloth.* 2s

A GLOSSARY of the Dialect of the district of Cleveland in the North Riding of Yorkshire. By the REV. J. C. ATKINSON, *Incumbent of Danby.* Thick small 4to, 662 pages, *cloth.* £1. 4s

ON THE Dialect of Somersetshire, with a Glossary, Poems, &c., exemplifying the Dialect. By J. JENNINGS. Second Edition, edited by the Rev. J. K. JENNINGS. Fcp. 8vo, *cloth.* 4s 6d

A DICTIONARY of the LANGUAGE of SHAKESPEARE. By SWYFEN JERVIS, *of Darlaston Hall Staffordshire.* 4to, 378 pp., *in double columns,* 4to, *cloth (a cheap volume.)* 12s

The author died while the volume was in the press, when his friend the Rev. Alex. Dyce, the Shakesperian scholar, completed it from the materials he had left.

TRANSACTIONS of the LOGGERVILLE LITERARY SOCIETY. 8vo, pp. 174, *with many humorous cuts, extra cloth gilt edges.* 7s 6d

GENEALOGY of the Family of COLE, of Devon, and of those of its Branches which settled in Suffolk, Hants, Lincoln, Surrey, and Ireland. By JAMES EDWIN-COLE. 8vo, *cloth.* 5s

PORTRAITS of Illustrious Persons in English History, drawn by G. P. Harding, F.S.A., from Original Pictures, with Biographical and Historical Notices, by Thomas Moule, F.S.A. In a handsome roy. 4to volume, *bound in cloth extra, bevelled edges, and gilt leaves.* £1. 1s

Contents : King Henry VIII. and the Emperor Charles the Fifth. Sir Robert Dudley, *Son of the Earl of Leicester.* Queen Katherine of Aragon. Sir William Russell, Lord Russell *of Thornhaugh.* Sir Anthony Browne. Anthony Browne, *Viscount Montagu.* Margaret Cavendish, *Duchess of Newcastle.* Sir Anthony Shirley. Sir Charles Scarborough, M.D. Henry Carey, *Viscount Falkland.* Flora Macdonald, *the preserver of Prince Charles Stuart.* William Leuthall, *Speaker of the House of Commons,* 1640. Edward Vere, *Earl of Oxford.* William Camden, *Antiquary.* Sir Thomas Browne, *of Norwich,* M.D.

Separate prints may he had on folio, india paper proofs 3s 6d each.

EARLY ENGLAND and the Saxon English ; with some Notes on the Father-Stock of the Saxon-English, the Frisians. By W. BARNES, B.D., Author of Poems in the Dorset Dialect, &c., &c. Fcp. 8vo, *cloth.* 3s

ANCIENT ROLLS OF ARMS, No. 1., Glover's Roll of the Reign of Henry III. Edited by George J. Armytage. 4to, *with frontispiece of Shields, sewed. Price* 4s.

It is the intention of the Editor to bring out a series of these Rolls to the extent of a dozen or more, varying in price from 4s to 10s. No. II. will contain another Roll of the Reign of Henry III, in which nearly 700 Coats are emblazoned.

A HAND-BOOK to the Popular, Poetical, and Dramatic Literature of England, from Caxton the first English Printer, to the year 1660. By W. CAREW HAZLITT, *one thick vol,* 8vo, pp. 716, *in double columns, half morocco, Roxburghe style.* £1. 11s 6d

—— LARGE PAPER, royal 8vo, HALF MOROCCO, ROXBURGHE STYLE. £3. 3s

It will be found indispensable to Book-Collectors and Booksellers. It is far in advance of anything hitherto published on Old English Literature.

A MARTYR TO BIBLIOGRAPHY : A Notice of the Life and Works of JOSEPH-MARIE QUÉRARD, the French Bibliographer. By OLPHAR HAMST. 8vo, *cloth (only* 200 *printed).* 3s 6d

HANDBOOK for FICTITIOUS NAMES, being a Guide to Authors, chiefly of the Lighter Literature of the XIXth Century, who have written under assumed names ; and to Literary Forgers, Impostors, Plagiarists, and Imitators. By OLPHAR HAMST, Esq., *Author of A Notice of the Life and Works of J. M. Quérard.* 8vo, *cloth.* 7s 6d

—— THICK PAPER (only 25 copies printed). 15s

An exceedingly curious ... interesting book on the bye ways of Literature.